The Entrepreneurial Humanities

With AI, cryptocurrency, and more in the news, it seems that being an entrepreneur means being in IT, but humanities graduates are launching new businesses every day, turning a profit and having social impact. This book explores how a humanities background can enable entrepreneurs to thrive.

Across all levels of education, students are given the message that to change the world—or make money—the arts and humanities are not the subjects to study. At the same time, discussions of innovation and entrepreneurship highlight the importance of essential skills, such as critical thinking, storytelling, cultural awareness, and ethical decision-making. Here's the disconnect: the subjects that help to develop these vital skills are derided at critical points in any aspiring entrepreneur's education. This collection of perspectives from entrepreneurs in a range of fields and humanities educators illustrates what individuals, and the wider world, are missing when humanities are overlooked as a source of inspiration and success in business.

Featuring a foreword by *Sensemaking* author Christian Madsbjerg, this is a thought-provoking guide for aspiring entrepreneurs in all sectors, and for educators, a window on the practical value of the humanities in an ever more mechanized world.

Alain-Philippe Durand is the Dorrance Dean of the College of Humanities, Professor of French, and affiliated faculty in Africana Studies, Latin American Studies, LGBT Studies, and Public and Applied Humanities at the University of Arizona. He is the author and editor of five books: *Black, Blanc, Beur. Rap Music and Hip-Hop Culture in the Francophone World*; *Un Monde techno. Nouveaux espaces électroniques dans le roman français des années 1980 et 1990*; *Novels of the Contemporary Extreme* (co-edited with Naomi Mandel); *Frédéric Beigbeder et ses doubles*; and *Hip-Hop en français. An Exploration of Hip-Hop Culture in the Francophone World.*

Christine Henseler is Professor of Spanish and Hispanic Studies at Union College, NY. She earned her BSJ in Journalism and BA and MA in Romance Studies from the University of Kansas and her PhD from Cornell University. She co-leads 4Humanities and has published several books, volumes, and articles on the topic of the humanities, interdisciplinary learning, Generation X, and literature and digital media. Her most recent edited volume is titled *Extraordinary Partnerships: How the Arts and Humanities are Transforming America* (Lever Press).

The Entrepreneurial Humanities

The Crucial Role of the Humanities in Enterprise and the Economy

Edited by
Alain-Philippe Durand and
Christine Henseler

NEW YORK AND LONDON

Designed cover image: © Getty Images

First published 2023
by Routledge
605 Third Avenue, New York, NY 10158

and by Routledge
4 Park Square, Milton Park, Abingdon, Oxon, OX14 4RN

Routledge is an imprint of the Taylor & Francis Group, an informa business

Library of Congress Cataloging-in-Publication Data
Names: Durand, Alain-Philippe, editor. | Henseler, Christine, 1969– editor.
Title: The entrepreneurial humanities : the crucial role of the humanities in enterprise and the economy / edited by Alain-Philippe Durand, Christine Henseler.
Description: New York : Routledge, 2023. | Includes bibliographical references and index. | Identifiers: LCCN 2022057680 (print) | LCCN 2022057681 (ebook) | ISBN 9781032462301 (hardback) | ISBN 9781032462264 (paperback) | ISBN 9781003380665 (ebook)
Subjects: LCSH: Entrepreneurship. | Decision making. | Critical thinking. | Humanities—Economic aspects.
Classification: LCC HB615 .E59728 2023 (print) | LCC HB615 (ebook) | DDC 338/.04—dc23/eng/20230126
LC record available at https://lccn.loc.gov/2022057680
LC ebook record available at https://lccn.loc.gov/2022057681

ISBN: 9781032462301 (hbk)
ISBN: 9781032462264 (pbk)
ISBN: 9781003380665 (ebk)

DOI: 10.4324/9781003380665

Typeset in Bembo
by codeMantra

Dedicated to Jacquelynn and Bennett Dorrance and all other generous donors of the Humanities.

Contents

Foreword

Let's Engage

One of the most successful investors in Silicon Valley, Marc Andreessen, was asked a few decades back what he thought about the humanities. He, of course, is the founder of Netscape, which brought the Internet to the world in the early 1990s. Marc Andreessen also built a wildly successful investment firm called Andreesen/Horowitz, which funded many successful companies we know and whose services and products we all use today. His answer was that people who wanted to study topics like math, engineering, and science would get a lot out of college. But he was less enthusiastic about people who tried to do their studies in the humanities. He said: "*I'm sure it's fun, but the average college graduate with a degree in something like English is going to end up working in a shoe store*" (Shontell 2012).

This rather snarky comment is a version of the joke that the only question you get to ask after finishing a humanities degree is: "do you want fries with that?". It is also a general sentiment in technology circles over the past 30 years. The ideology is that the people who *build* things are valuable to society, and these builders are mostly science or engineering majors. Humanities and social science graduates are "talkers" who don't contribute with anything other than being what they themselves call "critical." The ideology of people, like the early Marc Andreessen, calls this general attitude to what is valuable "build it, and they will come." Mark Zuckerberg calls the approach "move fast and break things." The idea is that thinking happens by doing and making rather than pontificating and criticizing.

I know that most of the readers of this book will disagree with these statements and remind us that Zuckerberg did indeed break things—like the election process in the United States or the self-confidence of our daughters. But think about it for a moment; the "*builders*" of the past decades created the Internet with all the services we use. They build social media that makes it possible to stay connected with people all over the globe. The phone in your pocket, with its ability to look up all knowledge ever created and call any human alive today, was made by builders. The creativity to make a new global supply chain—a kind of nervous system—that connects us all to all the things we need didn't come out of an art history or philosophy department. Historians didn't invent video calls, vaccines, VR headsets, or venture capital. A group of university music theory people didn't create the James Webb telescope, touch ID, or Tesla. In a way, the technologists with their math and physics degrees have some right to be self-confident and unimpressed by people from other fields such as the humanities. Perhaps we deserve to work in a shoe store?

As someone who spent decades trying to defend and show how helpful the humanities can be, the challenge from *the builders* is slightly arrogant but not entirely dismissible. In fact: are people who like me belong in the humanities truly helpful? Are we just talking to ourselves? Is the reason no one—and I mean *no one*—reads papers from scholars in the humanities that we are irrelevant to the rest of the world? The answer is *mostly* yes. But the answer is also that the ideas and particularly the methods of the humanities have the potential of being as powerful as any method from the STEM fields. This might be why the same Marc Andreessen said the following to Tyler Cowen in June of 2022: "*I spent the first 25 years of my life trying to understand how machines work. Then I spent the second 25 years, so far, trying to figure out how people work. It turns out people are a lot more complicated.*" *Physicist and communicator extraordinaire Neil DeGrasse Tyson said something similar on Twitter in 2016*: "*In science, when human behaviour enters the equation, things go nonlinear. That's why Physics is easy, and Sociology is hard.*"

I am convinced that understanding people and the world they operate in can be beneficial if you want to build. It is also the case that many mistakes can be avoided if the study of humans is part of the equation when we make things for them.

As far as I know, we are all humans, which is helpful. If you want to understand the human condition, we have a leg up over machines. We intuitively relate to what it means to be human. Anyone, engineers included, has this skill. But studying human worlds, our stories, language, songs, and the meaningful world of objects, equipment, emotions, goals, and identities gives people from the humanities an edge over people from different fields like design, science, and engineering. It is obvious to me that a historian's skill in making sense of disparate forms of information to piece together what it might have been like to live in another time or place gives depth and clarity to any understanding of us. Philosophy can inform how we—at a deep ontological level—exist in the world and how we know things and learn about the human condition. Art history gives us a way to understand the role of images, and ideas shape who we are. The study of languages is a prism into different cultures, how we are different, and what we share. The same is the case for comparative literature when it comes to how we tell stories to organize ourselves. All topics of the human sciences share this powerful tool of sensemaking. The problem is that we hide these skills very well with tortured and cryptic language and our self-referential culture. This is very unfortunate because we are needed. We need to have philosophers and anthropologists in the technology labs of Los Angeles, Seattle, Shanghai, and São Paulo. The new frontier technologies will impact our lives, and we can't leave that job to engineers and designers alone. We risk ending up repeating the mistakes of the past without us. We also need to understand not just use-cases but misuse cases of these technologies. To create new artificial intelligence, we need to understand what *artificial* and *intelligence* means in the first place and the system of human activities it will impact. Just like we need to scrutinize how we migrate to a carbon-neutral world. Humans are a piece of the puzzle of all of these problems. The social and environmental problems we face can't be solved effectively without us. At its root, all these issues are about the human world, which is the very core of expertise in the humanities. We are toast if we don't help understand those worlds and imagine their futures.

It is comforting to know that there are pockets of initiatives, like the book you are reading, to start this necessary process of engaging and putting our tools to work. Projects like this should comfort us that there are new networks of scholars who want to work. I highly recommend that university researchers redirect their effort toward these topics and make themselves available to solve these problems. The questions are deep, intricate, and exciting. This book could be part of a new start and direction for the humanities. So, let's open the humanities to the world and accept the invitation from people like Marc Andreessen to invest in and create the future.

Christian Madsbjerg

Work Cited

Shontell, Alyson. "ANDREESSEN: If You Get An English Degree In College, You're Going To End Up Working At A Shoe Store." Dec. 12, 2012, https://www.businessinsider.com/sorry-english-majors-but-youre-all-soft-and-destined-to-work-in-a-shoe-store-2012-12

Acknowledgments

We would like to thank our editors Meredith Norwich and Bethany Nelson at Routledge for believing in the project and for their advice, support, and patience. We also want to express our gratitude to the many people who contributed directly or indirectly to this team work: all the contributors of this volume, as well as Christian Madsbjerg for the beautiful and convincing foreword. We also want to acknowledge the support we received from the various institutions that gave us the time, resources, and networking to complete this volume: the University of Arizona, Union College, Universidade Federal de Campina Grande, Universidade Federal de Santa Catarina, the Universidade Federal do Rio Grande do Norte, Universidade de Macau, American College of the Mediterranean, Université Le Havre Normandie, and the Modern Language Association Academic Program Services Leadership Institute. Other colleagues and friends were very helpful and supportive in completing this book: all colleagues and students at Union College and in the College of Humanities at the University of Arizona; and Shane Burgess, Jacquelynn and Bennett Dorrance, Daiana Dula, Béatrice Galinon-Mélénec, Jim Hensley, Sylvie Leleu-Merviel, Fabien Liénard, Ronaldo Lima, Julie Cavignac, Paulo Goes, Paula Krebs, Dennis Looney, Shelly Lowe, Josilene Pinheiro-Mariz, Jason Rhody, Lydia Tang, and University of Arizona's President Robert C. Robbins, Provost Liesl Folks, and all who attended the UA College of Humanities' Humanities Leadership Summit on April 27, 2022 at the University of Arizona's Center for Outreach and Collaboration in Washington DC.

Finally, we wish to thank our family for their constant support, love, patience, and non-stop inspiration. They are the most important to us, always.

Contributor Bios

Joanna Carey is Associate Professor of Earth & Environmental Science at Babson College. Her research focuses on answering fundamental questions regarding ecosystem processes in the context of global change, and she teaches courses related to ocean systems and climate change, among other topics to business majors at Babson College. Joanna received her PhD in Earth Science from Boston University (2013), her MS in Environmental Science from Yale University (2007), and her BS in Environmental Policy & Planning from Virginia Tech (2005). Before joining Babson in 2017, Joanna completed several post-doctoral fellowships, including an NSF Earth Science Fellowship and a USGS Powell Center Fellowship, both hosted at the Marine Biological Laboratory in Woods Hole, MA.

Roseanne Chantiluke is an Executive Leader, Researcher and Facilitator based in the UK. Roseanne earned both her BA in French and Spanish and her MSt in French from the University of Oxford. She has since worked with a range of schools, universities, and companies in England, France, Chile, and the United States in educational program design and research, with a view to providing more equitable access to educational opportunities for all learners. Most recently, Roseanne initiated and designed the University of Oxford's first longitudinal teacher engagement program for the Department of Undergraduate Admissions and Outreach and was a member of the project team for Penguin Random House and the Runnymede Trust's nationwide research into diversity in literature teaching.

Alain-Philippe Durand is the Dorrance Dean of the College of Humanities, Professor of French, Professor of Applied Intercultural Arts Research, and affiliated faculty in Africana Studies, Latin American Studies, LGBT Studies, and Public and Applied Humanities at the University of Arizona. He is the author and editor of five books: *Black, Blanc, Beur. Rap Music and Hip-Hop Culture in the Francophone World* (Scarecrow Press); *Un Monde techno. Nouveaux espaces électroniques* *dans le roman français des années 1980 et 1990* (Weidler, preface by Marc Augé); *Novels of the Contemporary Extreme* (Continuum, co-edited with Naomi Mandel); *Frédéric Beigbeder et ses doubles* (Rodopi); and *Hip-Hop en français. An Exploration of Hip-Hop Culture in the Francophone World* (Rowman & Littlefield). He has published chapters and articles in journals such as *PMLA, The French Review, Romance Notes, Contemporary French Civilization, L'Esprit créateur, Romance Quarterly*, and *Contemporary French and Francophone Studies: SITES*, among others. He is Associate Editor of the journal *Contemporary French Civilization*.

Jana Fedtke, PhD, is Assistant Professor in Residence in the Liberal Arts Program at Northwestern University in Qatar. Her research and teaching interests include science and technology in fiction, gender studies, and transnational literatures with a focus on South Asia and Africa. Dr. Fedtke's work has been published in, for example, *Online Information Review, Asian Studies, Journalism Practice, South Asian History and Culture*, and *Asexualities: Feminist and Queer Perspectives* (Routledge).

Susan M. Frost is Associate Lecturer at the University of Wisconsin—Green Bay (WI) in the Humanistic Studies and Business Departments, teaching Humanities, Business & Critical Thinking and Critical Thinking, Not Business as Usual for the MBA program. Recently retired as president of Frost Marketing Communications, Inc., she devotes her time to teaching and writing focused on the humanities as a unifying force for all other disciplines. For the past 20 years, her work has focused on the application of traditional humanities content as a foundation for dynamic thinking. She provides workshops in application for public servants throughout the country. Ms. Frost holds a BA from the University of Wisconsin—Green Bay and an MA in English/Modern Studies from the University of Wisconsin—Milwaukee.

Christina Goldschmidt is an award-winning design leader who is known for transforming product design teams to work at enterprise scale while fostering cultures that drive both business and social impact. Before joining Etsy as Head of Product Design, Christina spent 25 years gaining cross-functional experience driving digital innovation at Fortune 500 companies like Accenture, Morgan Stanley, American Express, Omnicom Media Group, The Discovery Channel, and others. Christina's expertise extends beyond design into product and tech, helping teams innovate by focusing on the intersection of desirability, viability, and feasibility. With an equal leadership in management, her key to helping designers unlock and empower themselves and their careers is a strong foundation in anthropology and customer behavior. As an advocate for mental health, she works to help managers lead from a place of authenticity. Christina received her MBA from NYU

Stern and a BS in design from Rensselaer Polytechnic Institute. She is passionate about education and is a leading instructor and guest lecturer at NYU Stern and General Assembly, to name a few. She has also been featured at SXSW, the Better Product Podcast, Fortune Magazine, Ecommerce Design Summit, InVision's Inside Design, and HR Transform. Outside of work she loves to focus on craft, be it in millinery, ikebana, cooking, or the perfect cocktail.

M. André Goodfriend retired from the Department of State in 2022 as a member of the Senior Foreign Service with the rank of Minister Counselor after a career lasting over three decades. Serving as Director of the State Department's Office of eDiplomacy, Mr. Goodfriend coordinated preparation of the State Department's Open Government Plan and worked to facilitate the conduct of diplomacy with technologies, promoting knowledge sharing and transparency. In Budapest, Hungary, in the absence of an ambassador, he served as Chargé d'Affaires a.i., engaging in an open conversation on approaches to implementing shared values. As Consul General in Damascus during the years prior to the closure of the US Embassy, Mr. Goodfriend utilized increased public engagement and collaborative effort to safeguard the welfare of the US citizen community in an increasingly hostile environment. Other overseas assignments have included Israel, India, Russia, and the United Kingdom. Born in California and raised in Arizona, Mr. Goodfriend has studied Hungarian, Hebrew, French, Russian, Greek (classical and modern), Spanish, Hindi, Arabic, and Yiddish.

Christine Henseler is Professor of Spanish and Hispanic Studies at Union College, NY. She earned her PhD from Cornell University and her BSJ in Journalism and BA and MA in Romance Studies from the University of Kansas. She co-leads 4Humanities and hosts a website called *The Arts & Humanities in the 21st Century Workplace*. She has published several books, volumes, and academic articles on the topic of the humanities, interdisciplinary learning, Generation X, and Spanish literature and digital media, including *Generation X Goes Global* (Routledge, 2012), *Spanish Fiction in the Digital Age* (Palgrave, 2011), and *Extraordinary Partnerships: How the Arts and Humanities are Transforming America* (Lever Press, 2020), which has been viewed over 40,000 times. She has also published opinion pieces in the HuffPost, Inside Higher Ed, and other outlets, often in collaboration with colleagues from different fields and professions outside of academia (for more info www.christinehenseler.com).

Mohammed Ibahrine, PhD, is Professor of Innovation and Entrepreneurship and the coordinator of IEN 301 Innovation and Entrepreneurship Mindset in the School of Business Administration at the American University of Sharjah, United Arab Emirates (UAE). He has worked at several universities in Germany, Morocco, the United Kingdom, the United States, and the UAE. Over the last 25 years, he has been doing research and consultancy work on technology, business, and human interaction in cultural, political, social, economic, and organizational contexts. He has won several teaching, research, and creative awards.

Simone Kliass is an international ambassador for Women in Voice, vice-president of the Brazilian extended-reality association, and creator and curator of the Pixel Voice voiceover conference. Simone Kliass has given talks at SXSW and VO Atlanta in the United States; The VoiceOver Network in Europe; and Rio2C, Path, HackTown, and Pixel Show in Brazil. She hosts Brazil's leading virtual reality conference, works as a voice consultant for the New-York–based Edge Studio, narrated the Primetime Emmy-award–winning VR experience "The Line," and can be heard in hundreds of TV and radio commercials in Brazil.

Christian Madsbjerg is the co-founder of the global advisory firm Red Associates. He teaches twentieth-century continental philosophy and the practical application of the Human Sciences. Latest as a Professor of Applied Humanities at The New School for Social Research. He is a Senior Fellow at The Health and Global Policy Institute in Tokyo, Japan, and a distinguished visitor at The Buffett Center for Global Affairs at Northwestern University. His work has been featured in publications such as *The Economist, The Wall Street Journal, Financial Times, The Washington Post, Der Spiegel*, and *Foreign Affairs Magazine*. He is also on the board at Fritz Hansen, Bjarke Ingels Group: BIG, The Metals Company, US board of Kvadrat, and Red Associates Holding.

Ajay Major is Assistant Professor of Medicine at the University of Colorado School of Medicine, specializing in lymphoma and myeloma, and a physician-publisher in the medical education and narrative medicine spaces. He is a Class of 2016 graduate of Albany Medical College and completed a residency in internal medicine at the University of Colorado in 2019 followed by a hematology/oncology fellowship at the University of Chicago in 2022. He and Aleena Paul founded Pager Publications, Inc. in 2014, a 501c3 non-profit literary corporation that curates and supports peer-edited publications for the medical education community.

Matthew M. Mars, PhD, is Associate Professor of Leadership and Innovation in the University of Arizona College of Agriculture and Life Sciences. His research focuses on how entrepreneurial logics and strategies become embedded in and influence academic cultures, community development initiatives, and social movements. In addition to being a widely published interdisciplinary scholar, Dr. Mars is currently the co-editor of *Advances in the Study of Entrepreneurship, Innovation and Economic Growth* series, associate editor of *Community Development*, and a member of the editorial board of *Local Development & Society*.

Ken S. McAllister is the Associate Dean for Research and Program Innovation for the University of Arizona's College of Humanities. Ken is a Founding Professor in the Public & Applied Humanities Department. His administrative area of expertise is training humanities faculty to be active grant and contract seekers, and he has helped change the College's sponsored projects culture from one that produces thousands of dollars in external funding to one that produces millions. As a researcher, Ken co-founded and co-directs—with his colleague Judd Ethan Ruggill —the Learning Games Initiative Research Archive (LGIRA), one of the world's largest publicly accessible computer game collections.

Leah N'Diaye is a Management Consultant in Organizational Effectiveness and an expert internal change and transformation practitioner. She earned her Master's degree in HR Management and Organizational Science from the Université Paris-Dauphine, which is one of Europe's leading academic and research institutions in the Organization and Decision Sciences. She is known as someone who leads with empathy, curiosity, and everything human. Today, Leah is heading up the organizational change management practice at Silicon Valley Bank (SVB), the financial partner of the innovation economy. She is the original founder and leader of the Organizational Effectiveness Center of Excellence which she built from the ground up, significantly supporting SVB's growth. Some of this work has involved organizational transformation, process and technology adoption, and leading change efforts for an acquired east coast private bank. She recently published a case study with Gartner, the world's leading information technology research and advisory company, entitled "Experience-Focused M&A Integration Management."

Aleena Paul is an internal medicine and pediatrics primary care physician and a clinician-educator at New York Medical College. She earned her MD from Albany Medical College and MSEd from Hofstra University. She completed her med/peds residency at the University of Massachusetts Medical School, and subsequently a joint General Internal Medicine and Academic General Pediatrics Fellowship at the Zucker School of Medicine at Hofstra/Northwell Health. Her research interests include developing and assessing the impact of health humanities curricula on professional identity formation. She is co-founder with

Ajay Major of Pager Publications, Inc., a non-profit literary corporation that curates and supports peer-edited publications for the medical education community.

Judd Ethan Ruggill is Professor and Head of the Department of Public & Applied Humanities at the University of Arizona. He is also the co-founder and co-director (with Ken McAllister) of the Learning Games Initiative Research Archive (lgira.mesmernet.org), an organization that preserves and lends game-related materials to video game researchers, museums, galleries, and media production companies around the world.

Hope J. Schau is Eller Professor of Marketing at the University of Arizona's Eller College of Management. Hope's research focuses on market practices, consumption journeys, brand building, integrated marketing communications, the impact of technology on marketplace relationships, and collaborative value creation. She is President-elect of Consumer Culture Theory Consortium, an Associate Editor at the *Journal of the Academy of Marketing Science*, an Area Editor for the *Journal of Public Policy and Marketing*, and the *Journal of Business Research*.

Shivaike Shah is a producer from London, and the founder of Khameleon Productions. He was recently the Visiting Artist at the Brown Arts Institute, Brown University, where he completed his 12-state 30-college *Uprooting Medea* tour, visiting institutions from Rhode Island to Texas. He is also the creator and host of the Khameleon Classics Podcast series. Shivaike has also worked in the West End, Film, TV, and fashion, and currently works for Netflix.

Eric Touya de Marenne is Professor of French at Clemson University. He received his PhD in Romance Languages and Literatures at the University of Chicago, the John B. & Thelma A. Gentry Award for Teaching Excellence in the Humanities in 2012, and the Dean's Award for Outstanding Achievement in Service in 2017. His research and teaching interests include 19th–21st-century French and Francophone literature and culture, and interdisciplinary approaches to literature, art, economics, ethics, and society. His most recent publications include *Simone de Beauvoir: le combat au féminin*, Paris: Presses Universitaires de France, 2019, and *The Case for the Humanities: Pedagogy, Polity, Interdisciplinarity*, Lanham: Rowman & Littlefield, 2016.

Introduction

Open for Business: The Entrepreneurial Humanities

Alain-Philippe Durand and Christine Henseler

Equipped with degrees in French and Romance Philology, respectively, Bennett Dorrance co-created DMB Associates, a real estate development firm with several affiliated companies; and Brandon S. Lee and Garrett Christian are the founders of Terra Dotta, the leader in higher education software. With a Bachelor's degree in History and a Certificate in Chinese, Megan Reilly Cayten founded and led an ethical fashion accessories company called Catrinka, which financially empowers women and girls and provides education and mentoring. Should we be surprised when our Google searches discover thousands more individuals with humanities degrees who endeavor in the building of new, and often social, enterprises?

For- and non-profit companies are launched every day by graduates of the humanities who are not only making a social impact but are also turning a profit. And, yet, when the general public hears words like "innovation" or "entrepreneurship" and reads articles and magazines that sell us on the "100 Most Innovative People in __________ *(fill in the blank)*," they usually think of technologists and scientists. Words like "innovation" and "entrepreneurship" are rarely driven by conversations that focus, let alone include the humanities.

But why not? Humanities disciplines have always intersected in professional fields as wide-ranging as environmental studies, engineering, computer science, neuroscience, biology, the health professions, and more. But when students think about the role of the humanities in their careers, they are stunted by very narrow understandings of what these disciplines teach, and what they can do.

The problem is a systemic one. Our K-12 schools clearly send the message that science, technology, engineering, mathematics, and medicine (STEMM) defines excellence, that some humanities courses, such as Spanish, French, Classics, or Religious Studies, are core to being an educated human being but generally lead to limited career success, and, equally important, that the arts are considered "nice" electives for which students get partial credit. From the moment students place a foot into our public schools, they are told that if you want to change the world,

DOI: 10.4324/9781003380665-1

if you want to become "successful," focusing your professional sights on the arts or humanities is not the way to go. For example, none of the 16 career clusters or pathways to college and career readiness outlined in the National Career Clusters® Framework mentions a single humanities discipline. Worse, in at least one instance, the humanities are listed this way:

> **Liberal Arts, Languages, History**
> **Not an official cluster.** These programs are officially assigned to Education & Training, but have been placed here to identify education majors from other liberal arts majors. Includes programs in area, ethnic, cultural and gender studies; English language and literature; foreign languages and linguistics, history, liberal arts and sciences, general studies and humanities; and multi/interdisciplinary studies in liberal arts.
>
> (Minnesota Office of Higher Education 2017)

Our K-12 schools also reflect the lack of knowledge from the general public when it comes to the humanities. Yet their sentiments contradict the findings of the Humanities Indicators project by the American Academy of Arts and Sciences, who recently found positive news regarding the total number of credits taken by high school seniors in the humanities, including, but not limited to, these figures:

- Throughout the period of 1990–2019, English was the most studied subject among high school students in the United States
- Among all broad subject areas, the biggest percentage increase in credits taken, 53%, was in visual and performing arts.
- World history course taking increased dramatically over the past several decades. In 1990, 73% of graduating high school students took the course, but by 2019, that share increased to 94%.

Despite this high school exposure, the vast majority of Americans (especially politicians and journalists) are quick to portray the studying of humanities as useless and the perfect pipeline toward unemployment.

As anyone who has attended a high school's Career Day event knows, when the local university's deans of Business, Science, Engineering, Law, Medicine, and Humanities are introduced, only one of them (guess who!) has to start their speech by first defining the field they represent. In fact, in some instances, the presentations differ starkly: STEM is asked to speak about job prospects, while the humanities are asked to talk about everything else.

Worse still, even higher education publications and some people within the humanities disciplines often disagree on a common definition or have a tendency to limit the humanities to the studying of English, history, and philosophy. To illustrate and support this repeated partial description of the humanities disciplines, one can just search the *Chronicle of Higher Education's* database of past articles with the key word "humanities" to see that the vast majority of these pieces only provide examples, quotes from English, history, and philosophy experts.

Not to speak of what you might find, or rather, not find, when you conduct a search for the word "humanities" in one of the most influential journals in innovation and entrepreneurship: *The Stanford Social Innovation Review*. In June of 2022, a search yielded 55 articles. Exactly 0 included a title with the word "humanities." They included words like "storytelling," "ethics," "value," "social impact," but not "humanities." Why not? Aren't the humanities referenced as central fields for the learning of creative and critical thinking and communication skills, cultural awareness, ethical decision-making, and more? And aren't the best (social) innovation and entrepreneurship studies centered around multidisciplinary teams?

Could it be that by focusing on skills alone, we have been limiting our impact, suggesting that the humanities function "at the service" of other disciplines (i.e. good writing skills are good in business or in marketing, etc.). But, contrary to this belief, and as one of our contributors, Roseanne Chantiluke argues, "the study of Modern Languages is about more than developing proficiency in the functional skills of a different language. It's about developing a critical engagement with the world around us." Through first-hand experience in the field of non-profit education, Chantiluke has found that, "studying Modern Languages demands self-awareness, deepens humility, and develops empathy as it privileges the process of meaning-making and storytelling over attaining 'fluency' in functional skills."

Part of the problem derives from the humanities themselves. Those of us who have contributed to their defense in public conversations (articles that appear in mainstream media and social media sites) have been far too narrow in focus when it comes to talking about the humanities in the fields of innovation and entrepreneurship, in part because their study has lacked an expansive and embracive view of the role of what the humanities actually *do*.

The important data mining project funded by The Mellon Foundation, *WhatEvery1Says*, and directed by professor Alan Liu at the University of California, Santa Barbara has found that public narratives about the humanities focus on communicating activities in academic circles through "events, courses, and projects" instead of "concrete humanities research and discoveries" in ways that do not tend to leave "students with a clear idea of the day-to-day practicalities of applying the content or methods of humanistic study to jobs" (27) By contrast, "articles about scientific research often rivet the public's attention on actual *things* observed or discovered, like exoplanets, particle accelerators, or genes" (27). In essence, there is little to no discourse of what the humanities *do*.

M. André Goodfriend worked for many years for the US State Department and was a member of the Senior Foreign Service (the diplomatic corp.). He is also the author of "Diplomacy as Entrepreneurial Humanities" in this volume, and he believes that the humanities is, actually, one of the most practical degrees that a student can obtain. You don't hear that very often, do you? He explains that,

> Throughout my career, from the earliest days of adjudicating visa applications to being the top-ranking U.S. diplomat in a country, from considering how one's perception of nationality affects one's approach to the U.S. to considering how effectively the design of technologies is human-centered, I've been fortunate to have the opportunity to apply my humanities studies.
>
> As human beings, we play a role in shaping societies, creating communities and establishing our own individual careers; and we apply our understanding of languages, literature, philosophy, history, archaeology, anthropology, human geography, law, religion, art… all the disciplines of the humanities in order to flourish in those endeavors.

Goodfriend understands first-hand that the humanities afforded him the

> flexibility to navigate societal and organizational cultures, and helps one motivate a team as a leader. Using the humanities foundation to recognize potential and assess the risk to turn potential into reality opens up the opportunity to take applied humanities a step beyond, into the realm of the entrepreneurial.

The arts suffer far less from such abstractions and one-sided conversations given that there is a much more concrete approach to *doing*, with a strong turn toward cultural and creative economy entrepreneurship and creative impact investing. In addition, it is far easier to assess how much the arts have been contributing to the nation's GDP. In case you're curious, in 2020, "the cultural economy accounted for 4.2% of the gross domestic product in the United States, or $876.7 billion dollars" ("Arts" 2022). Try a similar search for the "humanities" at the same site, the Bureau of Economic Analysis by the U.S. Department of Commerce, and this is the response: "Sorry, no results found for 'humanities.' Try entering fewer or more general search terms."

Alan Webber, co-founder of Fast Company magazine provides food for thought for those working in both the arts and humanities. He argues that

> creative entrepreneurship lives in the overlapping zones of technology, experience, entertainment, and design thinking. It is more likely

> to be a verb than a noun, a way of being or doing or thinking or experiencing than a single product. Or service. It defines who we are and what we value much more than what we buy or own or consume. It springs from a creative urge—to make, to tell, to show, to fashion, to perform. It rarely comes about because of a four-box matrix that reveals an open space in the competitive landscape.
>
> (xviii)

In this volume, we hope to jumpstart a "Humanities-as-Verb" movement. We believe that the humanities have real, transformative potential in today's day and age, one that defines who we desperately need to become and how we need to get there. Process matters, because

> Any place where a verb is more important than a noun, you'll find a creative entrepreneur. Any place where experience is valued over ownership, you'll find a creative entrepreneur. Any place where meaning and purpose are elevated above status and celebrity, you'll find a creative entrepreneur.
>
> (Webber xix)

Susan Frost in this volume challenges us by asking:

> What if we dumped old theories of liberal education based on class-laden nineteenth and early twentieth century perspectives, and approached the humanities as a cluster of highly pliable topics, with the understanding that thinking through the humanities is thinking in the very biosphere that creates this new world?

Those of us working in and through the humanities have a crucial role to play in making our disciplines more "verb-like," in partnership with an array of disciplines and professional fields, and in collaboration with the for and non-profit business industries. We must better understand and break down the deep-seated suspicions about building alliances between the humanities and the for and non-profit sectors. Because we believe that the humanities can have real, transformative potential.

Let us be clear: we are not advocating for more business-oriented education for students, although we do believe in the need to integrate more foundational humanities learning into these programs. With this volume, we hope to expand how to think about the applications of humanities and point toward a space—that of innovation and entrepreneurship—that provides fertile ground across a wide range of disciplines and professional fields. *The Entrepreneurial Humanities* aims to dismantle the too common narratives depicting the humanities as siloed and self-interested, useless, a thing from the past, only valuable for those interested in an academic career or the life of the mind. *The Entrepreneurial Humanities* specifically develops a dialog between two traditionally disconnected groups: humanities scholars and professors and employed humanities entrepreneurs. This volume distinctively focuses on a group of academics and professionals from around the world who, directly or indirectly have embraced and applied, as students and/or in their careers and across a variety of industries, the knowledge and essential transformational skills of the humanities across a wide range of enterprises.

Our goal is to provide what we see as an essential disciplinary translation if politicians, journalists, donors, educators, administrators, and members of the public are going to associate humanities contributions with actions that make industries, innovation, and life better. This book intends to engage readers about the work that humanities do in the world in and beyond the academy and how a new generation of professors and administrators are changing the teaching and branding of the humanities.

We believe that the humanities have not been recognized sufficiently for the role they play in the world of innovation and entrepreneurship, understood broadly. This lack of attention to what the humanities can *do* across different professions and disciplines provides us with an opportunity to develop new and exciting partnerships and programs. As Alain-Philippe Durand and Ken S. McAllister have argued (2022),

> in some academic circles, unfortunately, leadership built around entrepreneurship—work that always happens at the nexus of risk and reward (especially financial risk and reward)—conjures images of Wall Street wolves and Silicon Valley profiteers rather than academics aiming to make the world (or at least their campus or discipline) a better place.

In this book, you will hear from academics and non-academics in fields as varied as national security and diplomacy, medicine, marketing, leadership training, global educational programming, climate change, design thinking, voice and human speech, and, yes, higher education. These essays are not presented as comprehensive to the subject, but rather as openings for further dialog and discussion.

In this volume, we use the word "entrepreneurial" as both a noun that refers to a disciplinary field (innovation and entrepreneurship), and as an adjective (the *entrepreneurial* humanities) that describes a process of thinking, understanding, learning, and applying. We use these terms to expand on how to talk about the humanities in ways that are more flexible, adaptable, and open to plurality. In essence, we see the term as leading to heightened attention and application of diversity, equity, and inclusion (DEI) through the building of more global, cultural, and linguistic awareness, human history and expression, and engagement with individual and community values, beliefs, and ethics. In essence, to build contextual awareness. Our hope is that the term serves to emphasize the need to gain deep knowledge of others and increase reflective thinking about ourselves for the betterment of society and the building of new opportunities and innovations through more human-centered lenses.

And, despite the deep learning that the humanities can provide, we suggest moving beyond the term "entrepreneurial mindset." We suggest speaking more about the concrete and applied role that humanists play in the field of innovation and entrepreneurship, not just the ways in which we contribute to an entrepreneurial state of mind. What's missing when students speak of their impact on the future is excitement around their potential role through the learning of the humanities. By extension, the lack of concrete assessments of the impact of the humanities largely erases our (economic) contributions, as the above-mentioned empty searches suggest. This needs to change.

The "entrepreneurial humanities" are also infused with a dose of hope. Because, as a *Forbes* article from 2014 argues,

> Being entrepreneurial is essentially about thinking and doing something that we have not done before, in order to achieve a desirable goal or outcome. It is about assessing a situation, designing alternatives, and choosing a new way – or perhaps a combination of ways – that we hope will lead us to something better; however we happen to define "better" at that moment.
>
> (De Carolis)

Ken S. McAllister and Judd Ethan Ruggill agree. They state that "The humanities, however, are in fact an ideal locale for training entrepreneurs, as they prize and promote the creative, interpersonal, and intercultural intelligences crucial for bringing ideas into being." The other contributors in this volume also add to the hope that the humanities can provide in the building of future entrepreneurs as readers will see.

Several sections comprise *The Entrepreneurial Humanities*, starting with "Why the Humanities & Entrepreneurship?" Christine Henseler's "Sparking a Movement: Cross-Disciplinary Innovation and The Humanities" argues for the development of more cross-disciplinary and diverse learning experiences to increase innovation, entrepreneurship, and sustainable human-supportive change. Through personal experiences, specific case studies, and recent reports, her essay explores how young entrepreneurs, industry leaders, and educators are applying knowledge and skills learned in the arts and humanities to challenge assumptions, offer new perspectives and practical paths moving forward. Referring to reports, such as the GII Innovation Index, the Business Roundtable, and Deloitte, Henseler points to the need for additional investment in the building of human capital and the innovation of educational institutions, departments, and programs.

Retired diplomat M. André Goodfriend's chapter, "Diplomacy as Entrepreneurial Humanities," provides a personal narrative of Goodfriend's long career in the US Department of State that argues that diplomacy can be seen among the most entrepreneurial of professions. He describes how his humanities education, focusing on languages, philosophy, history, and religion, provided him an understanding of the power of language to create and shape the world around us.

The following chapter, "Entrepreneurship: A Radically Relational Undertaking?," conjures up a workshop that the author, Executive Director of the Oxford's Centre for Tutorial Teaching Roseanne Chantiluke, delivered at secondary schools in London in 2018. Chantiluke structures the essay around the key learnings of the workshop to reflect on how her formation in Modern Languages literally and metaphorically lies at the heart of their understanding of what entrepreneurship can do and mean for the work they perform as the Executive Director of a UK-based educational services company. The essay calls for an expanded understanding of all that "entrepreneurship" contains as a concept by reflecting on the cornerstones of Modern Languages Teaching (MLT) and what MLT can teach us about "undertaking" complex relational work in different contexts.

Next, Jana Fedtke and Mohammed Ibahrine, respectively, Assistant Professor in Residence in the Liberal Arts Program at Northwestern University in Qatar and Professor of Innovation and Entrepreneurship at the American University of Sharjah, present a case study they developed for the course they teach on Innovation and Entrepreneurship Mindset. They argue that cultivating an entrepreneurial mindset in the arts and humanities as part of the university curriculum in an environment that traditionally privileges STEM fields and business enables and motivates students to apply their social entrepreneurship skills in creating future jobs, solving pressing social issues, and building sustainable futures.

Susan M. Frost is a lecturer at the University of Wisconsin-Green Bay (WI) in the Humanistic Studies and Business Departments. In her essay, she also advocates for the importance and needs to incorporate the critical thinking of the humanities across the curriculum. Rather than decrying the waning humanities, her essay presents them as regenerative and transformative, advocating that they should be taught as a fresh, exciting, and productive garden of ideas.

The second section of *The Entrepreneurial Humanities*, "Creating Change and Designing for Transformation," includes five chapters. In the first, "Voice Entrepreneurs: Making a Career in Human Speech," Brazilian voice talent Simone Kliass demonstrates how artificial intelligence (AI) and other technologies have disrupted the voice industry, while also suggesting that critical thinking, problem-solving, and strategic planning can bolster a freelance artist's chances of achieving economic stability. Her essay addresses questions such as: How can human talent compete against AI? What are the ethical implications of letting AI substitute human talent? How will AI and other technological novelties shape the future of the arts and humanities?

In the next chapter, Joanna Carey, an Associate Professor of Earth & Environmental Science at Babson College, addresses climate change challenges and how entrepreneurial mindsets and the humanities can help. Specifically, climate change presents society with ample opportunities to do better, *if* we have the courage to act. Finding such courage to act requires broad-scale recognition that addressing climate change is not about "saving the Earth," but rather about saving humanity.

In "Collaborative Humanities: Creativity, Classics, and Being a Chameleon," theater and film producer Shivaike Shah recounts his own personal experience with one of the most important humanities skills: collaboration. As part of Khameleon Productions *Uprooting Medea* tour, Shah took his work with *Medea* to 30 US institutions across 12 states. Collaboration was at the core of these visits—between professors, departments, centers, and even whole institutions. Shah views collaboration as the core mode of operation with which to develop and generate new ideas. He argues that it is through collaboration, between people inside and outside the academy, that the humanities can reimagine their future while grappling honestly with their exclusionary colonial history.

Christina Goldschmidt is the Head of Product Design at Etsy, and she examines design thinking techniques in her piece "Healing Trauma at the Intersection of Entrepreneurship and Design." She shows how design thinking is foundational in complex industries such as financial services and management consulting. In addition, Goldsmith explains how elements of design thinking can have a positive treatment effect on those symptoms associated with posttraumatic stress disorder (PTSD). Indeed, as Goldschmidt argues in her chapter, there are many medications and therapies that help PTSD, but a notable subset of such therapies are also covertly present in the practice of design thinking.

The last essay of this section, "Liberal Arts Approaches to Teaching Women Entrepreneurship in Senegal: Narratives, Ethics, Empathy," focuses on professor Eric Touya de Marenne's experience teaching business, economics, and culture at Clemson University in the context of French-speaking Africa. Touya de Marenne deals with three companies that are founded and managed by women in Senegal. The essay explores specifically how students develop critical competencies through the course "French for International Business" that enables them to broaden their awareness of others through storytelling, enhance their capacity to rethink ethical issues pertaining to entrepreneurship, and become more empathetic toward gender inequalities.

Kicking off "The Humanities@Work" section, University of Arizona's professors of Public and Applied Humanities Ken S. McAllister and Judd Ethan Ruggill examine internships as an entrepreneurial act. They are interested in how humanities internship programs are able to vivify the act of bringing ideas into being. McAllister and Ruggill argue that the creative, interpersonal, and intercultural intelligences at the heart of the humanities make for an excellent entrepreneurial foundation. According to them, humanities interns are able to draw on their understanding of the human condition to see, design, and advocate for institutional, interpersonal, and cultural change.

As a founding leader on Silicon Valley Bank's (SVB) Organizational Effectiveness Center of Excellence, Leah N'Diaye focuses on SVB's ability to drive internal organizational change. Her essay argues that, for long-term success, a business must also focus on the Employee Experience (EX). Start-ups need to create an EX that will attract, retain, and engage the masses. The goal is about making the workplace, or the EX, more human, especially in this post-pandemic world.

Internal medicine and pediatrics primary care physician and clinician-educator at New York Medical College Aleena Paul and Assistant Professor of Medicine in Hematology at the University of Colorado School of Medicine Ajay Major outline their entrepreneurial framework in founding the publication *in-Training*, the decisions they made to enable organic evolution of the publication to meet the changing needs of the medical student community, the steps they took to ensure long-term sustainability, and the impact of the publication on the intersection of the humanities and medical education. Since its launch, *in-Training* has now published over 2,000 works by medical students across the globe, from narrative medicine reflections to poetry to opinion pieces, with over 6 million pageviews in that time.

Finally, in this section's last chapter, University of Arizona's Associate Professor of Leadership and Innovation Matthew M. Mars and Professor of Marketing Hope J. Schau illustrate the relevancy and influence of the arts and humanities to progressive forms of entrepreneurship that help counter the perpetual pursuit of uniform precision, colloquially termed "perfection," that is too often the norm among global mega-brand businesses. Mars and Schau introduce a growing community of humanist entrepreneurs who work to offset the power of perfection by offering consumers unique experiences and handcrafted products that are intentionally imprecise, inherently imperfect, and ultimately irreplicable. These artists, craftspeople, and cottage creators foster more sustainable consumption through unique blends of creativity, ingenuity, and entrepreneurial skills that transcend conventional business logics.

Works Cited

Bureau of Economic Analysis. "Arts and Cultural Production Satellite Account, U.S. and States, 2020." Bureau of Economic Analysis. 15 Mar. 2022. https://www.bea.gov/data/special-topics/arts-and-culture#:~:text=Arts%20and%20cultural%20 economic%20activity%20 accounted%20for%204.2%20percent%20 of,or%20%24876.7%20billion%2C%20in%202020.

De Carolis, Donna M. "We Are All Entrepreneurs: It's a Mindset, Not a Business Model." *Forbes*. 9 Jan. 2014. https://www.forbes.com/sites/forbeswomanfiles/2014/01/09/we-are-all-entrepreneurs-its-amindset-not-a-business-model/?sh=1a486e2ed84f

Durand, Alain-Philippe and Ken S. McAllister. "Humanities = Jobs. The Tactics of Contrarian Entrepreneurial Humanists." Co-authored with Ken S. McAllister. *ADE Bulletin* 159 & *ADFL Bulletin* 47.2. 2022, 82–98.

Humanities Indicators. "Credits Earned by Graduating High School Seniors." https://www.amacad.org/humanities-indicators/k-12-education/credits-earned-graduatinghigh-school-seniors

Liu, Alan, Drogue, Abigail, et al. "What Everyone Says: Public Perceptions of the Humanities in the Media." *Daedalus* Summer 2022. Pgs. 19–39.

Minnesota Office of Higher Education. "What is a Career Cluster?" 2017. https://www.ohe.state.mn.us/dPg.cfm?pageID=1989

Webber, Alan. "Foreword: The Disruption of Creative Entrepreneurs." In Alice Loy and Tom Aageson. *Creative Economy Entrepreneurs: From Startup to Success.* Global Centre for Cultural Entrepreneurship DBA Creative Startups, 2018.

Part I

Why the Humanities & Entrepreneurship?

Chapter 1

Sparking a Movement

Cross-Disciplinary Innovation and the Humanities

Christine Henseler

Ten years ago, I first attended the NYC Games for Change Festival, a conference that explores the intersection of game design and social impact.[1] The event radically, and delightfully, disrupted my professional path. I met designers, illustrators, artists, writers, musicians and sound designers, classicists, historians, educators, film directors and leaders of government organizations, foundations, and, yes, entrepreneurs from both the for- and non-profit industries. Sandra Day O'Connor even gave the keynote. Before me stood the first woman to serve on the Supreme Court for the role she played in creating a video game called iCivics. I knew I was experiencing a turning point in my career. So I hit the Play button.

I was sitting in the front row (a most uncomfortable spot), when I first heard the team of Native Alaskan elders talk about their collaboration with E-Line Media game designers to develop the video game Never Alone. The path toward creative innovation between these two unlikely visionaries led to dozens of prizes, accolades, and yes, dollars. Their entrepreneurial approach animated the stories of the Iñupiat people in ways that never before connected and built cultural pride in their communities' heritage. The Cook Inlet Tribal Council said that their video game became "a bold, risky idea that had paid off" and that also "sparked a movement" (Henseler 15, 2020).

I couldn't help but wonder: could unexpected partnerships like this one also spark a movement and bring new cultural pride to the Humanities? Their story reminded me of a basic need: the need to hear from artists and humanists who engage in highly creative and innovative endeavors to change the way we see, interact, and act in the world. So, I endeavored to find a few of these voices. And three years later, born was an edited volume titled *Extraordinary Partnerships: How the Arts and Humanities Are Transforming America*. The book compiled the creative risks and careful partnership-building from academics and non-academics across a wide range of fields, including social circus culture, art and urban design, astrology and poetry, engineering and radio, marketing and literature. And yes, in case you're interested, the volume includes the full story of what started

DOI: 10.4324/9781003380665-3

it all: Never Alone, told by the members of the Cook Inlet Tribal Council themselves. I published the volume open source through Lever Press, a Liberal Arts consortium publisher, and as of this moment, the book has been downloaded over 40,000 times.

It was at the Higher Education Maker Summit at the ASU Chandler Innovation Center a few years back that I first connected with Jae Rhim Lee, visual artist and designer of the Infinity Burial Project. I also met Ryan Holladay, a new media curator of Artisphere and TED Fellow, and Alicia Eggert, an interdisciplinary artist and TED Fellow. I shouldn't have been surprised by their work. But I was. These artists and humanists made me more aware of a world of young professional innovators. Not only were they using knowledge and skills learned in the arts and humanities, but they were also applying them to reimagine our realities, our lives, and, yes, even our deaths. Did my students know about them? I found out they didn't, but when introduced, their beliefs about the role of the arts and humanities altered their educational pursuits and professional ambitions.

It was also at this Maker Summit where I observed that most maker initiatives were driven by engineering and entrepreneurial venture creation—how tinkering can lead to business building—as well as policy development in the fields of science and technology. Connections to the world of art were clear, visible, and exciting, but I was one of the only humanists in attendance (with a slight tilt of the head my fellow attendees would ask: "what are *you* doing here?"). At this conference, I found that conversations and programing, even NSF grant solicitations, lacked connections and conversations about human contexts and cultures, ethics, and impact. That said, grants in my own field, in the humanities, tended to be equally narrow and limited to ideas that fit into pre-defined boxes.

All too often, I found myself at gatherings where similar people from similar backgrounds talked about similar ideas, all usually agreeing with one another in fierce opposition to the outside world. Where were the surprising and different conversations and viewpoints to challenge my assumptions, open my mind to new ideas, and offer new perspectives and paths forward? Whether I was at a deans meeting, a humanities meeting, or a Modern Languages meeting, conversations tended to repeat well-worn trends; even good ideas fell into oblivion and isolation.

That's when I started using my yearly conference allowance (thank you Union) to attend events outside my own field. I attended the Solutions Journalism Network conference in Salt Lake City Utah, at which hundreds of journalists from around the world engaged in interactive conversations about writing for social change. I attended the Ashoka conference in San Diego to meet more changemakers working in different communities around the world. Invigorated, I stood in long lines to enter panels at South by Southwest in Austin, Texas. There, I was inspired by Melinda Gates whose work focused on supporting women in the workplace; I met

Antionette Carroll, President and CEO of the Creative Reaction Lab, who taught me that we are not paying enough attention to diversity and inclusivity in the design thinking process. And, yes, I admit it, I was most excited (and took lots of pics) of the cast of the television series *This Is Us*. (A girl's gotta have her vices.)

In some ways, the television series *This Is Us* is a good metaphor for us humanists, isn't it? The show asks us to take a good hard look at the real struggles affecting our disciplines, inside and outside the academy. Who are we?—The Humanities—in the eyes of our viewers, now really? In the eyes of my students, we are "soft," "lacking financial viability," and "lacking application in the real world." We are a series of disciplines often too abstract to be able to define—most students have no idea what the "humanities" are and which disciplines they include—and too useless to spend precious tuition dollars. They are so impractical, aren't they? But when I started to share examples of young innovators working at the intersection of disciplines, my students' eyes started to light up.

Have you ever heard of Mike Ford, the "Hip Hop Architect," I'd ask? They hadn't. Ford created what he calls The Hip Hop Architecture Camp®, which "positions Hip Hop culture as a catalyst to introduce underrepresented youth to architecture, urban planning, and design." Have you ever seen the underwater sculptures sunken by artist Jason deCaires Taylor? These structures have become both tourist attractions and coral and reef substrates for regrowth. Yes, art can have a concrete and real impact on the environment. Quirky, funny, and odd, my students laughed and reflected when they heard the TED Talk by Kate Hartman on "The Art of Wearable Communication." Hartman's work questions, as she asks at the end of her talk: "how can we maintain a sense of wonder and a sense of criticality about the tools we use and maintain to relate to the world?"

How can we, in the humanities, I subsequently wondered, further this sense of wonder in our students as well? Through sustained cross-disciplinary research, reflection about the purpose of education in their lives, and student-centered conversations, the young minds before me, in fact, began to reevaluate their own professional futures, with "us" in mind.

With Us in Mind

When I myself started to expand where I looked, I found that both the arts and humanities were already actively involved in an exciting array of enterprises across a vast number of disciplines that invigorate, re-humanize, contextualize, and pluralize our life experiences. Is it any wonder that we have been witnessing a rise in programs in the public humanities, environmental humanities, sustainable design, data visualization, creative entrepreneurship, digital humanities, business ethics, medical humanities, creative investing, geohumanities, and more? Yes, our enrollments in traditional humanities majors may be going down, but would our data suggest otherwise if we included all of the inter-, cross-, and transdisciplinary schools and programs in existence today?

I started noticing that there are industry leaders in fields as varied as bioengineering, cybersecurity, and health care who are already recognizing that success in their fields is looking more humanistic every day. For instance, Craig Martin, president and CEO of Jacobs Engineering Group, Inc., told students at a talk on ethics in engineering at my alma mater, the University of Kansas, that "It takes courage and conviction to put ethical considerations at the forefront of [your] work and to never be complacent about integrity or sacrifice [your] principles." In essence, leaders like Martin are finding evidence that those individuals who have gained deep and defining knowledge from the study of philosophy and ethics, global cultural understanding, or religious studies are most able to lead us into a future that can sustain humanity across various sectors of society.

And there are specks of light on the horizon. Increasingly, students are gaining valuable skills *and* knowledge in the development of their humanistic abilities: in the field of ecospheric studies, students are exploring the importance of contextualizing environmental impact and energy use in human histories, cultures, and communities; in the field of criminal justice reform, they are examining work innovations that humanize prisons and build holistic education-to-work pipelines. In the health professions, they are examining the impact of storytelling on the well-being of both patients and practitioners.

Engineers are also more consistently asked to consider contexts, cultures, and the impact of their work on living environments. This means that they need to know and respect, humbly, a communities' religious and spiritual beliefs, the artistic, economic, and environmental elements that define the past and present history of their lives, which include their building materials and crafts, the role of women and children in their social spaces, their communities' linguistic idiosyncrasies, and, among others, the rituals that define their births, lives, and deaths. To that end, Union College offers Liberal Arts and Engineering for students who want to amplify their engineering coursework with broader study in the visual arts, sociology, philosophy, foreign languages, and more.

Many medical institutions are starting to pay attention to the ways in which the arts and humanities provide not just "added benefits" but integral knowledge to future medical professionals. Although no Arts + Humanities + STEM program data exists, a quick survey reveals there are over 40 undergraduate and graduate programs in the medical humanities alone, including Baylor University's Medical Humanities Program, Stanford's Medicine and Muse program, and the University of Virginia's Law and Humanities.

Rita Charon, pioneering leader of the Narrative Medicine program at Columbia University, chairs the Department of Medical Humanities and Ethics in the Vagelos College of Physicians and Surgeons. The department, states its webpage, helps medical students and practitioners "understand and address the complex human experiences inherent in health, illness, and death" (Division of Narrative Medicine). To do so, the program covers several areas of study, including philosophy, literary studies, history, religious studies, law, social sciences, and the arts. It's become one of the most well-known programs in the world.

And as our disciplines open up to one another, we also find more entrepreneurs affecting change at the intersections. For instance, did you know that noise tops all hospital complaints and can negatively affect patient recovery? In fact, The Archives of Internal Medicine found that in 2012, noise level in hospitals peaked at 80.3 decibels, far exceeding the recommended 35 decibels recommended by the World Health Organization (Sparacino). Electronic musician Yoko Sen learned this first-hand when she found herself sick in a hospital bed disquieted by the vexing noises of alarms, beeps, and screams around her. Compassionate about alleviating suffering, this perceptive ambient electronic musician created a company called Sen Sound. She then spent her time transforming the sound experience in hospitals by humanizing and dignifying patients' and staff experiences. Her question to you is: what is the last sound you want to hear at the end of your life?

The benefits of addressing not just complex, but also daily, small, and impactful responses to human experiences are just as important in the growing field of environmental studies. Take the TED Talk of social entrepreneur Jae Rim Lee. She is an artist and MIT graduate who brought together fashion and flesh-eating mushrooms to reimagine funeral practices. Her goal is to shift how society thinks about our environmental impact not just on earth, but quite literally *in* earth. To that end, she developed a more ethical alternative for the postmortem body's decomposition called the "Infinity Burial Suit," which she is selling through her company Coeio.

I showed this TED Talk in a research-based course I teach at Union College on the arts and humanities. What I thought was going to be a quick show-and-tell, took over the entire hour and 40 minutes. The burial suit collided with the core cultural values of individuals with different religious and spiritual backgrounds and engagements with their own material bodies. Even those students who were avid environmentalists grappled with this organic decomposition practice.

While many schools of entrepreneurship might hail the work of Jae Rhim Lee as an extraordinary example of thinking outside the box—please forgive the pun—in actuality, the real-life reaction to the Infinity Burial Suit is a stark reminder that every entrepreneurship program should include core courses in religious studies, sustainable design, human culture, and ethics; because our severe environmental problems need to be reappraised, quite literally, from the underground up. And we can start by reevaluating the core requirements of our majors and minors.

In fact, I would argue that in this era, every innovation and entrepreneurship program needs to be removed from business and economics departments and placed in more multidisciplinary centers and collaboratives with strong representation of arts and humanities programs and area studies programs such as LatinX Studies, Africana and Asian Studies, Indigenous Studies, and Women and Gender Studies. Why? In an article titled "A holistic person perspective in measuring entrepreneurship education impact," scholar Tine Lynfort Jensen quoted a study from Brock and Steiner that found that "75% of 107 [entrepreneurship] courses in the U.S. and Europe were placed in business schools" (355, 2014). By removing and recentering our programs, we clearly communicate that our future should be driven by an inclusive and integrative thinking and learning approach that is not only driven by financial success; because we can't find solutions to problems in (human) isolation. Yes, economic success and knowledge matter greatly in the building of a for- or non-profit enterprise, but so does the impact that our work will have on our communities. And those solutions are always driven by their impact on real people.

"Humanitarian Competition"

The problem is that the economic priority of most innovation and entrepreneurship programs correlates to our nation's overarching investment philosophies. Over the past 20 years, the United States has invested in economic productivity over its education system and the well-being of its citizens. The results, of course, have become painfully visible during the COVID pandemic.

The GII 2019 Innovation Index, which provides innovation performance metrics of 129 countries and economies worldwide, ranked the United States in the third place according to comparable income groups, after Switzerland and Sweden, but before the Netherlands, the United Kingdom, Finland, and Denmark (15). In stark contrast, an extensive study titled "Measuring Human Capital: a Systematic Analysis of 195 Countries and Territories, 1990–2016" examined the investment in education and health care as measurements of a country's commitment to economic growth. The United States ranked in an embarrassing 27th place, with Finland in first. In 1990, the United States was ranked sixth (Lim et al., 2018).

So, what happened? US ranking dropped because of its minimal investment in educational attainment and human capital, which according to the President of the World Health Organization, Jim Yong Kim, is defined as "the sum total of a population's health, skills, knowledge, experience, and habits" (Unprecedented Study, 2018). Without strategic investments in more human capital generally, and in education more specifically, researchers believe that the United States "risks falling behind even further" while China, among other countries, clearly appears to be "on an upward trajectory" ("Education", 2022).

The worrisome cost of this economic path has been met by non-profit leaders who are working to better align political, economic, and social actors. To that effect, the sector has grown 20% in recent years compared to the 2–3% of the profit sector. In addition, hiring in this sector has grown more than 50% because the non-profit industry is enjoying more financial and public support ("Non-Profit", 2022). According to the Urban Institute, "the sector contributed $985.4 billion to the US economy in 2015, composing 5.4 percent of the country's gross domestic product" ("Global Innovation", 2019). In 2022, it contributed 5.9% ("Health").

In the for-profit sector, there are also clear signs that they too are realigning their priorities. In August 2019, a roundtable of 181 CEOs published a new "Statement on the Purpose of a Corporation" ("Business Roundtable"), through which they committed to leading their companies for the benefit of all stakeholders—customers, employees, suppliers, communities, and shareholders. In this document, Jamie Dimon, Chairman and CEO of JPMorgan Chase & Co. and Chairman of Business Roundtable, made a bold statement. He said that "the American dream is alive, but fraying" ("Business Roundtable"). I don't think I am alone when I say: *I couldn't agree more.*

To restitch our fraying American dream, more and more executives are determined to drive their businesses in inclusive, sustainable, and purposeful ways. Darren Walker, President of the Ford Foundation noted how essential these practices are to achieve "shared prosperity and sustainability for both business and society" ("Business Roundtable"). Sure, there is still a lot of work before us. But, the tide is turning. Sustainability and equity are driving the business industry, even investment practices, and change is coming.

Any futurist can see the writing on the wall: the road before us must be driven by what Japanese educator Tsunesaburo Makiguchi over 100 years ago called "humanitarian competition." He foresaw a time when the word "competition" would return to its original meaning of "seeking together" to contribute to individual and social happiness and well-being. In essence, he believed that it is possible to, "choose those methods that profit ourselves while profiting others," and that this philosophy would be "manifested in the creative forces of our cultural achievements, which would be a greater force than military prowess, political or economic determination" (Daisaku 7, 6, 2001).

The 2019 Deloitte Human Capital Trend survey provides evidence that this vision is materializing today. They polled nearly 10,000 respondents in 119 countries and found that social enterprises are in fact achieving both social and financial impact. These enterprises are advancing a vision of "humanitarian competition" by measuring success through shareholder returns and self-identified measures like their impact on income inequality, diversity, and the environment.

It's clear that achieving these goals needs some major rethinking. Broad-based reinvention is hard, and it doesn't happen overnight, especially when the workforce is also becoming more diverse every day. That's why 86% of Deloitte respondents believed in the need to reinvent their ability to learn. They wanted to learn how to improve the lives of their workers, customers, and communities in which they live and work.

To achieve these goals, Deloitte suggested reinvention with a human focus through five principles: purpose and meaning, ethics and fairness, growth and passion, collaboration and personal relationships, and transparency and openness. And they argued for attention to not only *why* these changes were needed, and *what* needed to change, but also *how* to change. Deloitte proposed three approaches to change: by *refreshing* organizations (updating and improving), *rewiring* them (creating new connections that change the strategic direction), and *recoding* (designing from scratch). But the aim for all should be, they argued, human-driven reinvention on a broad scale.

Demographic changes in the workplace are a major component to driving a rethinking of who, exactly, employers and employees are, how they behave, and what matters to them. Why does this matter to those of us working in education? Because, like it or not, we are in the business of developing future employees and employers. Therefore, if we believe in a version of "humanitarian competition," then we must also determine how to refresh, rewire, or recode our own institutions, departments and programs, our scholarship, and teaching. And to engage more directly with "the human element," we must build our children's human capacity, i.e., their ability to think through the arts, humanities, and ethnic and area studies. No matter the discipline and program, we must ignite the next generation's capacity "to shape and create change."

Us Humanists. Are We Changemakers?

Deloitte spoke about a paradox. They said that while we live in a world of amazing technology, it is—and always will be—human potential that moves us forward. Richard Florida, a well-known (and admittedly controversial) American intellectual, agrees. He focuses on social and economic theory, stipulating in *The Rise of the Creative Class*, that "the deep and enduring changes of our age are not technological but social and cultural" (22, 2019). Social and cultural changes are harder to see. They don't grab headlines. They are not published in MIT's top "30 Under 30" or the top ten tech innovations of the year. Because they result, says Florida, from the gradual accumulation of small, incremental changes in our day-to-day lives.

These changes have been building for decades and, as mentioned above, are now clearly coming to a head. They involve, explains Florida, habits of thinking and behaving found in the individual, our values, our beliefs, and our communities. They reshape, says the author, how we see ourselves as economic and social actors. By extension, it is we, as staff members, faculty members, administrators, who can also shift these core values where it matters most: our own habits of thinking and learning, which infuse how we build programs and infrastructures.

Thought leader in sustainability studies and education, professor emeritus Stephen Sterling, at the University of Plymouth, UK, noted how in the past, "the mechanization of knowledge building favored educating people to adapt to change, rather than building their capacity to shape and create change" (Leicht, 2018). This begs the question: how do we expand our children's (and our own) knowledge, habits of thinking, beliefs, values, and behaviors in ways that can reinvent "the human element" from the (under-)ground up, for years to come?

To answer this question, we must pay more attention to the contributions *and* limitations of the fields of study that advance today's education curricula. For example, should every Environmental Science program include a class on environmental justice? Should every humanist learn to code? Which questions and knowledge drive each discipline? How can they provide a mutually beneficial set of foundational skills and knowledge to develop the full spectrum of human capacities? What do the arts and humanities contribute to student learning that no other discipline can? And what is lost when we view the arts and humanities as mere add-ons in this process?

Let's take the case of language learning. At Stanford University, journalist Alex Shashkevich published a set of essays on "The Power of Language: How Words Shape People, Culture". The series conveys how language use underscores stereotypes, how foreign languages can inform our own idiom, and how language serves as a lens into behavior. Essentially, Shashkevich reveals that "studying how people use language – what words and phrases they unconsciously choose and combine – can help us better understand ourselves and why we behave the way we do" (2018). The impact of language on behavior, and behavior on matters as diverse as climate change and justice reform, leads us to conclude that foreign language study, English, and linguistics have an important role to play in the development of the next generation's human capacities, of innovation and enterprise.

Only through deep and sustained learning through the disciplines that comprise the arts and humanities, can we build the human capacity needed to affect change on a broad scale. Because words, images, and sound are the human elements that connect us to one another. And nowadays, that connection is dreadfully fraying the American dream (whose dream exactly?). That's why we need creatives like Adong Judith, a Ugandan author and director who writes plays that move her audiences to conversations about disagreeable or taboo topics. Adong believes that stories can change mindsets; they can humanize and teach us to empathize. She says in her TED Talk "How I Use Art to Bridge Misunderstanding" that writing and acting can amplify voices and topics. She brings silenced voices to the stage to challenge people to reach beyond their own comfort zone and open themselves to exploring the different views and experiences of those around them.

Adong's work is one of thousands of examples of the powerful impact the arts and humanities have on open and inclusive relationship-building, elements that we need to transform educational programs, workplaces, and communities. There is no better example of this than the chapter in this volume written by M. André Goodfriend about "Diplomacy as Entrepreneurial Humanities." Goodfriend reminds us that the world turns based on the color of our skin, by the religious, spiritual, and cultural rituals and traditions that define our countries, by the words we use to describe our plights, and the images and sounds that connect with our emotions and describe our beings. By how we connect to one another, and how not. We don't call these elements that define our existence, the meaning, and purpose of our lives "hobbies," "soft," or "a waste of time," as so many critics characterize the arts or humanities, do we? Then let's not cut the flesh and blood—our humanity—from our bones. Lest we want to become a society of robots.

While effective, and, yes, I dare say trendy, the approaches most talked about to affect social change, such as innovation and design thinking, team-building, business leadership training, and skill-building, often overlook core understanding only found in the knowledge and skills we gain through the enduring study of our histories, our cultures, our values, or our languages. I dare argue that the arts and humanities are the missing ingredient to build more equity-oriented results. In fact, I am constantly shocked by the fact that most social enterprises and innovators pay little to no attention to the educational role of the arts and humanities in building the next generation's capacity to affect equity-oriented change.

Granted, I think the arts and humanities have a PR problem. Most students, as I mentioned above, wouldn't be able to identify the 40+ unique disciplines under this general umbrella, not to speak of articulating what one can learn in each individual discipline, what questions they ask, and what knowledge they impart, and how. Not to speak of how they can be measured. To most, the diversity of answers can be surprising; the practical applications of the arts and humanities even more unexpected, as seen in *The Arts and Humanities in the Twenty-First Century Workplace* (www.

ah21cw.com) project, on *4Humanities* or *Humanities for All*. But there is still a clear disconnect we must address. We need a slow, steady, and strategic culture change.

To build the capacity to shape and create change, then, as stipulated by Stephen Sterling, we need to strategically shift the direction of learning to more deeply and seriously engage with our collective plurality. In 1999 and 2002, Waddell and M.D. Mumford hypothesized that "social innovation occurs when new forms of social relations between disparate groups or individuals create new organizational processes that meet common goals" (quoted in Ayob et al., 2016). We desperately need more of this type of social innovation in higher education, in our business, and humanities programs alike. Thinking with and through the humanities, as Susan Frost in this volume suggests, can build frameworks for broad and bold changes that can be mutually beneficial.

To build intergenerational and multidisciplinary human capacity, then, we must all be open to rewiring our brains and de- and recentering ourselves, stepping outside our *Weltanschauung*, to use a term from my own German heritage. As the contributors in this volume propose, the humanities play a significant role in developing tomorrow's innovators and entrepreneurs in everything from climate change, diplomacy, marketing, health and trauma, medicine, and more. To expand how we think and work, we need to expand who we talk to, who we partner with, and why and how. Can we change the game? I think so. I think we can spark a movement.

Note

1 https://www.gamesforchange.org/.

Works Cited

Ayob, Noorseha, et al. "How Social Innovation 'Came to Be': Tracing the Evolution of a Contested Concept." *Journal of Social Policy*, vol. 45, no. 4, Cambridge University Press, 2016, pp. 635–53. https://doi.org/10.1017/S004727941600009X.

Business Roundtable Redefines the Purpose of a Corporation to Promote 'An Economy That Serves All Americans'. Aug. 19, 2019. Accessed March 15, 2022. https://www.businessroundtable.org/business-roundtable-redefines-the-purpose-of-a-corporation-to-promote-an-economy-that-serves-all-americans

Daisaku, Ikeda. *Soka Education*. Santa Monica, CA: Middleway Press, 2001.

"The 2019 Deloitte Human Capital Trend." https://www2.deloitte.com/us/en/insights/focus/human-capital-trends/2019.html

"Division of Narrative Medicine at Columbia University." https://www.mhe.cuimc.columbia.edu/division-narrative-medicine

"Education". *Science Daily*. Accessed March 15, 2022. https://www.sciencedaily.com/terms/education.htm

Florida, Richard. *The Rise of the Creative Class*. New York: Basic Books, 2019.

Global Innovation Index (GII) 2019. https://www.wipo.int/edocs/pubdocs/en/wipo_pub_gii_2019-chapter1.pdf

Kate Hartman. "The Art of Wearable Communication." https://www.ted.com/talks/kate_hartman_the_art_of_wearable_communication?language=en

Henseler, Christine. *Extraordinary Partnerships : How the Arts and Humanities Are Transforming America*. Lever Press, 2020. https://www.fulcrum.org/concern/monographs/cv43nz67c

"Health of the U.S. Nonprofit Sector Quarterly Review." *Independent Sector*. Sept. 12, 2022. https://independentsector.org/resource/health-of-the-u-s-nonprofit-sector/#:~:text=Nonprofits%20make%20up%205.9%25%20of,points%20from%20the%20previous%20year.

"Jacobs Engineering Leader to Examine Ethics With Students." University of Kansas. School of Engineering. Nov. 6, 2013. https://engr.ku.edu/jacobs-engineering-leader-examine-ethics-students

Jensen, Tine Lynfort. "A Holistic Person Perspective in Measuring Entrepreneurship Education Impact – Social Entrepreneurship Education at the Humanities." *The International Journal of Management Education*, vol. 12, no. 3, Elsevier Ltd, 2014, pp. 349–64. https://doi.org/10.1016/j.ijme.2014.07.002.

Leicht, Alexander, Heiss, Julia and Won Jung Byun. "Issues and Trends in Education for Sustainable Development" UNESCO. Assistant Director-General for Education, 2010–2018, 2018.

Lim, Stephen, Rachel Updike, et al. "Measuring Human Capital: A Systematic Analysis of 195 Countries and Territories, 1990–2016." *The Lancet*, vol. 392, no. 10154, 2018, pp. 1217–34.

Martin, Craig Martin. "Jacobs Engineering Group Inc. Announces Retirement of President and CEO at Year-End." Nov. 23, 2014. https://www.jacobs.com/newsroom/press-release/jacobs-engineering-group-inc-announces-retirement-president-and-ceo-year-end

Shashkevich, Alex. "The Power of Language. How Words Shape People, Culture." Aug. 22, 2019. Accessed September 2021. https://news.stanford.edu/2019/08/22/the-power-of-language-how-words-shape-people-culture/

Sparacino, Diane. "Dangerous Decibels: Hospital Noise More Than a Nuisance." *rn.com*. 2015. https://www.rn.com/nursing-news/hospital-noise-more-than-a-nuisance/

"Unprecedented Study Finds US Ranks 27th Among Nations Investing in Education, Health Care." *Science Daily*. September 24, 2018. https://www.sciencedaily.com/releases/2018/09/180924190303.htm

Chapter 2

Diplomacy as Entrepreneurial Humanities

M. André Goodfriend

Views expressed within are my personal views and not necessarily those of the U.S. Government. This is a personal perspective, drawn from a humanities-grounded career as a diplomat. That being said, it's less about diplomacy, or even humanities, and more about the power of narrative and what it means to be entrepreneurial. It is also not intended to be an authoritative, research-based treatise, but more of an exploration of a concept – that perhaps more than any other academic focus, the humanities are entrepreneurial, providing those who study them with the understanding necessary to identify what is of value and the confidence and expertise to take risks and succeed. And, diplomacy, perhaps more than any other career, relies on entrepreneurial humanities.

Making It Real

In 1979, when I first applied to join what was then called the U.S. International Communication Agency, I began the essay that accompanied my application with: "Wherever there are people, there are ideas and emotions which want to be understood."

My family, like many families in the United States, had ventured to America from elsewhere. Those who established their lives in the United States brought their histories and their cultures with them, infusing them into the American story, while at the same time continuing to share a narrative with relatives who were building their lives in other homes. There was never any question in my mind that languages had a very practical application. They were how I could communicate with family. But, communication requires more than simply stringing words together; it requires an understanding of how people think, of the cultures, the histories and the beliefs that shape them.

My application to become a diplomat continued by laying out why I had chosen to study the humanities at university. I was 22 years old, and this is how I phrased my learning paths:

> One gains understanding not only through involvement but also through study. I saw human ideas and was fascinated by them; so, I

DOI: 10.4324/9781003380665-4

> studied Philosophy. And, through all of our ideas runs the thread of our beliefs, religious and cultural; so, I studied these beliefs too. By the end of my sophomore year at the University of Arizona, I was majoring in Philosophy and Classical Greek as well as minoring in Religious Studies. And yet there were so many cultures; and, they each thought in a different way. I was intrigued by the patterns of their thoughts and their turns of phrases. One of the best ways to gain insight into the way a culture thinks is to study its language; so, I studied languages. Besides majoring in Greek, I added a major in French, as well as taking courses in Russian, Yiddish and Spanish. Like a sponge, I was absorbing the thought of humankind, relating one idea to another, one culture to another. I was rooted in the world of humanity, rooted in its thought, rooted in its beliefs and idiosyncrasies, and rooted in its history. But what sort of plant would grow from such roots? The answer was one sown in the field of communications.

While today, over 40 years later, I might phrase things differently, my sense that the understanding we gain from the study of humanities can be applied practically in shaping a career and shaping a society hasn't changed.

It wasn't until nearly a decade after my initial application, however, that I was taken on as a diplomat by the U.S. Department of State. The name of the agency to which I had initially applied had reverted back to its original name: the U.S. Information Agency, highlighting the value of semantics and the importance ascribed to names. Were we engaged in communicating or informing? Now, in the era of the Internet and "social media," being able to engage and interact with the public seems crucial, but approaches to communication in the twentieth century often focused on the strength of the messenger and the message, rather than on establishing a rapport and facilitating engagement (Wikipedia crowdsourcing 2021).

Communication, to me, however, has always involved engagement and interpreting feedback. Shortly before joining the Department of State, I had merited a footnote in a volume on political communication for having suggested that "the process of message selection and presentation encapsulates the notion of audience feedback" (Negrine 2004, 15). I had been looking at various communication models and noting that prior to communicating, one must first establish that one's messages are being received and understood. This could be by saying something simple, like "Hello," and gauging the response. Are we speaking the same language? Do we understand the same cultural references? Only after we have received and adjusted our messaging based on this feedback can we begin to communicate.

Applying Humanities

Diplomats rely upon the ability to communicate effectively in a variety of cultures and an array of languages. For every non-English-speaking country in which I served: Israel, India, Russia, Syria and Hungary, the State Department provided me time to study the local language and achieve conversational proficiency. As the U.S. Government Accountability Office noted to Congress in a March 2017 report:

> Proficiency in foreign languages is a key skill for U.S. Foreign Service officers (FSO) to advance U.S. foreign policy and economic interests overseas. Effective diplomacy requires the ability to communicate clearly and persuasively with host-country interlocutors and local populations in their languages.

The report further notes that diplomats said that "foreign language proficiency facilitates greater cooperation, enhanced communication, appreciation, rapport and respect, and better access and helps them build and improve relationships with their host-country contacts" (United States Government Accountability Office (USGAO) 2017).

Certainly, for me, being able to have a conversation with someone in that person's language not only opened doors, but also opened windows into different perspectives and attitudes. And when those conversations are about who we are as individual human beings or as communities and nations, understanding the cultural perspective can be key to understanding the entire conversation. Some of my first conversations, as an entry-level diplomat conducting visitor visa interviews, focused on why it was that visa applicants were responding to the question about nationality by providing their religion or their ethnicity. However, when I would tell them that the response should be the nationality that is listed in their passport, their response would be "but that's my citizenship, not my nationality." Every conversation about a visa application had, under the surface, a differing perspective with regard to the nature of nationality and citizenship. Every application for a U.S. passport, or to register the birth of a child as an American citizen, also included the philosophical question about what it means to be an American. But, these were just the basics, the entry-level questions for an entry-level diplomat.

Throughout my career, from the earliest days of adjudicating visa applications to being the top-ranking U.S. diplomat in a country, from considering how one's perception of nationality affects one's approach to the U.S. to considering how effectively the design of technologies is human-centered, I've been fortunate to have the opportunity to apply my humanities studies. And, over the past few decades, "Applied Humanities" has itself been the subject of study and discussion. It's been gratifying to see that the University of Arizona, the university which enabled me to apply a solid foundation of humanities in my career, has itself instituted a degree program in "applied humanities" (https://pah.arizona.edu/). As human beings, we play a role in shaping societies, creating communities and establishing our own individual careers, and we apply our understanding of languages, literature, philosophy, history, archaeology, anthropology, human geography, law, religion, art… all the disciplines of the humanities in order to flourish in those endeavors.

There is a complexity in the definition of a diplomat that is partially captured in the word "diplomat" itself. The words "diploma" and "diplomat" stem from the same ancient Greek root: a document that has been folded in half. An authority authorized to issue credentials might issue a diploma, and a diplomat has been issued the appropriate credentials to be able to act on behalf of the issuing State or authority. In a formal sense, a diplomat requires credentials to be able to carry out the required role, yet less formally, being diplomatic requires more than credentials, it also requires that the person be able to engage tactfully and effectively with others.

The attributes that the U.S. government looks for in its diplomats are (U.S. Department of State 2020)

- Composure
- Cultural Adaptability
- Experience & Motivation
- Information Integration & Analysis
- Initiative & Leadership
- Judgment
- Objectivity/Integrity
- Oral Communication
- Planning & Organization
- Resourcefulness
- Working with Others
- Written Communication
- Quantitative Analysis

And, unsurprisingly, these all readily stem from a humanities foundation.

Knowing how to draw upon a humanities foundation and apply it to life gives one the flexibility to navigate societal and organizational cultures, and helps one motivate a team as a leader. Using the humanities foundation to recognize potential and assess the risk to turn potential into reality opens up the opportunity to take applied humanities a step beyond, into the realm of the entrepreneurial.

Humanist Entrepreneurs or Entrepreneurial Humanities?

Interest in becoming an entrepreneur has grown significantly in the past few decades. In the early 1970s, only a small number of universities offered an entrepreneurship program. By the beginning of the twenty-first century, at least 1,600 universities offered 2,200 entrepreneurship courses (Murphy, Jiao, and Welsch 2006, 13). A decade later, the number had doubled to over 3,000 institutions worldwide offering courses, degree programs and/or concentrations in entrepreneurship (Cornwall, Morris, and Kuratko 2013, 6). Along with the range of courses, there is a range of types of entrepreneurs one can aspire to be… social entrepreneurs, technology entrepreneurs, research entrepreneurs, imitative, solo etc., each with entrepreneur as the subject, modified by whatever adjective best describes the qualities of a person who is seen as an "entrepreneur."

One could say that diplomats are humanist entrepreneurs. Whether in negotiating to end conflict or working with allies to create a framework to safeguard human rights, diplomats regularly take on risk to create something of value to their country and often to humankind overall. Diplomacy has also long been a tool for the U.S. to influence the global economy and encourage jobs, trade and lower consumer costs for Americans. This happens through negotiating multilateral and bilateral agreements to foster stability in global business, as well as through a range of programs to encourage entrepreneurship worldwide (U.S. Department of State 2017). However, rather than looking at the wealth of examples regarding how diplomacy facilitates entrepreneurship and economic growth, let's look at how diplomacy itself is entrepreneurial.

Increasingly, whether in discussing the role of technology, the nature of work or the impact of the "fourth industrial revolution" (Schwab 2017, vii), we recognize the need to be human-centered. Diplomacy, by its very nature, is inherently human-centered, focused on relations not just between governments, nations and cultures, but also between the people within those entities. We, as diplomats, it can be argued, are more effective when we study the humanities because we are better able to spot opportunities to create understanding where there was none, and better able to assess risk, due to our deeper understanding of human nature. Most importantly, a foundation in the humanities helps us see where these things intersect with national interests.

In a human-centered world, humanities is not the modifier, but the subject of the sentence. If entrepreneurship is the ability to recognize hidden or undeveloped value matched by the willingness and expertise to take the necessary risks to turn potential into reality, diplomacy is the application of the humanities to identify enough common ground to build peace.

A Word at the Beginning – The Power of Words to Create Reality

"A speech act is something expressed by an individual that not only presents information but performs an action as well" ("Speech act", n.d.). That we can create something solely through words may be a hard concept to grasp (Green 2007). There are numerous humorous renditions in which God creates light not simply by saying "Let there be light" but by uttering Maxwell's equations pertaining to electric and magnetic fields, because, after all, words don't have causal power, regardless who speaks them:

> *And* ***GOD*** *Said*
> "$\nabla E = \rho / \varepsilon 0$
> $\nabla \boldsymbol{B} = 0$
> $\nabla \times \boldsymbol{E} = \partial \boldsymbol{B} / \partial t$
> $\nabla \times \boldsymbol{B} = \mu 0 \left(\boldsymbol{J} + \varepsilon 0 \partial \boldsymbol{E} / \partial t \right)$"
> *...and there was LIGHT*!

And yet… diplomacy regularly creates and shapes reality, sometimes through words, sometimes with music or through many of the other arts and sports that bring people together. Diplomacy itself is often described as "an art," but more often, it uses art. In its various descriptions, the diplomat is often seen as drawing upon an understanding of the ways in which people understand each other, the ways in which people establish a rapport, in order to advance foreign policy and economic interests. Diplomats are drawing upon the subjects that generally make up the humanities curriculum and applying them professionally to achieve goals.

Writing on the State Department's "Dipnote" blog, Sunsariay Cox and J.P. Jenks note that

> ….the State Department set out to connect American Jazz artists directly to international artists and foreign audiences to share this music, confront false narratives, and improve the public image of the United States in light of racial tension and inequality. Beginning in 1956, the State Department sent American artists and Jazz Ambassadors abroad – as it still does today – understanding that Jazz evolved from and mirrors the diverse and imperfect fibers of American life and democracy.
>
> (Cox and Jenks 2021)

With regard to sports, the State Department's Bureau of Education and Cultural Affairs states on its website that

> We believe that if we can sweat it out together on the field or court, then we can see eye-to-eye with one another. When leveraged thoughtfully and strategically, we know that sports can be a platform to champion foreign policy priorities—inclusion, youth empowerment, gender equality, health & wellness, conflict resolution, and entrepreneurism.
>
> (U.S. Department of State Bureau of Educational and Cultural Affairs 2022)

International music festivals, art shows, sports competitions (e.g. the Olympics) and beauty pageants are all ways in which we draw on culture to find common ground for people to engage peacefully. We are using words, sounds, images and recreational activities to create reality.

Entrepreneurialism – Assuming Risk to Create Value

In a discussion of entrepreneurship, it's hard to escape the notion that an entrepreneurial entity is focused on setting up a for-profit business to monetize an idea. And while a grounding in humanities and diplomacy might help a would-be entrepreneur lead a team in establishing a profitable business, can the actual focus of diplomacy and by extension humanities be entrepreneurial if that focus is not the establishment of a profitable business? It's hardly a rhetorical question. As the call for essays for this volume noted, "When the general public hears the word 'entrepreneurship' and reads articles and magazines that sell us on the '100 Most Entrepreneurial People in ______ (fill in the blank),' they usually think of the fields of technology and the sciences. 'Entrepreneurship' is rarely driven by conversations centered on the arts and humanities." But, this was not always the case.

Just as we noted the significant rise in the number of institutions offering programs in entrepreneurship, Google Books Ngram viewer indicates a steady increase in the use of the word "entrepreneur" beginning at the end of the nineteenth century. By the mid-1940s, the use of "entrepreneur" continued to increase at an accelerated pace through the end of the twentieth century (Figure 2.1).

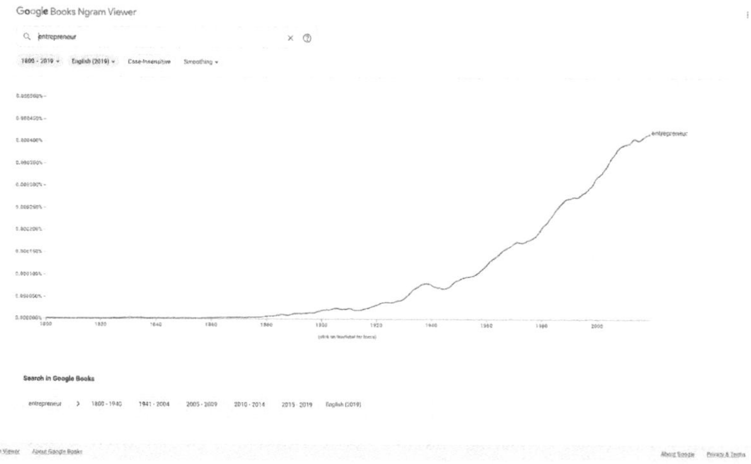

Figure 2.1 Use of the word "entrepreneur" (Google Books Ngram Viewer).

Yet, while the use of the word "entrepreneur" was increasing, its meaning was changing. Wikipedia was launched in January 2001, and the first definition for "entrepreneurship" posted in September 2001 was, "the practice of starting new organizations, particularly new businesses" (2001 Wikipedia definition). However, the current Wikipedia definition, 20 years later, is "the creation or extraction of value. With this definition, entrepreneurship is viewed as change, generally entailing risk beyond what is normally encountered in starting a business, which may include other values than simply economic ones."

This current, more expansive definition of entrepreneurship ironically seems more similar to the definition provided in 1922 by F.M. Taylor (Taylor 1921, 84):

> The Entrepreneur. – The primary, central factor in production is responsibility-taking; hence the primary, central agent in production is the person, natural or legal, who supplies this factor.
>
> Adam Smith (1776) called this person the undertaker, a designation now out of vogue. Recently some writers have taken to using a newly – coined term, enterpriser. But most writers using the English language nowadays employ the French equivalent of Adam Smith's term, the word 'Entrepreneur.'

The Entrepreneur is the agent who assumes responsibility in productive undertakings (*emphasis added*). If our analysis of economic factors has been understood, little further exposition will be required at this point.

> The entrepreneur is not a laborer but an employer of labor; is not a landlord, but a renter of land; (The entrepreneur) is not capitalist, but a borrower of capital. (The entrepreneur) rents from the landlord, borrows from the capitalist and hires a body of laborers; and, marshaling together the elements obtained from these, (the entrepreneur) institutes production.
>
> (Taylor 84)

The New World Encyclopedia's 2020 definition of "entrepreneur" (New World Encyclopedia Contributors 2020) is also expansive:

> a person who undertakes and operates a new enterprise or venture and assumes some accountability for the inherent risks involved. … Most commonly, the term entrepreneur applies to someone who establishes a new entity to offer a new or existing product or service into a new or existing market, whether for a profit or not-for-profit outcome.

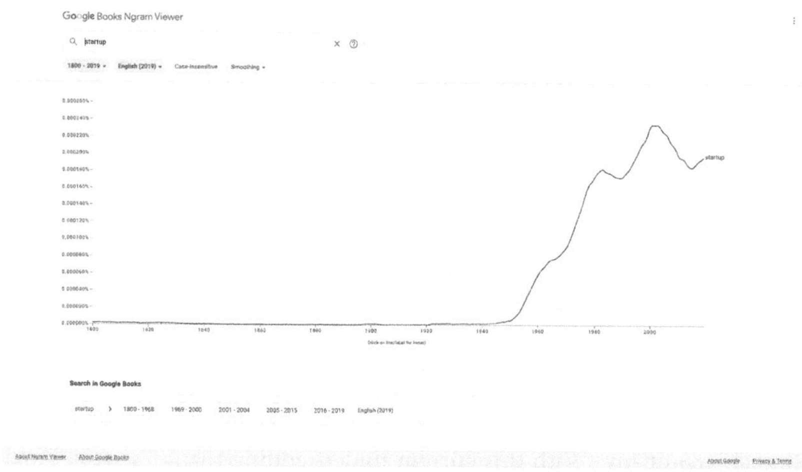

Figure 2.2 Use of the word "startup" (Google Books Ngram Viewer).

And this brings us to how that new business entity, often called a "startup" might be defined. The word "startup" has only been used in the sense of a new business since 1976 (Rodriguez 2019), but its use skyrocketed in the 1980s and 1990s, peaking in 2000, but beginning to rise again within the past few years (Figure 2.2).

Looking at the evolution of the definition of "start-up" on Wikipedia is enlightening.

From

> A start-up (or startup) company is a company recently formed. The word has been much used in the late 1990s, during the dotcom boom, where much stock market speculation and hype surrounded small hitech start-up companies seeking early IPO and promising enormous future profits. Many such start-ups were spin-offs from university research groups.

in 2002, when the first Wikipedia definition was contributed.

...to

> A startup company or startup is a company with a limited operating history. These companies, generally newly created, are in a phase of development and research for markets. The term became popular internationally during the dot-com bubble when a great number of dot-com companies were founded.

a decade later in January 2012.

...to

> A startup or start-up is a company or project undertaken by an entrepreneur to seek, develop, and validate a scalable business model. While entrepreneurship refers to all new businesses, including self-employment and businesses that never intend to become registered, startups refer to new businesses that intend to grow large beyond the solo founder. At the beginning, startups face high uncertainty [4] and have high rates of failure, but a minority of them do go on to be successful and influential. [5]

in January 2022, the most recent definition at the time of this writing.

As with the much older word "entrepreneurship," the word "startup" has also matured, taking on a fuller meaning than a recently formed "hitech" company. With this current understanding that a "startup" may be a project undertaken by someone determined to take on risk to create something of value while validating a scalable business model, let's take a look at a diplomatic startup.

The United Nations as a "Startup"

In June 1941, when nearly all of Europe had fallen to the Axis powers, nine exiled governments (Belgium, Czechoslovakia, Greece, Luxembourg, the Netherlands, Norway, Poland, Yugoslavia and General de Gaulle of France) as well as Great Britain, Canada, Australia, New Zealand and the Union of South Africa met and declared

> That the only true basis of enduring peace is the willing cooperation of free peoples in a world in which, relieved of the menace of aggression, all may enjoy economic and social security; and that it is their intention to work together, and with other free peoples, both in war and peace to this end.
>
> ("1941: The Declaration of St. James' Palace", n.d.)

Two months later the President of the United States and the Prime Minister of the United Kingdom took this vision for a better future further, stating that

> they believe all of the nations of the world, for realistic as well as spiritual reasons, must come to the abandonment of the use of force. Since no future peace can be maintained if land, sea or air armaments continue to be employed by nations which threaten, or may threaten, aggression outside of their frontiers, they believe, pending the establishment of a wider and permanent system of general security, that

> the disarmament of such nations is essential. They will likewise aid and encourage all other practicable measures which will lighten for peace-loving peoples the crushing burden of armaments.
>
> ("'The Atlantic Charter' – Declaration of Principles issued by the President of the United States and the Prime Minister of the United Kingdom" 2018)

At the beginning of January 1942, 26 States at war with the Axis powers signed a document titled "Declaration by United Nations" in which they "subscribed to a common program of purposes and principles embodied in ... the Atlantic Charter."

With this vision statement and the support of a growing number of States, statesmen and diplomats took on the risk and

> the supreme responsibility resting upon us and all the United Nations to make a peace which will command the goodwill of the overwhelming mass of the peoples of the world and banish the scourge and terror of war for many generations.

Subsequent meetings, still taking place while the world was in the throes of war, focused on establishing the type of "World Organization" necessary to implement this ambitious vision. By March 1, 1945, 21 additional states had signed the "Declaration by United Nations" ("Foreign Relations of the United States: Diplomatic Papers, 1942, General; the British Commonwealth; the Far East, Volume I", n.d.).

The Charter of the United Nations was signed on June 26, 1945 by the representatives of the 50 countries. World War II ended on September 2, and the UN officially came into existence on October 24, 1945. The establishment of the United Nations was an initiative undertaken with significant investment and risk, in the hopes that its innovative and ambitious approach would realize something of great value – world peace.

The Ever-Present Question of our Humanity and What we Value

There was much more to the establishment of the United Nations, however, than the development of a scalable business model. One element that distinguished the United Nations from the League of Nations, which had been formed in the aftermath of World War I, in an effort to prevent the future outbreak of war, was not only the scale of its vision, but also the manner in which nations were perceived. A principle promoted by President Wilson and accepted by the allies was that of national "self-determination," i.e., that a "people, usually possessing a certain degree of national consciousness, should be able to form their own state and choose their own government" ("self-determination | Definition, History, &

Facts | Britannica" 2021). So, empires were dismantled and new nation-states were created. But, not all members of the peoples who identified as nations were living in the same newly-formed states. Some peoples also found that they continued to be without a nation-state in which they could choose their own government. The League of Nations established a series of guarantees to safeguard the rights and culture of these "national minorities" as separate communal entities within the States where they resided. Whereas the League of Nations saw its mission as primarily to prevent the outbreak of war, the vision of the United Nations was less to prevent war and more to promote a global system of peaceful coexistence in which member States acknowledged a universal set of human rights and agreed to safeguard the rights of all their citizens, not as members of a separate national minority, but as citizens of the State in which they lived (Jackson Preece 1998, 95).

The diplomatic effort to establish the United Nations drew heavily upon an understanding of what it means to be a human being, what is a cultural heritage and what are the human rights that could be considered universal ("Universal Declaration of Human Rights | United Nations", n.d.).

And if the establishment of the United Nations can be seen as an entrepreneurial endeavor, could not also the establishment of a political state or the consolidation of a people behind a national identity?

The preamble to the U.S. Constitution reads:

> We the people of the United States, in order to form a more perfect union, establish justice, insure domestic tranquility, provide for the common defense, promote the general welfare, and secure the blessings of liberty to ourselves and our posterity, do ordain and establish this Constitution for the United States of America.

Could this not be seen as the vision statement for the startup nation that was being established through the words that follow? And when Abraham Lincoln references that the founders had "brought forth on this continent, a new nation, conceived in Liberty, and dedicated to the proposition that all men are created equal," how different is that than a CEO referencing the founder's vision, yet arguing that the value of sustaining this enterprise was not for financial profit, but for a principle that stems from an understanding of the humanities?

Why Not? And the Art of the Possible

Perhaps it was the serpent in the Garden of Eden who was the first entrepreneur, saying to Eve (according to George Bernard Shaw): When you and Adam talk, I hear you say "Why?" Always "Why?" You see things; and you say "Why?" But I dream things that never were; and I say "Why not?" (Shaw 1921, Part 1, Act 1).

Entrepreneurs look around them, at people, at objects, at ideas... and recognize value. Even when the value of what they perceive is hidden or undeveloped, entrepreneurs recognize its potential. And, while those who are not entrepreneurs may also see the same indicators of potential value, they are dissuaded from turning the potential into reality because the obstacles seem too daunting and the risks seem too great. But entrepreneurs, after asking "why not?" are willing to take those risks.

But, the "why not?" question is essential in order to assess the risks and turn a vision into a reality, to engage in what, as Count Otto von Bismark framed it "die Lehre des Möglichen" often translated as "the art of the possible," but more accurately meaning the doctrine of achieving the most possible (von Waldeck 1867). And, while Bismark ascribed this doctrine to politics, he was describing the manner in which war was being avoided and relationships between Russia, Prussia, Austria and France were being established. He was describing diplomacy.

Epilogue – An Enterprising Word at the End

In this chapter, I realize I've focused a lot on words, their meanings and their ability to shape our perspectives, events and reality. Languages, literature, history, cultural identity all draw on words and our ability to create a narrative, turn the world around us into a story that can inspire.

We've already seen how the words "enterprise" and "entrepreneur" are connected. An entrepreneur shoulders risk in the hopes of launching a successful enterprise.

And "Enterprise" is also a well-known name for a ship. The U.S. Naval Institute relates that

> the first American ship named 'Enterprise' was a 70-ton sloop which originally belonged to the British and cruised on Lake Champlain to supply their posts in Canada. The ship was captured for the Americans by Benedict Arnold on May 18, 1775. He fitted her out with 12 long 4-pound carriage guns and ten swivels and renamed her 'Enterprise'.
>
> (Jorgensen 2011)

As if this were a parable, I like to think that Arnold renamed the sloop the Enterprise after he had it fitted out with the armaments necessary to succeed in the face of risk.

Over the course of the next nearly 200 years, there were seven more American navy vessels named "Enterprise" before the name of a fictional starship with a mission to boldly go where no one has gone before (Jefferies, Jaeger's, and Guyett, n.d.). The story of the fictional U.S.S. Enterprise from Star Trek so inspired the public that hundreds of thousands wrote letters to NASA asking that the first space shuttle also be named "Enterprise." And so it was. President Gerald Ford acknowledged the impact of the vision portrayed in "Star Trek" when he proclaimed at the naming ceremony for the space shuttle that "To explore the frontiers of space, there is no better ship than the space shuttle, and no better name for that ship than the Enterprise" (Edwards 2018).

The mission of the U.S.S. Enterprise in the original Star Trek series seemed like that of a naval vessel exploring uncharted waters, but by "Star Trek: The Next Generation," the U.S.S. Enterprise was structured like a traveling embassy engaged in diplomacy (Grech and Abercrombie-Winstanley, n.d.).

The ability to shape the narrative is the ability to shape reality and, as the ever-diplomatic Captain Picard of the U.S.S. Enterprise would say, to "Make it so."

Works Cited

"1941: The Declaration of St. James' Palace." n.d. United Nations. Accessed February 5, 2022. https://www.unsecretariat.net/sections/history-united-nations-charter/1941-declaration-st-james-palace/index.html.

Cornwall, Jeffrey R., Michael H. Morris, and Donald F. Kuratko. 2013. *Entrepreneurship Programs and the Modern University*. N.p.: Edward Elgar Pub. Limited.

Cox, Sunsariay, and J. P. Jenks. 2021. "Jazz Diplomacy: Then and Now – United States Department of State." *State Department*. https://www.state.gov/dipnote-u-s-department-of-state-official-blog/jazz-diplomacy-then-and-now.

Edwards, Amy H. 2018. "What's In a Name? American Vessels Called Enterprise." *The Unwritten Record*. https://unwritten-record.blogs.archives.gov/2018/09/04/whats-in-a-name-american-vessels-called-enterprise/.

"Foreign Relations of the United States: Diplomatic Papers, 1942, General; the British Commonwealth; the Far East, Volume I." n.d. Foreign Relations of the United States: Diplomatic Papers, 1942, General; the British Commonwealth; the Far East, Volume I – Office of the Historian. Accessed February 5, 2022. https://history.state.gov/historicaldocuments/frus1942v01/d18.

Green, Mitchell. 2007. "Speech Acts (Stanford Encyclopedia of Philosophy)." *Stanford Encyclopedia of Philosophy*. https://plato.stanford.edu/entries/speech-acts/.

Jackson Preece, Jennifer. 1998. *National Minorities and the European Nation-states System*. N.p.: Clarendon Press.

Jefferies, Matt, Alex Jaeger's, and Roger Guyett. n.d. "USS Enterprise (NCC-1701)." Wikipedia. Accessed January 14, 2022. https://en.wikipedia.org/wiki/USS_Enterprise_(NCC-1701).

Jorgensen, Janis. 2011. *Naval History*. U.S. Naval Institute. https://www.navalhistory.org/2011/05/18/ the-first-enterprise-2.

Murphy, Patrick J., Jianwen Jiao, and Harold Welsch. 2006. "A Conceptual History of Entrepreneurial Thought." *Journal of Management History* 12, no. 1: 12–35. 10.1108/13552520610638256.

Negrine, Ralph. 2004. *Politics and the Mass Media in Britain*. N.p.: Taylor & Francis.

New World Encyclopedia. 2020. "Entrepreneur." New World Encyclopedia. https://www.newworldencyclopedia.org/p/index.php?title=Entrepreneur&oldid=1039119.

Rodriguez, Telmo Subira. 2019. "What Exactly is a Startup? Startup VS SME: Learn the Difference." *Medium* April 15, 2019. https://medium.com/swlh/what-exactly-is-a-startup-5ba629d7a0f7

Schwab, Klaus. 2017. *The Fourth Industrial Revolution*. N.p.: Crown.

"self-determination | Definition, History, & Facts | Britannica." 2021. Encyclopedia Britannica. https://www.britannica.com/topic/self-determination.

Shaw, George B. 1921. *Back to Methuselah – A Metabiological Pentateuch*. N.p.: Project Gutenberg.

"Speech act." n.d. Wikipedia. Accessed January 14, 2022. https://en.wikipedia.org/wiki/Speech_act.

Taylor, Fred M. 1921. *Principles of Economics*. University of California: Rondal Press. n/a.

"'The Atlantic Charter' – Declaration of Principles issued by the President of the United States and the Prime Minister of the United Kingdom." 2018. NATO. https://www.nato.int/cps/en/natohq/official_texts_16912.htm.

"Universal Declaration of Human Rights | United Nations." n.d. the United Nations. Accessed January 14, 2022. https://www.un.org/en/about-us/universal-declaration-of-human-rights.

United States Government Accountability Office (USGAO). 2017. "Department of State Foreign Language Proficiency Has Improved, but Efforts to Reduce Gaps Need Evaluation," Report to Congressional Requesters. No. GAO-17–318. U.S. Government Accountability Office. https://www.gao.gov/assets/690/683870.pdf.

U.S. Department of State. 2017. "Entrepreneurship Efforts." US Department of State. https://2009-2017.state.gov/e/eb/cba/entrepreneurship/index.htm.

U.S. Department of State. 2020. "13 Dimensions – Careers." U.S. Department of State Careers. https://careers.state.gov/work/foreign-service/officer/13-dimensions/.

U.S. Department of State Bureau of Educational and Cultural Affairs. 2022. "Sports Diplomacy." Bureau of Educational and Cultural Affairs. https://eca.state.gov/sports-diplomacy.

von Waldeck, Friedrich M. 1867. "Seite:Die Gartenlaube (1876) 858.jpg – Wikisource." Wikisource. https://de.wikisource.org/wiki/Seite:Die_Gartenlaube_(1876)_858.jpg.

Wikipedia crowd sourcing. 2021. "Hypodermic needle model." Wikipedia. https://en.wikipedia.org/wiki/Hypodermic_needle_model.

Chapter 3

Entrepreneurship

A Radically Relational Undertaking?

Roseanne Chantiluke

I remember the very first time I was called an 'entrepreneur'. I was a curriculum developer and project manager for Reach University on a video call with my then supervisor. We were discussing the complexities of translating a small-scale academic programme I had designed into a long-term organisational project with communities from across the world. 'Rose, you're a hell of an entrepreneur!' my supervisor said, beaming, and I remember the dull discomfort I felt in that moment, the type you feel when someone mispronounces your name. In a way, my supervisor had done precisely that: I'm a Francophone and Hispanophone literature graduate, and I have spent most of my adult life working in classrooms and supporting grassroots social movements; the title of 'entrepreneur' felt like a misnomer to me.

At the time, it was difficult to grasp exactly why I felt uncomfortable with being considered an entrepreneur. Since then, I have not only begun to find the language to describe the source of my discomfort in that instance, but also the language to reframe what entrepreneurship can mean for me and others who might struggle to internalise the term. When I say that I 'found the language' to support my understanding and reframing of entrepreneurship, I mean this in the most literal sense: my entrepreneurial journey as the Executive Director of the Centre for Tutorial Teaching starts with and continues to evolve through a deep consideration of all the things that my Modern Languages degrees have taught me. Through my degrees in French and Spanish, I have learned the foundations behind how we communicate, about the role of languages in how we navigate the world, and, therefore, about what entrepreneurship can mean.

This piece aims to share the process I have undergone in digging through language and meaning to find the grassroots of entrepreneurship. Its structure takes the form of a workshop session that I delivered to a group of British teenagers. Through the session, questions about entrepreneurship and social change were foregrounded through critical tools that my Modern Language degrees bestowed to me: questioning, dialogue, and an analysis of the language we use every day.

DOI: 10.4324/9781003380665-5

Part I: Difficult Definitions

It took a 2021 online workshop with a group of 16–17-year-olds for me to begin to understand my reservations towards calling myself an entrepreneur. The students came from a school in West London that specialises in Business and Enterprise. The school also happened to be where I had worked my first job for two years after researching Black French women's writing at graduate school in 2016. I was asked to conduct a session about my experience of student activism with a group of 16–17-year-olds who would have been just 11–12 years old when I first met them nearly half a decade before.

They were no longer plucky pre-teens trying to navigate a large school building with a new school uniform and new social groups; they were young people trying to navigate their imminent post-school careers. I was no longer the school's young 'Realising Aspirations Coordinator', freshly graduated and feverishly memorising the names of students, teachers, and tutor groups in my new workplace; I was an inadvertent entrepreneur searching for clarity about how my work in global education might be defined. The workshop hour served to converge these critical moments of questioning, strategising, and reflection that the students and I were undergoing in our individual lives. So, as a collective, we agreed that the workshop would be an atelier of ideas through which we could chisel out understandings of how we wanted to show up in the world, taking stock of how the work of social movements could frame our understandings.

As we dove into the question of the students' post-school destinations, the theme of the conversation immediately pivoted towards entrepreneurship: many of the students in the workshop wanted to run their own businesses, start their own companies, and go their own way once out of the school gates. When asked about what they associated with the term 'entrepreneurship', they responded with a litany of shorthand references for big tech: 'Innovation'; 'technology'; 'science'; 'money'; 'Elon Musk' … We talked through these references together; it became clear that, for the students, these references offered a blueprint for what the core of entrepreneurship meant to them and for what the outcomes of entrepreneurship looked like: operating at the cutting edge and exercising social, intellectual, and economic influence at scale.

Yet, when probed for personal examples of people who had started their own businesses and what they meant to the students, they offered up symbols of community in the form of family members, local leaders, and organisations who were based close by. One student spoke proudly about her sister's cupcake company. Another gazed shyly at his desk while speaking about his uncle's shop. Students grinned as they spoke about their side hustles while others reflected on their experiences with a local company as part of their International Baccalaureate Business coursework. Here, they spoke of grit, culture, authenticity, and generosity. But they did not necessarily speak about these more localised ventures as entrepreneurship.

What I witnessed emerging in our discussion was a connotative disconnect in our understanding of entrepreneurship. By and large, the students agreed with the definition of entrepreneurship provided by The Cambridge Dictionary: 'Skill in starting new businesses, especially when this involves seeing new opportunities'. (Cambridge Advanced Learner's Dictionary & Thesaurus) However, local community ventures and big tech-fuelled companies appeared to be doing different things for different communities in different ways; it was seemingly difficult to speak of both domains under an overarching, connotative banner of entrepreneurship. When it came to understanding and defining entrepreneurship, the connotative disconnect appeared to be rooted in questions of scale.

I discovered during the workshop that this connotative disconnect was at the heart of my own discomfort with calling myself an entrepreneur in the past. I struggled to align the grassroots-centred approach to international educational programming that I was building, with the large-scale, tech-fuelled, figurehead-driven approach to entrepreneurship that I had internalised from popular culture, just as the students had. Unpacking language and meaning had helped us to define our hitherto skewed understandings of what entrepreneurship could look like. Perhaps it could support us in crafting an interpretation of the term that felt expansive enough to hold imagination and scale on the one hand, while grounded enough to feel connected to community on the other. We had established that entrepreneurship was not a fixed term, but an overarching banner; so, what meaning could this banner hold for us? To figure that out, I did what any good Modern Languages graduate would do: I asked the group to return to the root meaning of the word.

Part 2: The Grassroots of Entrepreneurship

Many of the students in the workshop had encountered French at school at one point or another and so were able to recognise that 'entrepreneurship' derived from the French verb 'entreprendre'. When it came to translating the verb into English, they inferred different meanings in a way that felt both playful and grave. One student suggested:

> I know 'entre' means 'between' and 'prendre' means 'to take'…so maybe, I dunno… it means to 'take between', like to take something from between something else?

The idea of 'taking from between' caught on quickly as other students chimed in suggesting that 'entreprendre' was about finding the necessary middle ground or finding a solution to a problem. As I revealed a common English translation for the verb – 'to undertake' – the students heard resonances with the meanings that they were already discussing. To them, 'to undertake' or to take something 'from under' was just like taking something 'from between': neither of those concepts were about 'taking *over*' something. We spoke about the top-down approach that was implicit in the verb to 'take over' and how it differed from the bottom-up approach that was potentially implicit in the verb 'to undertake'. I introduced a concept into the discussion that could anchor the 'bottom-up' potential of entrepreneurship more precisely: the grassroots. To do this, I used a recent podcast episode I had listened to which had supported my own understanding of how the two concepts could be connected.

At that point, the workshop presentation gave way to the deep timbre of Samia Abou-Samra's voice from their episode feature on the Healing Justice Podcast. Through the recording, Samia guided the students through the potential relationship – both connotative and practical – between entrepreneurship and grassroots organising:

> [...] the root of the word is a French word 'entreprendre' to undertake, so to take something from under... it's like a grassroots approach....to take matters into our own hands is the way I interpret that, so it's an undertaking, and the way we think of enterprise to me is just another word for a community with a collective mission...
>
> (Irresistible fka Healing Justice Podcast)

Samia's understanding of entrepreneurship was intrinsically linked to a collective-focused and grassroots undertaking. This understanding was antithetical to the large-scale tech ventures that the students had mentioned at the start of the conversation and felt more in-keeping with the local business ventures that the students described later. The local West London organisation, the grocery shop, and the cupcake company were all examples of entrepreneurship because they were spaces of possibility and mission that were rooted in a community. Samia's definition also resonated with my individual sense of what I wanted my company's work in global educational training services to achieve: a dynamic community rooted around a common mission.

Through the meticulous work of linguistic analysis, the students and I had begun to reframe connotations and denotations of entrepreneurship. In so doing, we were using language to carve out a collective space of meaning-making for what entrepreneurship could look like for each of us. As we considered what this understanding of entrepreneurship could look like in practice, we turned away from linguistic analysis and towards the philosophical cornerstones of impactful language learning itself.

Part 3: Language and Grassroots Undertakings

I believe that, at its heart, the study of Modern Languages is about more than developing proficiency in the functional skills of a different language. It's about developing a critical engagement with the world around us. Through the practice of French and Spanish translation, I learned how communicating meaning from one language to another is a process of negotiation between different times, spaces, and places. Through analysing literature written in French and Spanish, I considered how identities and histories are built, narrativised, and understood in different contexts. When I lived abroad in France and in Chile as part of my degree study, I was faced with the complexities of communication as a dynamic encounter between different established beliefs and cultural practices. Studying Modern Languages demands self-awareness, deepens humility, and develops empathy as it privileges the process of meaning-making and storytelling over attaining 'fluency' in functional skills.

As I spoke to the students in the workshop about my experiences of student activism, I mentioned practices in student activist spaces in which I participated most actively. These practices fell loosely under the 'public engagement' domain of activism. Given the complex relational skills that I had been learning through my Modern Languages degrees, it was natural that the public engagement side of activism drew me in the most. Much of the work that I performed as a student activist was around supporting friends and fellow organisers in building a collective story around our causes and thinking of different ways to share that story with the world.

I peppered this segment of the workshop with anecdotes about the discussions I had with local community leaders, educators, and business owners in Oxford about what student movements meant for Oxford city's community at large. I opened up about moments where sharing our story resulted in conflict, about how so much of the work of collective movement-building is about fighting the discursive battle for the ability to assert and maintain one's narrative. I explained how a movement's core tenets and objectives can be built through general assemblies where people from all walks of life can tell their own story. I talked through the methods of improvisation that were used to tackle logistical challenges, and the language we used to talk about internal group conflict and how to resolve it.

Student activism has been my training ground for operating within 'a community with a collective mission'. Yet, if student activism has provided me with entrepreneurial scaffolding, this scaffolding has been supported by the sturdy foundations of Modern Language learning. What I have learned from my degrees around relational dynamics and intercultural encounters has allowed me to enter student activist spaces with a clear focus on collective meaning-making. Together, my experiences of student activism and Modern Language learning lie at the heart of my understanding of what entrepreneurship can look like.

At the time of writing, I am the Executive Director of the Centre for Tutorial Teaching – an educational start-up company based in the UK that trains students and teachers across the globe. My present domain of entrepreneurship lies in the spaces of organisational building and programme delivery. In my work as a Director, I have been – advertently and inadvertently – imbuing my practice with the entrepreneurial cornerstones of relational work and collective mission-building. This process has helped to shape every aspect of the Centre for Tutorial Teaching's practice.

For example, we have embraced the complexity of collective meaning-making by focussing on the *process* of programme delivery and seeing which questions emerge from the ground in different contexts. We draw on these emergent understandings to inform strategy and KPIs, rather than making top-down assumptions about what works. When it comes to programmatic delivery, we tailor language, sequencing, and subject-specific references for different groups of learners in different countries, in collaboration with educators on the ground. In so doing, we recognise that our programmatic practice is about negotiating contexts and cultures rather than dictating approaches that feel most familiar to us. We co-create and negotiate evaluation methodologies with our educators based on what they are already familiar with in their classrooms and what progress and success might mean for them.

Focussing the Centre for Tutorial Teaching's entrepreneurship around community means placing emphasis on co-designing goals – both programmatic and organisational – that are equitable, inclusive, and that inform one another. It means mobilising these goals to establish a collective language around what we are doing and how it came to be. It means to ask questions such as: what power do we have and where does it come from? What is our mandate and how might it shift and be internalised differently in different international contexts? Who does our mandate truly serve and how? To do this, we have needed the self-awareness, humility, and empathy that I believe Modern Language learning fundamentally develops.

Part 4: Entrepreneurship: A Radically Relational Undertaking

The benefits of Modern Languages for the work of entrepreneurship go beyond the transferable communication and research skills that students develop through study. Modern linguists are relational practitioners who can act as bridges of meaning between different contexts. My work in social movements and in organisational leadership today are testament to the complex and impactful ways that languages work supports collective undertakings and offers frameworks for a collective mission. I believe that the workshop session that I led – while about social movements – was fundamentally about language and its connection to entrepreneurship. Practically, the students and I drew on etymology and analysis to experiment with the meanings of entrepreneurship. Metaphorically, the work that we performed was the foundational work of languages: co-creating meaning, sharing experiences and views on what entrepreneurship meant, and learning about/ articulating tools for collective action. The students left with an expansive and individualised understanding of what entrepreneurship could look like for them: that it could act as a shorthand for a range of ventures that go beyond technology and scientific innovation; that it could act as a banner of meaning that can hold ventures of any scale; that entrepreneurship starts with a collective and is sustained by a mission; that entrepreneurship is, at its grassroots, a radically relational undertaking.

Work Cited

Cambridge Advanced Learner's Dictionary & Thesaurus ©Cambridge University Press, https://dictionary.cambridge.org/dictionary/english/entrepreneurship [accessed: Friday 18th February 2022].

41. Sacred Work and Radical Purpose – Ije Ude & Samia Abou-Samra of Turtle Tank, Irresistible fka Healing Justice Podcast, July 17 2019, https://healingjustice.podbean.com/e/41-sacred-work-radical-purpose-ije-ude-samia-abou-samra-of-turtle-tank/ [accessed: Friday 18th February 2022].

Chapter 4

Developing the Entrepreneurial Mind

A Fresh Look at the Humanities

Susan M. Frost

Entrepreneurial vision sees a need and fills it, finds an opportunity and seizes it. This may appear to be a reductive concept, but it is the core of all entrepreneurial thinking. How do we develop the transformative minds needed to become these fearless leaders – innovators who are insightful, interdisciplinary, and empathic thinkers? And, if someone is already that kind of thinker, how do we nurture and expand that process?

Academic environments are built on specificity; highly focused disciplinary silos that encourage thinking *within* a topic. Rarely do academics and students venture outside of the ivory towers of their fields, often claiming that a particular subject is not within their major and therefore, not especially relevant.

Professors are under pressure to design courses that adhere to strict rubrics in an attempt to build uniformity in learning objectives. These quality-assurance measures make grading and explaining grades easier for professors. At the same time, already anxiety-ridden students plead for their professors to spell out exactly what is expected to earn an "A."

With the commodification of education, most have turned the university experience into a product: grades are prioritized over long-term, adaptable knowledge. The proliferation of online essay stores that, for a price, will produce an A-quality assignment, attests to productization of education rather than its truly transformative purpose. How will institutions of higher learning meet the expectations of students who come to education with fixed ideas of what they (and for that matter, their parents, university regents, and legislators), want for their future without knowing what that future looks like? Equally troubling in this rapidly evolving environment is that this educational model seeps from the classroom to the boardroom; what may have worked in the twentieth century may point to failure in the twenty-first with its parade of industrial revolutions. Where do we find the tools that give us the lens required to see beyond specificity and into the peripheral vision necessary for that future? The means to that end may be hiding in plain sight: the disciplines within the arts and

DOI: 10.4324/9781003380665-6

humanities teach discerning a new order in what at first glance appears to be either chaos or not evident to the untrained eye.

This new world where entrepreneurial minds will have a creative field day requires a radical approach. "Putting new wine in old wineskins" is a sorry bet, unless schools of the arts and humanities themselves become entrepreneurial with their content (Luke 5:36–39). What if we dumped old theories of liberal education based on class-laden nineteenth- and early-twentieth-century perspectives, and approached the humanities as a cluster of highly pliable topics, with the understanding that thinking through the humanities is thinking in the very biosphere that creates this new world? The only security to be found in the current maelstrom is that the human condition is the single *terra firma* on which we can find our footings. The landscape isn't as new or as foreign as we may think.

The highly focused, silo-thinking ingrained by our educational system is carried to our organizations. Applying humanities disciplines to our thinking processes instills the interdisciplinary style of thinking demanded by entrepreneurial pursuits which extends beyond the prevailing business focus on data and technology, beyond the latest popular business advice books, and onto the cutting edge where entrepreneurs thrive. Two primary prerequisite talents for entrepreneurship are empathy and vision – talents increasingly touted as modern management and leadership attributes. Here is where the applied humanities advance to the forefront as fundamental, durable topics that teach entrepreneurship.

We have become focused on the fixed answers and quick fixes – but popular business books, while sometimes helpful, are not lasting solutions. They ride a current wave but lack enduring answers because they are topical rather than offering innovation and transformation. The *10 Most Effective…*, or *the 10 Most Popular…* or *the 10 Most Successful…* are just that, fixed and quick. What is in vogue does not necessarily prepare our minds to go deep or to stay ahead of and out-think the pack. One has only to stop and think about past hot trends when everyone was reading a business bestseller, investing time, money, talent, and energy implementing an author's new principles. Where is it now? Does anyone remember? Was it effective? Or, has the magic waned, leaving us to question what was gained and what was wasted?

It is important to remember that the latest business books on the bestseller list usually move to the endangered species list quickly by the time a trend is recognized, examined, written and edited, promoted, printed, and distributed – it is no longer on the leading edge but behind the curve. A publisher's marketing buzz is created, and suddenly an author repeatedly appears on talk shows, and people are chatting the book up; "everybody" is reading it. It is not unlike the hot stock tip which, by the time most people invest in it, has already peaked and is no longer an attractive buy; the real winners are the author and publishers. One has only to check their own bookshelf to find quickly dated material that was sold based on buzz rather than valuable content; it is temporary.

Where does that leave us in higher education teaching the humanities? In a time of monumental "pivoting," flexible thinking is more than a survival technique; it puts us on the cutting edge. Current business literature can give us some insight into coping with change, but this is not new territory, we *have* been here before, and the landscape should look familiar. The human condition is a constant; it doesn't change. Four industrial revolutions have left us with volumes of history, literature, cinema, and philosophy that present comprehensive stories of how revolution becomes evolution, how society responds, and suggest resources for proceeding successfully with whatever transpires. Historical thinking asks what happened, what factors were involved, and what were the unintended consequences? Literature presents a biosphere, a landscape without barriers, and a flow of interrelated, intermingling topics. There will always be love, passion, hope, greed, anger, and fear; how do they affect business dynamics? And finally, philosophy exercises our thinking powers because the key is not knowing *what* to think but rather, *how* to think, how to break through accepted norms and create new and exciting opportunities.

Moving from What to Think to How to Think

Delving into fundamental principles of understanding what changes thinking processes from trendy to visionary is necessary. Where do we go for durable material that transcends time and prepares us for a lifetime of entrepreneurial insights? What will sensitize us to empathetic leadership, transcend aging, and prepare us to pivot in response to change? In a new world, we cannot rely on old, quick answers but must change our approach. This is where the value of the humanities in training minds for vision and empathy becomes apparent because they present enduring principles. The documentation of past cycles provided by writings in the humanities provides insight into the way other industrial revolutions played out, not only in business, but also as a comprehensive picture of the result of dynamic change. The stability we long for is found in the dialectic of past revolutions and today's world. Thus, we must keep our finger on the pulse of current culture, but only as a resource for sagacious application of past knowledge.

Unexpected sources have recently aligned with this idea and have begun shifting the focus of business texts, pushing away from the traditional quick answers. Suddenly, popular business books have begun directing us to the humanities in general and literature in particular as a fundamental resource.

First, in 2013, came Whole Foods founder John Mackey's *Liberating the Heroic Spirit of Business: Conscious Capitalism* with Raj Sisodia. Adding to the book's legitimacy was that it was not a self-published marketing initiative, but rather was published by the respected Harvard University Press. What was the source of these revolutionary business ideas and how were they transformed into an innovative and successful business philosophy? Where did he learn his forward-thinking if not from a business education track? In his confessional introduction, "Awakenings," he tells us that he attended two universities, accumulated 120 electives but *never* took a business course. Only enrolling in classes of interest, dropping classes that did not engage him, he focused on philosophy courses and on the meaning of his own life.

"I had nothing to unlearn," (1) Mackey coaches his readers. In other words, unfettered by traditional business thinking, he was able to create an original business plan based on philosophy, literature, and personal experience. Mackey's nascent vision of conscious capitalism began changing culture. It was not the traditional business paradigm he had followed to transform a formerly hippie concept for natural and organic foods into a trendy and expensive grocery boutique; it was an empathetic approach that catered to what customers wanted both in terms of ethics and beauty.

Conscious Capitalism continues to be a foundation for new directions in business management and leadership for now. Six years after Mackey's book appeared, in August of 2019, JPMorgan Chase Bank President Jamie Dimon announced that the Business Roundtable[1] had redefined the purpose of business. Shifting the focus exclusively from profit and stockholder returns to comprehensive goals, Mackey's conscious capitalism emerged as the darling of the business world. Tricia Griffith, president and CEO of Progressive Corp, in the same *Washington Post* article, observed, "CEOs work to generate profits and return value to shareholders, but the best-run companies do more. They put the customer first and invest in their employees and communities. In the end, it's the most promising way to build long-term value." The new philosophy aligns with Mackey's application of conscious, more humane capitalism.

A surprising new look at the humanities and the purpose of literature followed Mackey in 2014, when Paris School of Economics professor Thomas Piketty furthered the conversation. In his ground-breaking economic tome, *Capital in the 21st Century*, Piketty pronounced French and English literature as foundational to understanding how economies worked in the first two industrial revolutions – and the basis for making sense of today's economic track. "Money was everywhere," he asserts, "not only as an abstract force but above all as a palpable, concrete magnitude." (105)

There is no economic data from the eighteenth and nineteenth centuries; therefore, we must parse the literature of the time to understand the economic landscape. Piketty moves economics from abstract models to an historical context, essentially pairing economics and literature as sister-disciplines: cause and effect. When data does not exist, he tells us, story does, and literature tells the complete tale of what happens with economic change: inflation, global economics, the impact of manufacturing, and the rise of consumerism.

Piketty cites novels as providing almost a textbook – a resource for a detailed account of the impact of economic gain and loss while presenting memorable stories that teach the empathy needed in modern leadership. Reading writers Jane Austen, Charles Dickens, and Honoré de Balzac, he explains the First Industrial Revolution (1760–1840) played out in the lives of all socio-economic classes. If you've ever been mystified by Austen's preoccupation with the incomes of Mr. Darcy (*Pride & Prejudice*, 1813) and other suitors, it is because Austen, Piketty points out, writes economic novels; so too does Balzac detailing a downward spiral caused by inflation in his work, *Old Goriot* (1835).

Again, the question arises are these dated chestnuts with little passing relevance? Or can they produce the foresight needed in changing economic times? One has only to look at the annual theater production of Charles Dickens' beloved *A Christmas Carol* (1843), a work recounting the "old fashioned Christmas" so dear to the heart of business and that, until its publication, was a minor, little-observed occasion. In fact, Dickens is often credited with transforming Christmas into the consumer feast it is today.[2] While producing warm holiday feelings, the story is also one of conscious capitalism: it produces empathy and advocates the joy of "spreading the wealth."

In our current nth industrial revolution, we face challenges not unlike those cited by Piketty. Re-purposing the novel as a way of interpreting the big picture produces the vision needed to respond to similar changes. One could counter that technology today is so far advanced that old revolutions could not compare, yet in each case technology fundamentally challenged and threatened how people lived – the human response remains unchanged.

Beginning with the First Industrial Revolution in 1760, consecutive industrial revolutions have built upon one another with increasing complexity and shortening life spans. As Klaus Schram so rightly points out in his article, *The Fourth Industrial Revolution*, there is even a conflict as to whether we have completed the Third Industrial Revolution (digitalization) and whether it is appropriate to be identifying a Fourth (cyber/physical) or as is sometimes termed, Industrial Revolution 4.0, which, like a software edition, facilitates additions. It also raises the question of whether they slide from revolution to evolution and run concurrently. The outcomes of these dynamic changes portend enormous political, social, cultural, and economic earthquakes. The intrinsic danger is becoming so lost in the complexities of this quagmire, so engaged in the technology itself, that we become blinded to the impact on our society. It is a clarion call for the vision provided by the humanities biosphere, and the situation increases pressure on the humanities to sort out this morass.

The bottom-line question is how these revolutions worked out in the past, which leads us to present times and how seemingly small business decisions may echo throughout an entire culture. The invention of the I-Beam had far-reaching consequences in the evolution of the modern city just as today's iPhone is not simply a telephone, but a cultural revolution.

Solidifying Mackey and Piketty's positions, Joseph E. Aoun, president of Northeastern University, addresses the humanities from yet another perspective. In his work *Robot Proof: Higher Education in the Age of Artificial Intelligence* published in 2017, Aoun not only lays out a case for repositioning the role the humanities in the world of business and entrepreneurship, he also pleads the case for its necessity for survival and flourishing in the coming environment. Re-titling it "humanics," he urges institutions to "re-balance their curricula," advocating for its study as an essential component in developing entrepreneurial networked thinking for the twenty-first century. There is "a need to build on old literacies by adding three more: *data literacy, technological literacy,* and *human literacy*" (xix). He states that through writing within the study of humanics, students also learn communication and design. When students say they can't get a job in their field, it is because they haven't, in many cases, developed the agility for creative application of their field to other disciplines. They are thinking in the silo of a solitary discipline, when they need to be understanding how interconnected all disciplines are. An accounting student, after studying the uses of museums in a humanities course, told me she regretted her major, explaining she found museum studies so much more exciting. It never occurred to her the necessity museums have for accountants who are also passionate about their institutional goals.

Piketty's point, that pre-twentieth-century economics can only be understood through literature, is well-taken when considered in conjunction with Aoun's observation that among the three literacies needed in the future will be data, technology, and the humanities. These authors also raise the question of whether all, or most, novels are economic in nature – and confirm that literature and economics are sister-disciplines, with literature describing the cause and effect of economic movements.

Aging with Grace: Enduring Entrepreneurial Basics

The question arises frequently whether old humanities texts are outdated. "Are these old works still relevant?" a business executive recently asked. For years I have taught Herman Melville's short story, *Bartleby the Scrivener: A Story of Wall Street 1853.* The question I pose to students is how do we deal with difficult employees, and how did the narrator deal with Bartleby? Over the years of asking this, the responses have changed dramatically.

Only three years ago, students positioned themselves in the strident, top-down management approach saying summarily, "Fire him!" Another class showed downright apathy; I considered replacing the piece. The greatest turn-about came recently, in the midst of Covid, when Bartleby's response to his employer's direction, "I'd prefer not to," echoed what the many thousands of workers are saying today, 150 years later, as open discussions on work and its meaning continue to occupy our conversations and change labor dynamics. History repeats in myriads of ways. Depending on what we are seeking from them, literary and philosophical works open productive conversations based on how works are presented.

Reading – as discourse between author and reader, and among author and a discussion group – is an eternal font of new and productive interpretations, in part because the conclusions are found in what readers bring to the author, and also because the author is exploring the human condition. Piketty tells us that "by patiently searching for facts and patterns and calmly analyzing the economic, social and political mechanisms that might explain them," the right questions will emerge (3). Used in this manner, texts change, take on new meaning, and build new knowledge. One has only to look back at a beloved book – if you annotate your books – to find seemingly foreign ideas your younger self scratched in the margins, and a re-reading will produce an entirely different conversation. Textbooks become dated, literature does not; the real issue is how they are read for long-term application; our brains are not data-wired, they are story-centered.

When the Covid Pandemic hit in 2020, university course designers valiantly came to the rescue, moving face-to-face classes to online formats and training professors in online teaching methods almost overnight. Through this upheaval, the idea of teaching an already-established online university course in the applied humanities left me feeling secure in the content and delivery of Humanities, Business, and Critical Thinking. It appeared that the term would be business as usual with everything under control.

What I didn't expect was that the course would indeed change: students, now anxious, in quarantine and sometimes ill, often without jobs or in jobs that became increasingly demanding, would adapt the course materials to the situation. They began re-purposing literature and author intent, finding new meaning in new times. Using the humanities as an applied subject engaged students on a deeper level as the materials were a way not only to think through the crisis, but also to find clarity and comfort in the readings.

The next question that arises is what is classic and endures the test of time? Daniel Pink's *A Whole New Mind: Why Right Brainers Will Rule the Future* (2005) is the launch-pad for two humanities courses I teach. The book, which fosters new thinking approaches, spent 26 weeks on the *New*

York Times Best Seller List. It examines six concepts fundamental to "right-brain" thinking: Design, Story, Symphony, Empathy, Play, and Meaning – all values and processes taught within the humanities, but rarely examined as a feature of traditional business practice. It opens a discussion of the use of non-linear approaches to problem-solving required for entrepreneurial thinking – and seen in the study of literature – by challenging accepted concepts and aligns with the popular process of "design thinking," a system that is focused on the needs of end users.

Teaching Pink's concept of "right-brain" thinking is equally useful in understanding "historical thinking," a process examining the "5-C's, change over time, causality, concept, complexity and contingency." It produces integrated and intermingled aptitudes that foster entrepreneurial thinking by adding a new dimension, all of which is found in the content of the novel (Andrews and Burke, 2007). Querying historical movements, often seemingly unrelated, reveals clusters that in some way may reappear and be useful in cultivating an entrepreneurial mind. Considering a work within its interdisciplinary environment exposes these unforeseen social mechanics. What else was happening at the time of publication and how was the work received?

The book taught students critical thinking: they responded that it was the most transformational book they had ever encountered, often passing it on to their HR departments, their colleagues, and even to their therapists. Happiness reigned, comfort abounded; and so, it was for my business and the humanities critical thinking course based on unlocking business principles found in classic humanities texts. That is, until this book on "right-brain thinking" celebrated its fifteenth birthday, when some students began finding it a little long in the tooth and somewhat dated. What I once believed to be classic now left me at a crossroads: keep it or cut it? While some students continued to find the text amazing, others found it annoyingly *passé* depending on where they were in their own critical thinking development. The book's role was to prepare students to read their humanities assignments in a new way, thinking out of their formulaic and comfortable silo-thinking process, shifting their process from the quick "correct answer" format into a more thoughtful, somewhat less organized, but comprehensive process. I found myself asking, *Who Moved My Cheese?* (Johnson, 2018).

The students' challenge forced me to consider *when* books were published, if they were still relevant and what historical environment impacted the works. That should have been easy, since in literary studies we always consider the context in which a work is developed. I found myself weighing whether the work should be replaced – keep it or toss it? The book, which continues to be used, now teaches two lessons. The value of critical thinking is teamed with a consideration of how materials reflect a time in which they were written and offers lessons in how perspectives and values change over time, an archeological artifact of past thinking.

It was apparent to me that trend-oriented books serve an auxiliary role, working in conversation with the solid, timeless writing of classical literature. In the applied humanities, classic works frame dialogs that move us to think beyond trends and the popular business concept of 40-year cycles. They push us to see how revolutions unfold in much longer cycles of an epochal nature as long as 150 years and are necessary to more completely understand the bigger picture.

A Fearsome Threesome: Literature and Practice

If we must abandon trends, or at least put them aside, where do we go to develop futuristic entrepreneurial thinking? How do we develop the entrepreneurial mind and foster the empathic vision required for leadership and creativity? In reviewing texts for the University of Wisconsin – Green Bay's new Impact MBA program which centers on breaking with normative business programs offered at other institutions and using a new humanities-based foundation for expansive business thinking, I faced an audience-reception challenge. How would humanities readings be received by working adult students already steeped in established approaches to business skills? A colleague and I reviewed a number of texts that we felt worked, staying in somewhat familiar territory for students. Breaking new ground is never comfortable; in this case, it was just plain terrifying. Most concerning was the possibility that the literature or philosophy would scare students away, leaving them wondering whether we were luring them down some ultra-liberal propagandist path.

We chose three authors whose work is traditionally taught within the humanities and whose work could be applied to the course goals and that we felt would help transform students' thinking processes, nurture empathy, and move them out of the silo and into a holistic perspective: Karl Marx, Henrik Ibsen, and Émile Zola. Each text addressed some aspect of management; however, the more we worked with the content, the more we feared that the nuggets of information embedded in long readings would not be succinct enough for a business program. Coming from an environment that thrives on bullet-points and listicles, would they lose patience? Ironically, we soon realized we, too, had been led astray by siloed thinking; we were hung on our own petard. It was the *story* that produced what we wanted for them. For our students, the selections evoked curiosity. Why was Karl Marx, often considered anti-capitalism, anti-business appearing in a business program, they wondered?

When Karl Marx first began looking at the fallout of the First Industrial Revolution, he wrote a series of essays which have been compiled into *The*

Economic and Philosophic Papers of 1844. He was young, only 26, and the industrial revolution was gaining steam and beginning to show its fallout on society. It became the foundation for all of his later works. For the Impact MBA class, it opened new conversations about our own labor at a time when society is equally adjusting to economic and social up-ending. Today, instead of workers migrating to cities and moving from agrarian societies to clock-punching factories, we are moving from that type of clock-punching work environment to a virtual work world.

Students who have studied Marx in the past, dismiss him as an anti-capital, anti-business instigator. Those who have never personally encountered his work make the same assumption based on what they have heard from others. Focusing on Marx's work as an early commentary on the social result of capitalism and the industrial revolution revealed that we were in many ways at a similar point in history. Class discussion centered on the essence of labor; when viewed through this lens, new and deeper conversations in relevance and application ensued. Discussions took us outside the norm to the essence of work, values, compensation, and work-life balance, especially during the pandemic. Problems produced by technology in 1844 are not much different than those we face in our own twenty-first century because these challenges of meaningful labor are part of the human condition. Students were surprised that Marx holds as much – or more – relevance now than when he unpacked the essence of labor unrest in the mid-nineteenth century.

After critics silenced Henrik Ibsen for his social commentary play, *Ghosts* (1881), he wrote *An Enemy of the People* (1882) in protest. His point was that, while the play could be hounded off the stage, the content, the problem he pointed out, would not go away; he suggested that it was swept under the carpet. The play, when repositioned, however, offers in-depth perspectives on leadership, negotiation, and empathy. It becomes an applied humanities topic with his major characters transformed into teachers of empathy, negotiations, and leadership in confronting a community crisis. Each of Ibsen's leading characters becomes an empathic prototype for students.

As an exercise, students are each assigned one of the characters – Thomas Stockman, the town's physician, Peter Stockman, Thomas' brother and the town's mayor, Morton Kiil, Thomas' father-in-law and a factory owner, Hovstad, the town's newspaper editor, and Aslaksen, a community leader and business owner. The students are then instructed to follow their character carefully, to step into his shoes. Withholding personal judgment, they must dissect the character's motivation: who do they trust, who do they dislike, why would they react the way they do, and what are they afraid of? The emotionally charged play evokes strong feelings about characters; students are forced to understand them – even if they don't like these people – as they wrestle with the play's all-to-familiar community conundrum. Problems in 1882 eerily reflect those we face today. The work adapts to multiple problems that continue to hound us: pollution, education, or the lack thereof, and unethical financial dealings among them. Beyond this topicality, the underlying truth of the work is the dynamics of leadership.

Re-purposing old novels is a method of seeing the comprehensive landscape, the whole story of how economics impacts a society in times when there was no data. Entrepreneurs tread unknown ground, often with no solid data; and, as we explore a holistic picture of life and economic impact in uncertain times, novels become guidebooks. As the First and Second Industrial Revolutions went full throttle producing cheap goods cheaply in mass quantities, how did society respond? Piketty questions how changes in manufacturing also changed the distribution of wealth, population centers, and social values (3). As we stand amid another industrial revolution, our situation remains the same.

The Ladies' Delight (Au Bonheur des Dames), a French novel written in 1883, by Émile Zola was the third work chosen for the class. It addresses the effect of the department store on supply chain, employee relations, marketing, and public relations at the birth of modern retailing and consumerism – and how that all ripples through values, class, and culture. Disguised as an engaging love story, *The Ladies' Delight* shows the department store as a complex machine turning goods into money. Perfect for presenting interdisciplinary concepts, the novel shows all the moving parts of retailing and how they integrate. Zola's works are especially interesting to re-purpose: among his literary goals was to deconstruct the Second Empire of Napoleon III (1852–1870) by considering how various elements of it impacted modern Paris and its citizens. In his 21-book Rougon-Macquart series, he deconstructs social institutions and ills: banking, transportation, labor, religion, prostitution, and alcoholism among other issues that impact and are impacted by the modernization of Paris. Zola documents the rise of the department store – as today we witness its completed economic cycle.

Bridging Theory and Literature to Practice and Entrepreneurship

Months after the MBA course closed, we asked students at a gathering which reading they found most impactful. Almost unanimously they named Zola as an author who illustrated how subjects, usually taught as disciplinary silos, exposed the interrelationships among topics. Zola's novel presented an integrated retail business, social, and city model from the nineteenth century and had prepared students for their work ahead, to apply multi-faceted initiatives to their own business projects. It had provided a foundation for integrated thinking.

In developing the course, however, even considering Zola's extensive research in his presentation of the department store,[3] it remains fiction and occurs in another century. The difficulty was to find a teachable correlation to Zola's work. Students needed a twenty-first-century working model so that they could apply course elements to their own organizational impact project. The requirements were complicated and the challenges daunting. Where does empathetic leadership combine with interrelated disciplines that extend beyond silo-thinking, business or otherwise? Equally, how could the new Business Roundtable's definition of the purpose of the corporation – serving customers, employees, stakeholders, and communities – be implemented? Ironically, the cure for this malaise was discovered at the Mayo Clinic in Rochester, Minnesota.

The clinic's unique patient-centered team approach to medicine mirrored the interdisciplinary focus of the Impact MBA course. In the "Rochester Project" as we titled the assignment, students were advised,

> The Clinic's roots are a fascinating look at how interdisciplinary thinking not only affects how they practice medicine but how the Clinic's philosophy has changed the entire community. Patient-centered design and management has been adapted as a way of life in Rochester. In 2018, the City of Rochester lifted the clinic model and created a city-wide comprehensive plan, one that reflects the learning goals of this class. As we work our way through the course, they are an example of how to put integrated holistic thinking into action.[4]

Presented as a credible model, the Rochester model was a management system, supported by their reading of Zola, that could be lifted to fit other management systems. The clinic's comprehensive design, based in empathy, was adopted as a model for city development and applied to all aspects of the city including tourism and hospitality, housing and transportation, and the addition of the arts – theater, music, and art.

The course emphasis on empathy as a fundamental business and leadership principle was further supported by Rochester's designation as a "City of Compassion"[5] by the Charter for Compassion, an organization that "provides an umbrella for people to engage in collaborative partnerships worldwide."[6] With this, students had an example of how the Rochester management model could be successfully implemented and one that exceeded the empty old business slogan, "the customer is always right."

For their project, students were asked to formulate an integrated business plan, an adaptation of the Rochester model to an initiative in their own companies. It was an assignment highly suited to students who were corporate executives and department heads. They had both the means and the employee capacity to initiate company change. But how would this work out for a student who owned a small auto repair shop located in rural northern Wisconsin? Business education is designed for large corporate endeavors leaving small "Mom and Pop" businesses out of their wake. Even the SBA's[7] definition of "small business" far exceeds the average U.S. business in employees and income, leaving most businesses struggling to find useful information.

At the end of the course, project presentations were impressive but most impressive was a student, a small business owner, who explained how she planned to expand her company to better meet the needs of her customers, her staff, and her community. Her focus on an expansion initiative would not only increase her business, but also increase customer and staff satisfaction – as well as benefiting her community. It was innovative, integrated, insightful, and met multiple needs. Her final analysis of the course work opened with: "Who would have thought that business and the humanities would be so tightly mingled together in a woven web?"[8]

Risky Business: New Thinking for a New World

Pivoting from established rubrics in business pedagogy toward innovative and flexible thinking processes takes tremendous courage. However, while business leaders advise university deans that they want leaders who can think in creative and expansive ways, or "outside the box," when presented with bringing the humanities into curriculum as application, their courage often flags in the absence of recognized metrics.

Business schools attempt to meet these needs – yet often scoff at the idea of the humanities being the key to twenty-first-century business thinking. At the same time, humanities departments often hold business in unsavory regard. Aoun is correct in stating that we need to rethink curricula and how we both view and present the humanities as an applicable topic, key to nurturing new thinking processes (xvii). Current movements toward the digital humanities, creating content and social commentary, are important initiatives – bridging the humanities with society in general, and business in particular. Rather than just creating a bridge, however, *thinking through the humanities* is a much larger and integrated project.

Re-balancing curricula using the humanities as a foundation – or at least an equal partner to data and technology – brings stability in tumultuous times. Re-purposing texts written for one purpose may not sit well with those invested in a specific discipline. Releasing these authors from their prescribed silo, however, gives them new life and new respect. Their stories demonstrate how unusual clusters and patterns form, creating strong allies among disparate sectors that shift social paradigms – a requisite for entrepreneurial thinking.

Arthur Miller's tragedy, *Death of a Salesman* (1949), is a case in point. In the play, the protagonist, Willy Loman, is a down-on-his-luck, aging over-the-road salesman. His sales are down, he appears to be suffering from dementia or depression, is a philanderer in a seemingly empty marriage, and his kids, following their father's example, have been tutored for failure. The play opens after the death of company owner, Frank Wagner, and Willy, having spent a lifetime with the company, is let go by the owner's son, Howard, who has inherited the business. When taught as part of the literary canon, the play neatly fits into a conversation on the failed American Dream, the dehumanization of the corporate world, or into Marxist criticism. This is a study in failure without a doubt.

But, as a work in the applied humanities, a myriad of new questions surface beginning with "What is the long-term effect of poor management?" When considered in that light, the temptation to wallow in the piece is replaced by a lively discussion of management responsibility, work-life balance, and how the workplace influences home life, a much larger and far more comprehensive conversation. The late Frank Wagner has left his loosey-goosey management fingerprints all over the lives of Miller's characters. Frank's son, Howard, more enamored by having his name on the door and his new purchasing power than in management is also on a downward spiral. Only seeing Willy's lack of production, Howard fires him leaving his sales territory without representation and with a sullied reputation. Without a plan, no expectations can be set; without training, it is impossible for employees to meet expectations in changing times. Without Howard having been groomed for his position of ownership and management, what is the prognosis for this company? When presented as applied humanities, *Death of a Salesman* unfolds as a comprehensive HR story giving management teams a better understanding of their role and produces better all-around outcomes for employees, the company, and the community along with the stockholders. The new goals of the play align perfectly with the new goals of the corporation as set by Jamie Dimon and the Business Roundtable.

The humanities canon is filled with applicable works. Can Immanuel Kant's essay, *The Answer to the Question: What Is Enlightenment?* encourage brave, independent, and thoughtful reflection? In a rapidly changing world not unlike today, his eighteenth-century society was faced with the First Industrial Revolution and followers who took unquestioned advice from their priest, from their doctor, and others. Marketers can gain a much deeper and lasting understanding of consumer behavior, the fundamentals of desire, and the effect of media by unpacking Emma Bovary's shoes – which Gustav Flaubert used as a metaphor in *Madame Bovary*, explaining the growth and effect of consumerism. And along the way, through these works, we instill empathy.

The fundamental challenge of the twenty-first century is how to develop the transformative minds needed to become these fearless leaders: innovators who are insightful, interdisciplinary, and empathic thinkers. We live in a scary world, existing in the midst of global upheaval. The Covid Pandemic has torn open our institutions, revealing the cracks and crevices in our societal underpinnings that no longer hold fast to shaky ground. Technology is creating brave new worlds that both support and threaten society. It is a time when almost every trusted social institution needs to be re-thought. But – like those who faced other industrial and social revolutions – we also live at a time of immense opportunity. We've been here before. Thinking through the humanities offers insight through hindsight and finds new answers. If entrepreneurial vision is seeing a need and filling it, seeing an opportunity and seizing it, do we have the patience – and the courage – to take the risk of teaching as humanities entrepreneurs?

Notes

1 "The Business Roundtable is an association of chief executive officers of America's leading companies working to promote a thriving U.S. Economy and expanded opportunity for all Americans through sound policy." www.businessroundtable.org/about-us.
2 The Charles Dickens Page: https://www.charlesdickenspage.com/charles-dickens-christmas.html; Books Tell You Why: https://blog.bookstellyouwhy.com/a-christmas-carol-the-influence-of-charles-dickens-on-christmas-traditions.
3 According to Robin Buss in his Introduction to *Au Bonheur des Dames* (x), Zola and his wife spent five to six hours on consecutive afternoons observing the business practices and customer/clerk interactions at Bon Marche in Paris, the foundation for the book.
4 University of Wisconsin – Green Bay, MBA 702.
5 Compassionate Rochester, Minnesota: https://www.rochestermn.gov/about/city-of-compassion.
6 Charter for Compassion. https://charterforcompassion.org/.
7 Small Business Administration. sba.gov.
8 Sandi Banaszak. Banaszak Service Center/Auto Sales/Auto Body, Beaver Wisconsin.

Works Cited

Andrews, Thomas, and Flannery Burke. "What Does it Mean to Think Historically?" *Perspectives on History, The News Magazine of the American Historical Association*. 1 Jan. 2007. Accessed February 2023. www.historians.org/publications-and-directories/perspectives-on-history/january 2007/what-does-it-mean-to-think-historically.

Aoun, Joseph. *Robot-Proof: Higher Education in the Age of Artificial Intelligence*. Cambridge: MIT Press, 2017.

Austen, Jane, and Tony Tanner. *Pride and Prejudice*. Reprint. New York: Penguin Books, 2002.

Balzac, Honoré de. *Père Goriot/Old Goriot (Oxford World's Classics)*. Trans. A. Krailsheimer. Reprint, New York: Oxford University Press, 2009.

Dickens, Charles, and Coralie Bickford-Smith. *Major Works of Charles Dickens (Great Expectations/Hard Times/Oliver Twist/A Christmas Carol/Bleak House/A Tale of Two Cities) (Penguin Clothbound Classics), Box*. New York: Penguin, 2011.

Flaubert, Gustave. *Madame Bovary.* Trans. Paul de Man. New York: Norton, 1965.

Ibsen, Henrik, 1828–1906. Arthur Miller's Adaptation of *An Enemy of the People.* New York: Penguin Books, 2019.

Johnson, Spencer, et al. *Who Moved My Cheese: An A-Mazing Way to Deal with Change in Your Work and in Your Life.* New York: Penguin Audio, 2018.

Kant, Immanuel. *Answer to the Question: What Is Enlightenment? Readings in the Western Humanities.* 5th ed., volume II. New York: McGraw-Hill, 2004.

Mackey, John, et al. *Conscious Capitalism, With a New Preface by the Authors: Liberating the Heroic Spirit of Business.* 1st ed. Cambridge: Harvard Business Review Press, 2014.

Marx, Karl. *The Marx Engels Reader.* New York: W. W. Norton, 1978.

McGregor, Jena. "Group of Top CEOs Says Maximizing Shareholder Profits No Longer Can Be the Primary Goal of Corporations." *The Washington Post.* 19 Aug. 2017.

Melville, Herman. *Bartleby, The Scrivener, A Story of Wall-Street.* New York: SMK Books, 2012.

Miller, Arthur. *Death of A Salesman, Certain Private Conversations In Two Acts And A Requiem.* New York: Penguin Books, 1976.

Piketty, Thomas, and Arthur Goldhammer. *Capital in the Twenty-First Century.* Reprint. Cambridge: Belknap Press, Harvard University Press, 2017.

Pink, Daniel. *A Whole New Mind: Why Right-Brainers Will Rule the Future.* New York: Riverhead Books, 2006.

Schwab, Klaus. "The Fourth Industrial Revolution." *Encyclopedia Britannica.* 23 Mar. 2021. https://www.britannica.com/topic/The-Fourth-Industrial-Revolution-2119734. Accessed 23 February 2022.

Zola, Émile. *Au Bonheur des Dames.* Trans. Robin Bruss. New York: Penguin, 2002.

Chapter 5

Disruption in the Arts and Humanities

Promoting a Mindset of Innovation and Entrepreneurship

Jana Fedtke and Mohammed Ibahrine

Introduction

In this chapter, we critically analyze the changing nature of teaching the arts and humanities in the context of a post-Covid-19 world. We are specifically interested in innovative approaches to promoting a mindset of entrepreneurship. Our chapter presents a case study of the new required course *IEN 301 – Innovation and Entrepreneurship Mindset* at the American University of Sharjah (AUS) in the United Arab Emirates (UAE). An international American-style liberal arts institution in the emirate of Sharjah near Dubai, AUS is in the process of introducing the values of teaching innovation and entrepreneurship to all students across the university in its three colleges and one school: the College of Arts and Sciences (CAS), the College of Arts, Architecture, and Design, the College of Engineering, and the School of Business Administration (SBA). Based on the UAE-Stanford Innovation and Entrepreneurship Education Program, the Harvard- and Stanford-certified instructor Dr. Mohammed Ibahrine taught the pilot class of *IEN 301 – Innovation and Entrepreneurship Mindset* in Spring 2021 and has taught the class on a regular basis since then. Starting in Spring 2022, multiple sections of this class are taught each semester. The course focuses on design thinking, sustainability, innovation, lean strategy, and leadership among other topics.

Our chapter critically analyzes the results of teaching this class to diverse audiences as we pay particular attention to the intersections with the arts and humanities. We also suggest future applications of the mindset of innovation and entrepreneurship in executing business models, pitching ideas as storytellers, and presenting as entrepreneurs. We argue that cultivating an entrepreneurial mindset in the arts and humanities as part of the university curriculum in an environment that traditionally privileges STEM fields and business will enable and motivate students to apply their social entrepreneurship skills in creating future jobs, solving pressing social issues, and building sustainable futures. Teaching an innovation mindset in the arts and humanities as part of the entrepreneurial university will

DOI: 10.4324/9781003380665-7

eventually lead to necessary disruption in education, applied social innovation, and overall societal transformation.

Innovation and Entrepreneurship in the UAE

Given the dramatic changes in society, the economy, technology, and higher education in the twenty-first century, a post-Covid-19 world needs to engage in new and more innovative ways of teaching and learning. Our chapter explores these current changes in the context of the Arab World, specifically the UAE. Higher education policymakers in the country have started to draw on different disciplines to create the right fit to prepare students for the future. They have attempted to rethink the educational system to transform it in light of the challenges of a knowledge economy. One of the challenges is the striking lack of creative human capital. Combining human and creative capital, creative human capital on an individual level comprises "a mix of individuals' own innate talents and abilities as well as the skills and learning they acquire through education and training" (OECD, 2007, 2). The digital economy has become the driving force of the creative economy. The UAE has been undergoing a dramatic economic transformation from an oil-based economy to a "knowledge economy," or "creative economy."

As part of the UAE Centennial in 2071, the country has established a long-term strategy based on four pillars, including a sustainable and diversified knowledge economy that is driven by an excellent educational system. At the center of the pillar of education, the UAE aims to empower students by teaching them "mechanisms for discovering their individual talents early" (UAE Centennial 2071, 2022, "Excellent Education"). On a macro-level, "educational institutions are encouraged to be incubators of entrepreneurship and innovation" (UAE Centennial 2071, 2022, "Excellent Education"). The great challenge for higher education is to harness all that creativity and apply its lessons to the benefit of society. The notion of the creative economy requires us to expand beyond traditional, often separate disciplines such as the sciences, technology, design, literature, philosophy, and art. It is more meaningful to cultivate interdisciplinarity to explore the intersections of the various fields.

We propose to explore this mindset in the regional context of the UAE at an American-style liberal arts university. In the last few years, the UAE government has adopted several initiatives to trigger innovation, entrepreneurship, and economic and social development to face the implications and ramifications of the post-oil era in the region. Entrepreneurship was identified as a potential catalyst for technological progress, sustainable growth, and disruptive innovation. The government has taken policy initiatives such as its determination to make renewables account for 44% of its energy needs by 2050. Another goal to be achieved by 2026 is to turn the UAE and

Dubai into a home for tech unicorns, create 1,000 digital companies, and train 100,000 programmers and coders (UAE Energy Strategy 2050, 2022). Adding to all these initiatives, the UAE Strategy for Artificial Intelligence supports all these macro-infrastructural changes for the knowledge-based economy (UAE Strategy for Artificial Intelligence, 2022).

In light of the UAE's mission to further innovation and entrepreneurship at all its institutions of higher education, our research is interdisciplinary as it focuses on the role of entrepreneurship in the humanities. This chapter highlights the role of entrepreneurship in teaching humanities students in the UAE. Our contribution builds on existing scholarship on entrepreneurship, but it expands it to the context of the Arab World and specifically to the UAE. The UAE is fully aware of the importance of the role of universities as engines of innovation in the creative economy. In the UAE, universities are encouraged to train and cultivate talented and creative professionals.

One of the most visible initiatives is the UAE's National Innovation Strategy launched in 2014 to make the nation one of the world's most innovative countries. The strategy includes three key pillars: creating an "innovation-enabling environment," supporting "innovation champions" such as individuals, companies, institutions, and governments, and "stimulating innovation" in seven key sectors, which are renewable energies, transport, education, health, technology, water, and space (UAE National Innovation Strategy, 2022). In a short period of time, these programs have started to show promising results. In 2021, the UAE enhanced its standing in the Global Innovation Index as it was ranked 33rd globally (4). The UAE was listed among the top three innovative economies in the region in the second place (Global Innovation Index, 2021, 23). Recently, the BBC selected Sharjah among five emerging "art cities beyond the canon of Western art history" (BBC, 2019).

Basco and Hamdan (2019) suggest that students' intentions to create a new business are relatively low in the UAE at only 5%. However, the same students show higher entrepreneurial intentions for five years after graduation (41%) (Basco and Hamdan, 2019, 17). Like many local people in other Arab Gulf countries, Emiratis prefer working in the public sector thanks to the generous benefits, favorable working conditions, and higher salaries. The UAE has, however, recently encouraged young Emiratis to work in the private sector to support their country in its efforts to position the UAE on the global map with regard to prosperity and innovation. This is part of the "Emiratization" of the UAE.

Cultivating an Entrepreneurial Mindset

In light of these developments on a national level, AUS developed a class focused on teaching students the basics of innovation and entrepreneurship.

Among other concepts, the class focuses on design thinking, sustainability, innovation, lean and agile strategy, and start-up leadership.

One of the most acute challenges that new graduates face is whether they are prepared for a new creative economy that "builds on the interplay between human creativity and ideas and intellectual property, knowledge, and technology" (UNCTAD, 2022).

Purg, Cacciatore, and Gerbec (2021) call for the benefits of the profound cross-fertilization between the art world and the entrepreneurial world (3). The current education system still divides disciplines into majors, departments, colleges, and schools and sometimes even celebrates the compartmentalization of teaching and learning. At AUS, for instance, arts and business are taught in separate schools and colleges: the humanities and arts in the CAS and business in the SBA. Classes such as IEN 301 present new ways of overcoming such divisions in an effort to teach students from various backgrounds skills from various fields.

Coined by the psychologist Jean Piaget, the term transdisciplinarity is one of the most discussed concepts in this context (Bernstein, 2015). Erich Jantsch argued that transdisciplinarity marks a meta-moment that transcends disciplinary boundaries and attempts to surpass multidisciplinarity, cross-disciplinarity, and interdisciplinarity (Bernstein, 2015). The new challenge that the educational system faces is how to produce knowledge based on such transdisciplinarity. Any new approach should present a unique program that symbiotically synergizes "between, across and beyond disciplines" (McGregor, 2015).

One of the objectives of IEN 301 is to connect disciplines such as literature, history, language, philosophy, and the visual and performing arts. The class is designed to provide students with an entrepreneurial mindset on which they can draw throughout their personal and professional lives.

Under the combined impact of digitization and Covid-19, some experts advance the argument that higher "education does not need to be reformed; it needs to be reinvented" (Formica, 2020, 65). Such reinvention requires a new entrepreneurial mindset driven by a new approach to trigger creativity and cultivate curiosity and imagination (Formica, 2020, 65).

In the "post-truth" age characterized by misinfodemics and environmental challenges, a specialization of knowledge has increasingly failed. New approaches of interdisciplinarity are needed. Future skills will differ from the ones currently being taught. As *The Future of Jobs Report* (2020) points out, critical-thinking and problem-solving are among the top skills that employers will look for in the next few years (5).

Research has shown that teaching entrepreneurship can promote a growth mindset (Yeager and Dweck, 2012). Dweck (2016) distinguishes between two mindsets: a fixed mindset and a growth mindset. People, on the one hand, perceive their talents and abilities as set traits in a fixed mindset. They take constructive criticism personally and attribute the success of others to luck. In a growth mindset, on the other hand, people believe that their abilities can be developed through dedication, effort, and hard work. They see failure as an opportunity to improve their performance (Dweck, 2016). O'Keefe, Dweck, and Walton (2018) suggest that having a growth mindset supports students, business people, and innovators in developing new interests. A growth mindset of interest is a logical extension of Steve Jobs's statement that "[T]echnology alone is not enough—it's technology married with liberal arts, married with the humanities, that yields us the results that make our heart sing" (qtd in O'Keefe, Dweck, et al., 2018).

IEN 301 – Innovation and Entrepreneurship Mindset

IEN 301 – Innovation and Entrepreneurship Mindset at AUS adopts the original syllabus of Stanford University and contextualizes it with specific modifications to respond to the needs of students in the UAE. The first chapters of the textbook and teaching context cover design thinking, where students are introduced to the design thinking toolkits and empathy map. Subsequently, the students study sustainability principles and sustainable design. The students are asked to work in teams on the Point of View statement project to apply what they have learned. Further book chapters introduce the students to business model canvas, branding and marketing, customer development and personas, lean start-up leadership, and team building. The Opportunity Analysis Project challenges the students to work in any organization, whether private, public, or nonprofit, to use a why-why-why analysis as well as other analytical tools and frameworks to analyze the market. They explore to what extent there is a market gap so that the teams can come up with a creative concept, a clear mission, customer development, and a business model. Other teaching content prepares the students to learn how to present a pitch as storytellers. In the individual final project, the students are inspired to produce a business idea with an innovation that solves a problem and meets the demands in the market.

The class showcases the idea of the mindset in its title because it promotes an entrepreneurial mindset among graduates of the humanities to build a professional profile required by the current demands of the job market. Providing the students with entrepreneurial skills increases the possibilities of self-employment as a career option.

Two student projects from IEN 301 serve as examples to showcase the creativity and entrepreneurial mindset of students in the humanities. Both students are majoring in English and took IEN 301 with Dr. Mohammed Ibahrine in Fall 2021. The students kindly agreed to using their projects as examples for this chapter. As part of their final comprehensive projects, the students are tasked with developing a business idea and an innovative solution after identifying a significant problem. The Personal Plan and Reflection (PPR) is designed so that the individual students are able to harness all the learning material such as empathy map, the portfolio map, divergent and convergent thinking, the value proposition canvas, and the business model canvas. The students are asked to include their reflections on these items in the business model. Another pedagogical component of the PPR is a three-minute pitch in which the student is expected to act as an innovator, entrepreneur, and storyteller.

The title of the first project is "Logos." This start-up is about "providing the platform for the best and brightest minds of the MENA region to share their scholarly and creative work" (Student report, 2021). While Arabic is a major world language, it has produced little digital content. Much more content is available in English and other languages, for example. Digital content in Arabic is rare (Student report, 2021). The solution that the student suggested is to provide a platform that is catered to "languages that use the Abjad alphabet (Arabic, Farsi, and Urdu) and Latin alphabet (Turkish, some forms of Kurdish) in all aspects (design, layout, etc.)" (Student report, 2021). This business idea is innovative and digital in design because it decidedly adopts algorithms which "will recommend readers to more content that suits their tastes and the Fourth Industrial Revolution technologies, cryptocurrencies will be accepted for some transactions" (Student report, 2021). The team needed for this endeavor consists of "skilled individuals from across diverse fields of expertise. Writers, software engineers, advertisers, academics, traditional publishers, and more. Combining people from all disciplines will ensure the process runs smoothly for users and staff both" (Student report, 2021).

This digital platform connects content creators with consumers who are looking for such an all-in-one platform that promises e-commerce features and functions to facilitate any kind of transaction. The student proposes the adoption of digital technologies, particularly e-commerce, as a means of completing any transactions between scholarly and creative producers and their target audiences such as individual users or professional users in the creative industries.

The second project presented a business idea called "Writing to Heal." This business is a workshop designed to wield the powerful tool of storytelling to provide young adults with a medium through which to navigate and understand difficult and unsettling emotions (Student report, 2021). The business started with the identification of the problem that "individuals emerging into adulthood who may not want to face the rigidity and intimidation of formal therapy sessions have limited options in terms of working through their complicated emotions and experiences" (Student report, 2021). The project assumes that there is an urgent need to address issues of mental health. As the student points out,

> both individuals and larger institutions are centering conversations on mental health and realizing its importance. As the World becomes more competitive and demanding, young adults, more than ever, need a stable support system and a healthy way to communicate and express their troubles.
>
> (Student report, 2021)

The solution that the student suggested is to provide "an open, welcoming space, led by a team who intimately empathize with the same journey, allowing for a unique and thorough exploration of people's thoughts and feelings" (Student report, 2021). The student was aware of "the possibility of not having enough funds or an adequate team" for this project (Student report, 2021). The challenge is how to organize "the finances to afford such a team, as well as all the materials required in starting a workshop like this" (Student report, 2021). One of the solutions the student presented is "finding people who are as passionate and invested in helping people through storytelling as I am, and who have the skill set that I am missing" (Student report, 2021). This is an example of social entrepreneurship in its crudest sense in that the student is not interested in making a profit in the first place, but rather focuses on having a positive impact on people and communities.

Teaching students of the humanities business skills and an entrepreneurial mindset has a practical benefit in that it opens their perspectives of business opportunities. In the context of the rise of creative industries such as advertising, architecture, arts, crafts, design, fashion, film, music, performing arts, publishing, R&D, software, toys and games, TV and radio, and video games, students of the humanities will appreciate their majors as a driving force in the creative economy. After completing this course on innovation and entrepreneurship, the students will be able to apply these business and entrepreneurial skills that they learned in other contexts. Some of the students' evaluations and feedback support the fact that the course learning outcomes have been met. An example includes: "He helped me learn more about local entrepreneurs through class activities and projects, which helped inspire us and look at their steps to success in detail" (anonymous student evaluation Fall 2021). Another student summarized their learning experience with the following statement: "We were shown many examples via videos and essays about real life entrepreneurs, especially ones in the region which helped heighten my understanding of what it means to be an entrepreneur in the Arab world" (anonymous student evaluation Summer 2021).

The students were able to identify problems and gaps in the publishing sector. This awareness is helpful in two ways: the first one is localizing technology and contextualizing business ideas. The second one is that the students are fully aware of the importance of diversity of teams and that diverse teams have more chances of success in business life. By creating a diverse group, the students showed confidence in leading a team of students from other majors such as engineering and advertising as well as academics and publishers.

Conclusion

These findings suggest that the job market can be radically transformed with ideas from new graduates who are well trained and immersed in their respective fields. IEN 301 is a course that combines many disciplines such as innovation, entrepreneurship, design thinking, sustainability, marketing, management, and leadership. This course has a comprehensive scope, stressing the importance of creating and cultivating a mindset and creative confidence. This set of skills can be considered a source of personal and professional self-realization. One of the findings is that students of the humanities have started to look at the economic aspects of daily life, as is the case with the work of these two students who took this course in Fall 2021. This course provides students with a start-up culture. It can be extended to the establishment of minors in entrepreneurial humanities and eventually majors in entrepreneurial humanities. New related courses such as social innovation and social entrepreneurship can be designed and taught since students of the humanities are typically socially driven and ethically oriented. Such courses can enhance self-awareness and normative thinking among students of the humanities.

This chapter has positioned entrepreneurial education as an enabler. Providing students of the humanities with the required knowledge and skills can actively involve them in the entrepreneurial learning process. Higher education in the UAE has increasingly called upon entrepreneurial humanities to prepare students from various disciplines for sustainable careers and professional development. In response, teaching entrepreneurship is likely to grow in the coming years. This chapter can start a discussion about how students of the humanities can learn to develop an entrepreneurial mindset. These findings, though not generalizable, present some best practices to help policymakers and educators integrate the entrepreneurial humanities in curricula and to develop minors, majors, Master's degrees, and other programs in the entrepreneurial humanities, which can shape the future of the humanities and higher education at large. Courses that converge divergent topics from the three colleges and one school provide faculty members and students alike with opportunities to create better learning and teaching approaches that unleash their potential.

Works Cited

Basco, Rodrigo, and Rana Hamdan. "Student Entrepreneurial Ecosystem in the United Arab Emirates." *Family Firms in the Arab World*. Nov. 2019. doi: 10.13140/RG.2.2.31520.12804

BBC. *The five most creative cities in the world?* 2019. https://www.bbc.com/culture/article/20190715-the-five-most-creative-cities-in-the-world

Bernstein, Jay Hillel. "Transdisciplinarity: A Review of Its Origins, Development, and Current Issues." *Journal of Research Practice* 11.1 (2015): R1. http://jrp.icaap.org/index.php/jrp/article/view/510/412

Dweck, Carol S. "What Having a Growth Mindset Actually Means." 13 Jan. 2016. *Harvard Business Review*. https://hbr.org/2016/01/what-having-a-growth-mindset-actually-means

Formica, Piero. "Reinventing Education for an Entrepreneurial Culture." *Industry and Higher Education* 34.2 (2020): 65–68. doi: 10.1177/0950422219899538

Future of Jobs Report. 2020. https://www.weforum.org/reports/the-future-of-jobs-report-2020/in-full/infographics-e4e69e4de7

Global Innovation Index. 2021. https://www.wipo.int/global_innovation_index/en/

McGregor, Sue L. T. "The Nicolescuian and Zurich Approach to Transdisciplinarity." *Integral Leadership Review* 15.2 (2015). http://integral-leadershipreview.com/13135-616-thenicolescuianand-zurich-approaches-to-transdisciplinarity/

OECD. 2007. *Human Capital*. https://www.oecd-ilibrary.org/education/human-capital_9789264029095-en

O'Keefe, Paul A., Dweck, Carol S., and Greg Walton. "Having a Growth Mindset Makes It Easier to Develop New Interests." 10 Sept. 2018. *Harvard Business Review*. https://hbr.org/2018/09/having-a-growth-mindset-makes-it-easier-to-develop-new-interests

Purg, Peter, Cacciatore, Silvia, and Čuček Gerbec Jernej. "Establishing Ecosystems for Disruptive Innovation by Cross-Fertilizing Entrepreneurship and the Arts." 30 Aug. 2021. *Creative Industries Journal*. doi: 10.1080/17510694.2021.1969804

UAE Centennial 2071. 2022. https://u.ae/en/about-the-uae/strategies-initiatives-and-awards/federal-governments-strategies-and-plans/uae-centennial-2071

UAE Energy Strategy 2050. 2022. https://u.ae/en/about-the-uae/strategies-initiatives-and-awards/federal-governments-strategies-and-plans/uae-energy-strategy-2050

UAE National Innovation Strategy. 2022. https://u.ae/en/about-the-uae/strategies-initiatives-and-awards/federal-governments-strategies-and-plans/national-innovation-strategy

UAE Strategy for Artificial Intelligence. 2022. https://u.ae/en/about-the-uae/strategies-initiatives-and-awards/federal-governments-strategies-and-plans/uae-strategy-for-artificial-intelligence

UNCTAD. 2022. https://unctad.org/topic/trade-analysis/creative-economy-programme

Part II

Creating Change and Designing for Transformation

Chapter 6

Saving Humanity

The Courage to Act on Climate Change

Joanna Carey

You've seen the news headlines – warning after warning of pending climate disaster. At this point, someone not aware of the climate change crisis is simply not paying attention. As a whole, our society has largely moved past the unfortunately long period of climate denialism, onto a period of climate change acceptance and inaction. While this broader acknowledgment that human activities are causing global climate change is refreshing, the inaction in the face of our collective knowledge is disheartening, to say the least. How can we recognize this problem exists, but continue to sit idle on effective action?

This chapter is about the potential of the entrepreneurial mindset as a tool for addressing climate change, as well as a largely overlooked, critical motivator for addressing climate change: saving humanity. The entrepreneurial mindset provides a useful toolbox for tackling this grand challenge of our time. Neck and Murray (2020) define entrepreneurship as "a way of thinking, acting, and being that combines the ability to find or create new opportunities with the courage to act on them." There are two aspects of this definition that resonate with respect to climate change – opportunities and courage. Climate presents society with ample opportunities for averting disaster while improving quality of life – but only if we find courage to respond to this crisis. Doing so requires a cross-disciplinary effort that recognizes the inherent social and cultural aspects of this crisis that extend far beyond solely scientific and engineering expertise.

Does our society have the courage to act on climate change? So far, the answer to this question is a resounding "no." But the past does not dictate the future – and recognition that the entrepreneurial mindset may provide the tools necessary to solve crises help us move forward, as – fortunately for humanity – climate change is a highly solvable problem, *if* we have the courage to act.

As the UN clearly stated in 2018, the scale and pace transformation needed to avert climate catastrophe is unprecedented in the history of human civilization (IPCC, 2018). In other words, climate change presents human civilization with a system disturbance on a scale not yet experienced

DOI: 10.4324/9781003380665-9

since humans evolved on Earth. What does such a disturbance look like, from the human experience? We can look at the Covid-19 pandemic as one such example. The pandemic resulted in many lives lost (at the time of writing over 1,000,000 people have died in the United States alone, with over 15 million dead worldwide). Moreover, the pandemic exacerbated inequalities globally via a shift in wealth; the world's 2,755 individual billionaires now own 3.5% of global household wealth, up from 2% before the pandemic (World Inequality Report, 2022). Like Covid-19, climate change is another large-scale global disturbance that will increase marginalization and inequities across the globe – unless we change course.

Addressing Climate Change Is Not About "Saving the Earth"

Finding the courage to act on climate change requires a reframing of motivation for action toward saving humanity and recognition of the opportunities; such actions are created to increase global equity, standards of living, and socio-economic status across the globe. While Western environmental movements of the 1970s were incredibly successful at increasing awareness of environmental degradation and passing effective laws that restored natural resources, the movement mostly relied upon altruistic motivations to "save the Earth." The public was encouraged to "save the rainforests" and "save the whales" for the sake of the rainforests and the whales. While some people identified with such noble motives, many people did not. The rhetoric of "saving the Earth" perpetuated the false narrative that environmental stewardship is a selfless altruistic endeavor, when a stronger motivator is saving humanity. That is, by basing environmentalism on self-sacrificing encouragement to protect the planet, we missed the larger motivator for environmental stewardship: saving ourselves.

"Environmentalism" could indeed be termed "humanism." A well-functioning earth system is necessary for a well-functioning human society. Humans rely upon natural resources, such as clean air, clean water, food, and shelter, for our survival. Planet Earth is our life boat in this expansive and threatening universe – a lifeboat that needs to remain structurally sound for survival.

This is not to argue that environmental destruction is only problematic from a human-centric lens. Rather, the human-centric lens is a valid perspective that will attract more political buy-in (i.e., political courage). And while we are currently undergoing rapid rates of species extinction, it is important to remember that in reality – the Earth does not need saving. Our planet is over 4 billion years old and has survived five mass extinctions, prior to the current on-going mass extinction event. Planet Earth has remarkable resilience to withstand and recover from disturbance.

Human civilization, however, does not exhibit such resilience. Even robust civilizations fall, often as a result of environmental mismanagement (e.g., Mesopotamia, Easter Island, Maoris) (Diamonds, 1994). The Earth does not need saving. People need saving.

The Past, Present, and Future of Humanity Is At Stake

The scale of climate change touches all aspects of humanity – from our cultural past, to our present populations, to the unborn. Cultural icons from former human civilizations, such as UNESCO World Heritage sites, are directly threatened by the increasing intensity and frequency of natural disasters, such as hurricanes and sea level rise. Such cultural icons provide "intangible value" and represent "icons of human civilization" from past cultures. Their loss would be irreversible. As just one example, 37 out of 49 low-lying World Heritage sites in the coastal Mediterranean region will experience a 50% increase in flood risk by 2100 from increasing sea levels (Reimann, 2018).

Current human populations are clearly impacted by climate change, but the impacts will not be evenly distributed across society. The poorest and most vulnerable will be hit the hardest, making climate change the ultimate example of environmental injustice and racism. These disproportionate impacts are a function of both regional differences in climate change impacts across the globe and because adapting to climate change takes resources, which not everyone has.

For example, increased rates of sea level rise threatens low-lying tropical island nations. Two villages in the Solomon Islands have already been destroyed, forcing those subsistence communities to relocate. The capital of the Choiseul Province of the Solomon Islands, Taro, is also being forced to relocate, becoming the first global capital to be displaced as a function of climate change (Albert, 2016). A loss of human populations in a region, via displacement or death, is another example of permanent loss of culture that cannot be replaced.

Extreme heat is becoming more common with climate change, directly impacting billions of people in the Middle East and South Asia, where only a small subset of the population has access to air conditioning and many people labor outdoors. In 2015 during the holy month of Ramadan, extreme heat killed over 3,400 people across Pakistan and India, where just 12% of the population has access to air conditioning. And as recently as March 2022, temperature records broke again, reaching 49.5 °C (120 °F) in Nawabshah, Pakistan (Jeff, 2022).

The worst drought in over 40 years is currently (May 2022) putting nearly 17 million people at risk of severe hunger in east Africa, with the UN projecting this value to reach 20 million individuals by September

2022 (Reuters, 2022). Such food insecurity is partially due to the March-May 2022 rainy season being the driest on record in Ethiopia, Somalia, and portions of Kenya (Reuters, 2022).

These are just a few recent examples of the disproportionate impacts of climate change on the global poor. Taken together, extreme weather exacerbated by climate change has already caused forced, involuntary migration of roughly 20 million people annually since 2008. These trends are expected to continue, especially across the developing world; by 2050 roughly 31–85 million people across sub-Saharan Africa, south Asia, and Latin America are projected to be displaced as a result of climate stressors. Such forced displacement not only impacts individuals, but it often represents a permanent loss of cultural heritage. By and large these most severe impacts of climate change will impact people with darker skin. No doubt that the predominantly rich, white Western nations would have found the courage to act if we were the ones forced to migrate or die due to extreme heat, loss of land, and food shortages. Finding the courage to act on climate change is about increasing global equity, both from a social and financial perspective.

That said, the wealthy are not immune to the destruction of climate change impacts. Richer populations will spend a larger fraction of their income on food, water, and insurance, compounded by global mass migration and conflict. While recent reports indicate most climate migration will occur within countries, not across international borders, wealthy nations will still have to adapt to some degree of increased immigration pressure and incidences of global conflict. Nevertheless, the wealthy have the resources to allocate to such stressors. The poor do not.

The inequities surrounding the inaction on climate change do not stop with the poor. Young people and the unborn will also be disproportionately impacted. If we do not act to address climate change, future populations will be forced to live in a world ripe with climate instability (increased prevalence and severity of natural disasters, drought, etc.). Moreover, they will be forced to spend incredible amounts of money to retroactively attempt to clean up our former inaction on climate change. Each decade of action delay increases the cost of climate change by 40%, and these accruing costs will be paid by today's young people and the unborn. It is estimated that by 2090, United States taxpayers will spend ~$500 billion per year addressing the costs of climate change under a business as usual emission scenario (although moderate reductions in emissions would reduce those costs by almost half) (USGCRP, 2018).

Those individuals currently in power, largely the baby-boomers in their 70s, will be long dead by the time the more severe impacts of our inaction – and the hefty price tag – become apparent to all. Those in power often tout the expense of decarbonization as the reason for inaction. While it may be in the best financial interest of older generations to maintain the status quo (no one wants a large market disturbance to the 401 K when they are in their mid-70s), one must ask the question: too expensive for you who? Not young people, by any means.

The intergenerational inequities are compounded with the fact that much of the impacts of climate change are irreversible. That is, assuming that future generations find the political courage to address the issue, they will not be able to re-wind the clocks and mitigate all previous poor behavior. Despite future technological advancements that will hopefully make atmospheric carbon capture financially viable, we will not be able to undo all harm caused. Technological advancements cannot recreate lost cultures or villages, re-introduce extinct species, or refreeze the Arctic. Our current inaction is largely permanent, removing collective agency from future populations.

As an educator of young adults, it is often challenging to look students in the eyes and tell them such truths – their future will be so much more difficult as a result of the ineptitude of their elders, people who knew about the problem and – in spite of that knowledge – made the decision to do nothing. The science on this topic has been clear for decades, but we wasted time telling lies that it's too expensive to take another path.

Opportunities for a Positive Difference Abound

There is good news: we still have a choice of what the future holds. The poor and the young do not have to be relegated to an unjust, increasingly inhabitable planet. We have the science and the technology to address this problem. We just need courage to act. That courage will only occur when people recognize the opportunities climate change presents us to directly improve our quality of life and standards of living worldwide.

Our culture is not immune to rapid shifts in societal norms or ways of doing things. In just a decade (~1900–1910), we transitioned from the horse and buggy to the automobile as the dominant means for individual transport. In less than a decade, the Public Works Administration, created as part of the New Deal, a way to spur economic recovery during the Great Depression, spent billions of dollars creating new infrastructure, such as bridges and dams, across the United States that are still essential to economic livelihood. These activities occurred because United States citizens decidedly found the courage to act upon opportunities for a better way of doing things.

We already see examples of such courage in the climate change realm in the plethora of scientific and engineering innovation that has occurred in recent years with respect to decarbonization. Over the past year, renewable energy accounted for 90% of all new electric capacity installation. This trend is projected to continue into the near future, largely due to the fact that the costs of solar panels and wind turbines have dropped roughly

90% and 70%, respectively, over the past decade. Projections indicate that within a quarter century, global primary energy demand could fully be met with renewable energy (Abbott, 2022; Breyer, 2021; Haegel, 2019; Rockström, 2017).

This shift to renewable energy away from fossil fuels has benefits beyond the global climate, as the renewable energy transition will increase access to cheap energy for all, increase blue collar job opportunities, and provide health benefits from improved air and water quality. Not only is renewable energy now cheaper than fossil fuels, but also the decentralized nature of renewable energy grid shifts, combined with the lower capital costs, will allow individuals and small communities to supply their own energy. This shift to decentralized grids reduces reliance on large utilities and minimizes required capital investments. While not all individuals or municipalities have the capital or access to mine and process oil, they are better able to create their own solar fields or wind farms, improving access to clean cheap energy globally.

The shift to renewable energy will create jobs, especially blue collar jobs that are desperately needed within the United States and beyond. The World Resource Institute estimates that for every dollar invested in renewable energy, nearly double the jobs are created compared to a dollar invested in fossil fuels (Jaeger, 2021). This is largely due to the high labor needs, combined with lower capital costs, of renewable energy grid installation and maintenance compared to fossil fuels.

Fossil fuel extraction and combustion is dirty business, quite literally. Coal mining, fracking, and oil production pollute surface and groundwater systems, while the combustion of fossil fuels pollutes the air and increases ground level ozone. Once again – the poorest and most vulnerable are disproportionately impacted by such pollution. As such, transitions away from fossil fuels have human health benefits, which will largely help increase equitable access to cleaning air and water at the global scale.

Addressing climate change via the entrepreneurial mindset goes far beyond decarbonization. Social and humanist entrepreneurs are working to solve problems directly and indirectly related to climate change across a variety of sectors beyond energy, including the healthcare, fashion, and agricultural sectors. Such sectors contribute to – and are affected by – climate change. For example, the healthcare industry contributes to climate change by using large amounts of electricity to power hospitals, fuel for transport, and additional energy required for disposal of waste and medications. Healthcare is also directly affected by climate change due to expanding ranges of infectious diseases, compounding stressors on mental health, increasing incidence of asthma, and increasing severity of natural disasters. Several tech start-ups are directly addressing these issues; Ada and Patientory, founded by Daniel Nathrath and Chrissa McFarlane, respectively, are two distinct companies focusing on health data management and analytics. While differing in their approach, both companies share the common goals of providing customers with easier access to health data in order to improve care efficiencies and allow for more personalized health tracking.

The fashion industry also swings a heavy sword with respect to greenhouse gas emissions across the supply chain. Excitingly, several companies have begun to address fashion's carbon footprint while also mitigating another related environmental crisis – plastic waste. Using novel technology that turns plastic waste into high-quality clothing, several niche companies (e.g., ECOALF, Girlfriend Collection, Alternative Apparel) and larger brands (e.g., Adidas, Nike, Patagonia) offer exciting alternatives to consumers who want new clothes without the hefty carbon price tag.

Agriculture is responsible for roughly 15% of global greenhouse gas emissions, and is also directly impacted by changing climate patterns. A plethora of organizations are working to minimize agriculture's carbon footprint, while also increasing the resilience of global food systems and farming communities. Nuestras Raices is a grassroots farming organization based in Massachusetts that provides food system education programs for Latino youth and socially disadvantaged community members, among other programs. Started by Puerto Rican immigrants in 1992, Nuestras Raices now has over 600 members and includes a 30-acre farm and numerous community gardens that support racial equality, access to healthy foods, and local economic growth. Other organizations are working to reduce natural resource use through more efficient agricultural practices. Bowery Farming is one such firm, practicing vertical farming powered by renewable energy that allows for dramatic reductions in agriculture's environmental footprint, especially energy, water, and land use. These are just a few examples of organizations employing the entrepreneurial mindset to solve societal problems, both directly and tangentially related to climate change.

Hope for a Better Future

The problem with climate change is that it will impact every sector of society. However, there is beauty in this fact, as it corresponds to prospects for alternative ways – better ways – of doing just about everything – from travel, to food production, to healthcare, to clothing manufacturing, to building and heating our homes. And as a bonus, those who are at the forefront of these changes – the visionaries among us who harness the capacity for rapid innovation – will also reap great economic benefits. Such visionaries recognize that addressing climate change is not a burden, but rather an opportunity.

For some, it is far easier to have a cynical negative view of the future, relegating ourselves to the dismal projections of a business as usual climate scenarios. However, for the sake of those of us still living – and those yet born – I urge us to take a proactive entrepreneurial approach, envisioning a better future where climate change action reduces global inequities and provides a safer stomping ground for the amazing capacity for human intellect, creativity, and love. Remember – the future is not yet determined. A bright future awaits, but only if we find the courage to act.

Works Cited

Abbott, Benjamin W. et al. "We Must Stop Fossil Fuel Emissions to Protect Permafrost Ecosystems." *Frontiers in Environmental Science.* 29 June 2022. doi: 10.3389/fenvs.2022.889428

Albert, Simon, et al. "Interactions Between Sea-Level Rise and Wave Exposure on Reef Island Dynamics in the Solomon Islands." *Environmental Research Letters* 11.5 (2016): 054011.

Breyer, C. "Low-Cost Solar Power Enables a Sustainable Energy Industry System." *Proceedings of the National Academy of Sciences* 118.49 (2021): 1–8.

Diamond, Jared. "Ecological Collapses of Past Civilizations." *Proceedings of the American Philosophical Society* 138.3 (1994): 363–370.

Haegel, Nancy M., et al. "Terawatt-Scale Photovoltaics: Transform Global Energy." *Science* 364.6443 (2019): 836–838.

IPCC. Summary for Policymakers. In: *Global Warming of 1.5°C. An IPCC Special Report on the Impacts of Global Warming of 1.5°C Above Pre-industrial Levels and Related Global Greenhouse Gas Emission Pathways, in the Context of Strengthening the Global Response to the Threat of Climate Change, Sustainable Development, and Efforts to Eradicate Poverty* [Masson-Delmotte, V., P. Zhai, H.-O. Pörtner, D. Roberts, J. Skea, P.R. Shukla, A. Pirani, W. Moufouma-Okia, C. Péan, R. Pidcock, S. Connors, J.B.R. Matthews, Y. Chen, X. Zhou, M.I. Gomis, E. Lonnoy, T. Maycock, M. Tignor, and T. Waterfield (eds.)]. Cambridge University Press, Cambridge, UK and New York, NY, pp. 3–24. 2018. doi:10.1017/9781009157940.001.

Jaeger, J., Walls, G., Clarke, E. Altamirano, J-C., Harsono, A., Mountford, H, Burrow, S. Smith, S., Tate, A. "The Green Jobs Advantage: How Climate-friendly Investments are Better Job Creators." World Resources Institute. 2021. https://doi.org/10.46830/wriwp.20.00142

Masters, Jeff. "India and Pakistan's Brutal Heat Wave Poised to Resurge." 5 May 2022. *Yale Climate Connections.* https://yaleclimateconnections.org/2022/05/india-and-pakistans-brutal-heatwave-poised-to-resurge/

Neck, H. M., & Murray, C. P. *Entrepreneurship: The Practice & Mindset* (2nd ed.). Thousand Oaks, CA: Sage, 2020.

Reimann, Lena, et al. "Mediterranean UNESCO World Heritage at Risk from Coastal Flooding and Erosion Due to Sea-Level Rise." *Nature Communications* 9.1 (2018): 1–11.

Reuters. "Drought Threatens Starvation in Horn of Africa, UN, Agencies Say." May 31, 2022. https://www.reuters.com/world/africa/drought-threatens-starvation-horn-africa-unagencies-say-2022-05-31/

Rockström, Johan, et al. "A Roadmap for Rapid Decarbonization." *Science* 355.6331 (2017): 1269–1271.

World Inequality Report 2022. *World Inequality Lab.* https://wir2022.wid.world/

USGCRP. *Impacts, Risks, and Adaptation in the United States: Fourth National Climate Assessment, Volume II* [Reidmiller, D.R., C.W. Avery, D.R. Easterling, K.E. Kunkel, K.L.M. Lewis, T.K. Maycock, and B.C. Stewart (eds.)]. U.S. Global Change Research Program, Washington, DC, USA, p. 1515. 2018. doi: 10.7930/NCA4.2018.

Chapter 7

Voice Entrepreneurs

Making a Career in Human Speech

Simone Kliass

Preface

The Portuguese language doesn't have a good word for my line of work. Here in Brazil, I'm usually called a *locutora*, which translates to "announcer" and suggests that I might be a radio disk-jockey or a TV sportscaster. English has better options. My Anglo colleagues around the world call themselves "voice artists," "voice actors," or "voice talent." But even these labels miss the mark; they emphasize performance – and though recording a commercial tag line, movie trailer, public-service announcement, or on-hold message (to give just a few examples) does require performance skills, I actually spend just a fraction of my day in front of a microphone.

So, what do I do, really? Like other freelance artists – singers, dancers, musicians, painters, photographers, writers, etc. – I have undertaken an economic venture. It just so happens that this venture is me. And while my passion for the arts inspired my career, my financial independence depends on more than talent. To make a living in a gig economy, I need to study trends, manage risks, invest capital, and pursue innovation. When business is good, I take note of what is working. When it's slow, I course correct. The French language has the perfect word for people like me – and by coupling it with my line of work, I think I've found my answer. What do I do for a living? I'm a voice entrepreneur.

My goal is to offer insight and real-world guidance to others who work in the arts and humanities. In the conversations ahead, my focus on technological disruptions in my own industry will show how an entrepreneurial mindset is vital for survival in today's job market. Discussions about the arts and humanities sometimes exclude views on critical-thinking, problem-solving, and strategic planning. This needs to change. Treating your passion like a business doesn't make you any less of an artist. It simply proves that you will do what it takes to make a career out of something you love.[1]

DOI: 10.4324/9781003380665-10

The Industry

The production technique of voiceover is as old as storytelling. It's not hard to imagine one of our early ancestors gesticulating the action of a hunt, his face illuminated by fire, while another tribesman narrates their adventure from the shadows. In modern-day TV shows, movies, and plays, dialog spoken by an unseen narrator is labeled in scripts as VO, which is shorthand for voiceover, or OFF, since the voice is heard off-camera or off-stage. Traditionally, these performances are delivered inside a booth with the assistance of a sound technician and tens of thousands of dollars of equipment.

In recent decades, however, the industry has undergone a revolution. In a digital economy that considers attention a commodity, voice has suddenly become vogue. Our refrigerators talk to us, our dentists have podcasts, and advertisements once regulated to commercial breaks on the TV and radio, now barrage us non-stop online. The demand for new voices, the affordability of recording equipment, and the growth of pay-to-play platforms that put clients directly in touch with talent have given rise to unprecedented levels of jobs and competition.[2]

The revolution has also brought a new competitor to the industry: artificial intelligence (AI)-generated synthetic voices. Using TTS (text-to-speech) technology, software developers are able to build a database of pre-recorded phonemes, words, phrases, and sentences that mimic human speech and make written content audible. Siri and Alexa are perhaps the best-known examples of how this technology works and the ubiquity of synthetic voices in our day-to-day lives shows just how much voice synthesis has advanced.

As an artist, I was apprehensive about AI encroaching on my line of work. But as an entrepreneur, I knew I stood a better chance of navigating technological change if I had a clear idea of what I was up against. How can a human talent compete against AI, I wondered? How can human talent use technology to our advantage? What are the ethical implications of letting AI stand in for human talent? How can AI developers and voice talent work together to ensure space for all? And, finally, how will AI-generated synthetic voices shape the future of our industry? Looking for answers to these questions, I reached out to four fellow voice entrepreneurs: a developer, two voice artists, and a strategist.

The Developer

In 2016, while doing research for a talk on synthetic voices, I stumbled across a YouTube video called "What happens when you give your sister a voice." It shares the story of a family who worked with a team of developers to create a synthetic voice for a young girl with cerebral palsy. The girl's sister provided the speech input needed to build the database, but developers also considered how the girl herself sounded when she vocalized. The company behind the initiative was VocaliD, and they continue to lead the charge in voice synthesis today.

For my first interview for this chapter, I reached out to Rupal Patel, VocaliD's CEO and founder. Through her revolutionary work in the voice industry, Rupal has become an advocate of ethical AI, inclusivity, and accessibility. Synthetic speech continues to evolve and in certain, limited applications, is now nearly indiscernible from human speech. Rupal understands the implications for those of us who work in voiceover and so she created the platform VoiceDubbs, which offers professional talent a fair and equitable way to scale our businesses through AI.

"The human voice is an incredible instrument," Rupal explains.

> The nuances of vocal control – like modulation of pitch, loudness, and duration – are challenging for current synthesis, but the technology is getting better. Humans use linguistic and social context to vary speech and we attempt to synthetically model this variability. Still, unless there is some human manipulation of the AI voice, it can sound unnatural or out of place. Our most sophisticated neural models can reproduce rhythm, breaths, and voice quality – but vocal performance is still a human skill.

The big fear among voice talent is that AI will take our jobs. Rupal is helping me and my colleagues understand that this is not an accurate representation of current market dynamics. There are bigger threats out there. For instance, novice talent on Fiverr or other gig platforms are undercutting our business much more than AI. The jobs synthetic voices can do are the ones that require lightning-fast turn-around times and high-volume voiceover. Currently, most of these jobs are not coming to us at all. They are going to Amazon Polly or Google Text to Speech instead. So why not get a piece of that pie by creating our own AI voice as well?

By fortifying its talent roster, VocaliD is also helping to upend outdated stereotypes. We see one example in the IVR (interactive voice response) systems used by call centers, which tend to rely on a female, middle-aged voice with a neutral accent. Why does the notion of female "assistant" continue to permeate our society? Why do we still think of women when we hear words like "nurse," "telephone operator," or "flight attendant" – and of men when we hear "doctor," "manager," or "pilot?" In 2005, Stanford researchers Clifford Nass and Scott Brave published "Wired for Speech," a seminal work in the voice-tech industry that raised important questions of stereotyping and gender bias.

In the nearly two decades since the book's release, clients have finally started to realize that the safe choice when choosing a voice as an interface is not necessarily the best choice. If the voice industry is undergoing a revolution, why not take advantage of this moment to become an instrument of change? Finally, we have the technology to help companies effectively connect with their broad and diverse customer bases with unique voice interfaces. No longer is the choice as simple as gender. Numerous factors now shape the way companies engage their listeners.

"There is increasing interest in voice to have more diverse representation," Rupal explains.

> This makes sense from a psychological point of view, as there is a lot of evidence showing that trust and engagement improves when there is a greater alignment with the speaker in age, accent, and speaking style. For example, elderly listeners have a hard time with very fast talkers or those with strong unfamiliar accents due to auditory comprehension. In my opinion, there is a need for more research on listener preferences which can then be incorporated into product design.

We can hear these changes all around us. Audio-interface options on newer cell phones and smart speakers, for example, include male, female, and even gender-neutral voices. Users can choose among different styles of voices, in different languages, and different regional accents. Some apps, like Waze, offer downloadable packs with famous voices and simplified TTS dashboards that let you record a voice of your own. The market can no longer rely on research dating back to the 1950s and 1960s, when less emphasis was given to diversity. We need current data to guide product design for modern listeners.

What does this mean for the voice entrepreneur? Rupal sees us as instruments of change.

> One of the biggest challenges I see today is that companies are either followers that jump on a bandwagon and say they believe in diversity and yet have no clue how to do it or those that sit back and wait for regulation. Entrepreneurs, on the other hand, can lead by example. We can challenge current stereotypes; we can experiment more than large companies and we can lead the charge to create a more representative and accepting soundscape.

The Artists

The next two women I reached out to have been challenging stereotypes and leading by example since long before I met them. The first, Anne

Ganguzza, is a full-time voice talent based in Southern California. Her podcast "VO Boss" offers a forum for discussions on how AI voices have reshaped our industry. A self-proclaimed technology enthusiast, Anne strives to help her colleagues book more jobs by embracing change. She advocates synthetic voices that are here to stay. And the technology behind them will only continue to improve. However, she also understands that their applications are limited.

"AI has reached new heights with the ability to process vast amounts of information and learn by itself through machine learning," Anne explains.

> This has been a driving force behind the development of chatbots, virtual assistants, and other AI-powered technologies that we interact with daily. However, although AI has proven to be useful in these applications, it is still ineffective at replicating human qualities or characteristics such as empathy, personalization, and engagement.

By articulating text from tens of thousands pre-recorded sound bites, virtual voices create the impression of informative and authoritative deliverers of content. But that's about as far as the technology goes. Anne and I believe that only human talent has emotional passion for sharing content with listeners. The ability to engage and motivate listeners is not something readily recreated with a synthetic or AI voice at this time. And that means, from an entrepreneurial perspective, for us to grow our businesses, we must focus on what sets us apart as artists.

"Where a client is looking for quick delivery of short bursts of information, synthetic voices may be suitable," Anne argues.

> But where content is more complex and requires a voice that is more emotionally engaging and sensitive to the material and the listener's needs, the only choice is the nuanced emotional delivery of a human talent who can inspire, motivate, and create bonds with listeners.

Luciana Silveira, a Brazilian voiceover colleague and vocal advocate of racial and gender diversity in the industry, backed up Anne's points – and took our discussion even further by arguing that, whether choosing a human talent or synthetic voice for a project, we need to put money where the mouth is.

> Clients often claim to support diversity by putting avatars of different races, ages, and genders in their audio-visual productions. But when the time comes to record dialogue, little consideration is given to accurate voice representation. Voice doesn't have a race, they say. That's untrue. A black avatar should be voiced by black talent.

Most production companies prefer to stay in their comfort zones – especially when going in a new direction will impact their profit margin. The focus is usually to turn the job around quickly and within budget. Little thought is given to how many different voices are out there – and when the question of accurate representation comes up, it's usually because the end-client made the request. Luciana believes that is why it's so important for producers and talent to engage in this conversation. "If we want to defend diversity, the changes must be real. When I started my career in this industry as a black woman, I struggled to be heard. Today my voice is strong and unique."

The Strategist

Steve Keller, an expert in the field of sonic strategy and identity, is lending support to Luciana's views with research of his own. Steve and I met as mentors for South by Southwest in Austin, Texas. His work explores how sound shapes our perceptions and influences our behavior and he devotes a great deal of time to the "sonic color line" of racialized listening and its impact on marketing and industry practices, particularly in voice casting.

> When we think of race, we often describe it as a visual construct, ignoring the fact that race is a sonic construct as well – and one that is just as effective in drawing racial boundaries and creating hierarchical divisions between the perceived 'whiteness' and 'blackness' of sounds. These sonic color lines are derived from listening practices exerted by a dominant culture, drawn across vocal tonalities and timbres, musical rhythms and genres, and even community soundscapes.

Steve's company, Studio Resonate, launched the website standforsonicdiversity.com to encourage producers and clients to take inventory of their casting practices, their voice talent rosters, and their approach to audio creation and production.

> There's definitely evidence of 'digital discrimination.' Consider error rates for voice prompts from users of color and the lack of diversity heard in voice assistants. I'm encouraged to hear developers and talent talking about these sonic inequities and looking for ways to change our approach to voice interactivity and voice AI, both systemically and creatively.

Conclusion

Spoken language sets *Homo sapiens* apart from all other species. We are shaped by speech even before we leave the womb, by hearing the voice of our mothers. Speech connects us with each other, and how we speak impacts how others perceive us. So it's no surprise that more and more companies today have chosen voice as the ideal interface between the products they sell and those who use them.

According to Steve Keller, The Mean Opinion Score (MOS), a commonly used metric to measure the overall quality of a voice for professionally recorded speech is currently 4.58. It's nothing short of remarkable, then, that Google was able to score a nearly identical MOS of 4.53 by using WaveNet with their TTS system. We have a long way to go before we can reproduce this score with multiple voices at scale, but the technology is here. We just need the data and the training sets.

Nevertheless, Steve believes the final frontier isn't the sound of the voice itself – it's the quality of the voice interaction.

> As we speak, our brains are making countless calculations when we're speaking to each other, using context, sensory cues, familiarity, etc. to establish communication that is perceived as congruent, appropriate, engaged, and intimate. While we can code sonic cues that can telegraph emotion and respond to contextual data using biometrics and environmental cues, we have a lot more ground to cover before AI voices can truly engage us in meaningful conversations.

What does this mean for the future of our industry? In voice, as in other fields of the arts and humanities, the answer will depend on the actions of entrepreneurs – those who look forward, embrace change, break paradigms, and become instruments of innovation. I invite you the reader to stand with Christine Henseler, Alain-Philippe Durand, Rupal Patel, Anne Ganguzza, Luciana Silveira, Steve Keller, and with me, in whatever your field may be. Let's chart a new path, not as competitors, but as colleagues. Let's transform our markets and put our creativity to work not just to strengthen our business ventures, but to make our world a better place to be.

Notes

1 I want to congratulate Christine Henseler and Alain-Philippe Durand for curating and editing this collection of chapters – and to thank them for inviting me to contribute. I also want to thank my husband Jason Bermingham for helping me to organize my thoughts in a second language.

2 For further evidence, see https://www.businesswire.com/news/home/20200504005185/en/Voices.com-Reaches-1-Million-Registered-Users-on-Voice-Over-Marketplace.

Chapter 8

Collaborative Humanities

Creativity, Classics, and Being a Chameleon

Shivaike Shah

While sitting in North West Texas in the midst of a sand storm, surrounded by a group of young engineers, I was surprised to realize how much I was still to be tested on the interdisciplinary practice I had espoused across America on my *Uprooting Medea* tour. With my production company, Khameleon Productions, and co-sponsored by the Brown Arts Institute at Brown University where I was the Visiting Artist, I had toured seven Ivy Leagues, numerous private liberal arts colleges, and numerous large state universities. The tour was based around our reinterpretation of Euripides' *Medea*, originally adapted by Francesca Amewudah-Rivers while we were students at Oxford University. I led over 70 workshops, roundtables, and classes across 30 institutions in 12 states, starting in Rhode Island and finishing in Texas.

As I planned this tour during the third lockdown in the UK, and proposed it to nearly a hundred institutions across the US, I had a request that I asked all colleges to accommodate. Though I was often in conversation with a Classics or Theatre department, I asked for the visit to be planned in as interdisciplinary a way as possible. Practising interdisciplinarity led me to founding Khameleon Productions, and building this tour. What became apparent, though, was that in many university departments and centres there was little infrastructure in place for cross-departmental collaboration, and even less for collaboration between colleges. Schools with brilliant professors across different disciplines that I had been lucky enough to connect with had never collaborated with, or in some cases even met, each other. Central to the tour was bridging this gap, and central to my approach to the Humanities and to generating work more generally was, and still is, collaboration. And as the tour came to an end, there I was, sitting in TTU, truly challenged by the sheer scope of what using my creative practice to bridge the gap between different disciplines really looked like.

Throughout 2021, I also developed a 30-episode podcast series, Khameleon Classics, which interrogates and explores the legacy of the Classics, particularly in the context of race and colonization.[1] As I engaged

DOI: 10.4324/9781003380665-11

in the legacies of Classics and colonialism through the podcasts, it became clear how pervasive the structures of supremacist 'classical' thought are across the Academy. Misconceptions of 'Civilization', 'Western Thought', and 'Canon' – terms I had used freely and without question my whole life – are in fact a carefully sustained, and often unquestioned, framework around which the Academy is built. My method of trying to break this down was to be a chameleon, combining various media, collaborating across different parts of the Academy, and commissioning a diverse host of artists to reframe this narrative.

This chapter will explore that collaboration in three main strands. I will briefly illustrate my personal approach to working, how I built the tour, and the collaborative nature of Khameleon's work. I will explain, drawing on my experiences from the tour, why I believe a true interdisciplinary approach to the Humanities is the only means by which to keep its disciplines moving forward, and out of those misconceptions. Finally, I will put forward how this approach is central to radically (re)imagining the power and relevance of the Humanities.

Learning Collaborative Practice

I graduated in 2019 and had eight months between the beginning of my career and Covid shutting down the world. As the pandemic began to hit and all work opportunities evaporated, I gained some perspective on my next steps. I decided to look towards theatre, a form I had explored extensively as an undergraduate, as the space in which I could both build my career and try and respond to the pressing need to amplify global-majority voices and stories. To begin building those possibilities, I founded Khameleon Productions, a non-profit production company dedicated to platforming the creative power of global-majority artists.

It was untraditional (to say the least) to found a production company just as Covid took hold of the world. However, I saw it as an opportunity. With most of the world sitting at home – in particular, many artists who would otherwise have been permanently busy – I emailed hundreds of people across Europe and the US to set up meetings. People had the bandwidth to connect, so we connected! Through many months of conversations with people from all corners of the creative world, Khameleon's vision started to take shape. Funding was non-existent for most of the first year of working, as Covid has decimated most public funding opportunities, but with time, Khameleon Productions became a theatre and film company.

As the process of building Khameleon was taking shape (and I must add that it is ever continuing), the company stated five clear aims, outlined on our website, each dedicated to achieving aspects of our mission statement.[2]

It quickly became clear that one of Khameleon's aims in particular would shape our approach to amplifying diverse voices:

> To take responsibility for using the tools at our disposal to build collaborative and celebratory creative spaces for our histories and stories.

This aim highlights Khameleon's position: it is not only that we must create spaces to explore the complicated history and legacy of stories shared between our communities – we must do so in a collaborative manner.

It is also a statement of intention, the intention that fills Khameleon's whole approach to creating work: we must take responsibility, and use every tool and platform we can muster, to generate those spaces. The ultimate aim is to celebrate – celebrate stories, history, culture, and collaboration.

As Theatre learned to navigate the pandemic, I restarted work, and I observed attempts to make creativity and performance more 'inclusive' or 'diverse.' In all these attempts, there were two factors against which I often felt I was stuck. Processes to diversify or amplify global-majority voices, however genuine, did not *begin* with those voices. In most instances, an outreach or diversity initiative was organized and then presented to the group that had been designated as in need of inclusion. Even if loosely defined in scope, the structure of these initiatives struggled to address the nuances and needs of that community because the organizers were not in active conversation with that community from the get-go. The opposite approach, I came to see, was often equally troubled. Unlike the first scenario, where organizers came up with an initiative that was then unilaterally presented to a so-called minority group, I saw, instead, the responsibility to address issues of outreach or diversity within organizations thrust wholly upon the group actually in need of support. Organizers would relinquish control, and the in-need group was left in charge of changing structures to platform their voices and communities.

Though the latter approach places a lot of power from the organizers into the hands of the recipient group, there must be a level of teamwork between the two groups. Organizers are often still the individuals with the funding, the connections, and the necessary platform to get things moving. When organizers completely relinquish an initiative and do not work collaboratively, it often leaves the marginalized group without necessary support, and with a huge increase in pressure and responsibility to instead teach and support the organizers.

Neither of the above two approaches – the power being mostly in the hands of one group or another – seem successful, at least in my experience.

Therefore, the logical next step is to find a collaborative middle ground that attempts to bridge and connect the two groups so that they can build a structure together. This is not a radical stance, nor is it a particularly new idea, yet it is one that we often fail to implement (even when we think we are doing so). It requires genuine collaboration, for which I have found that there are three necessary ground rules, each harder to achieve than the last:

1 One must accept that there are necessarily facets of the other party that one cannot understand.
2 One must relinquish, and actively unknow, presupposed ideas about the other party and the previously built structures of practice.
3 One must trust in the other party, allowing their knowledge to breathe alongside yours, secure in its ability and direction.

These are ground rules that go in both directions, though that took me a while to understand, as I originally saw these to be solely the responsibility of an organizer. In fact, when acting collaboratively, I believe a truly *mutual* understanding of the above is necessary to allow full teamwork. The last point is often enacted by creatives, even if it is not verbalized. In an orchestra, you play with the belief that the person sitting across the pit from you, playing an instrument you cannot play, reading music in a clef you may not understand, is not only able to, but also will perform in collaboration with you. On a film set, you trust that the grips and standbys and focus pullers and the endless crew whose job titles one often barely understands are going to work effectively using equipment you are likely unable to even turn on, to create a product that could end up being viewed on a phone screen on a train halfway across the world. In Theatre, I believe this act is the most pronounced (though perhaps I am biased). One opens the curtain and hopes that the audience, in their seats, collaborate with the show to suspend their disbelief and allow themselves to be transported with the actors to wherever they need to be, on a static 30-by-40-foot stage. Creatives are used to collaboration based on a sort of 'blind' faith, and it is that spirit of collaboration that I wanted to capture in this new company.

Khameleon works only with global-majority artists and creatives, but even within that (extremely broad) group, these three ground rules of collaboration are constantly challenging, and we are constantly learning. There is a simple reason why this is such a core part of our structure. If as a company we aim to share experiences, combine different artistic practices, and draw on various cultural reference points, collaboration is the *sole* means by which this can be achieved. From lived experience to practical knowledge, there is simply a limit to how much one individual can know. To create anything that abides by those three ground rules, we must look for individuals who can work together to build such a product. To be diverse as a company, diversity of thought, knowledge, and practice is absolutely necessary. How diverse can one individual be in their own thought, knowledge, and practice?

As Khameleon began fundraising, rewriting our *Medea* adaptation (with six voices working on the script in some capacity), building a podcast series, planning an international tour, and shooting a short film, we took on a huge slate of work for a young company. We also realized the only way to survive and build, especially through the pandemic, was to act as a chameleon, trying all approaches to develop. In doing so, we always centred discovering and rediscovering a collaborative approach.

As the tour became a viable opportunity following the support of the Brown Arts Institute and other colleges who committed at the early stages to support the visit both financially and with their name power, I began trying to expand its scope as much as possible. How could I thread different departments together? How could I bring different colleges together? By the end of the tour, I had been hosted by Classics departments, Theatre programmes, Humanities centres, Critical Black Studies departments, Honours colleges, a Political Science department, Women's Studies departments, and in numerous public-facing events.

Part of this breadth was simply practical. For departments to fund a visit, resources needed to be pooled, funding applied for across colleges (for example the New York Six schools), and even professors' individual departmental or personal funding pots combined. Collaborative efforts for funding are often required and are inadvertently a very effective way to get numerous people involved. It is hard to express how grateful and in awe I am of the professors who, already overburdened by work and Covid, committed huge amounts of time and energy to coordinate a visit from Khameleon. But part of this variation of departments was also due to a core aim of the project and questions I would often ask host institutions: who could this project intersect with? Which different groups and subjects could this project bring into the same room? And, for me most importantly, how can we use that interdisciplinarity to build with each other, while learning actively from those collaborations?

Avery Willis Hoffman, the Director of the Brown Arts Institute and our incredible mentor at Khameleon, always reminded us to make the project a central point from which we could collect, unlock, and manoeuvre complicated questions about the intersections between identity, belonging, race, and creativity. We had to be the chameleon – able to adapt to every situation, using our work as an anchor, to test and explore the freedom of this collaborative approach. The tour became the first expansive opportunity we had to truly experiment with these practices.

Collaboration in Practice: Touring from Rhode Island to Texas

One of the first workshops we took on tour at Wellesley College took advantage of an already strong relationship between a Classics and a Theatre professor. We had actors acting out sections of *Medea*, while the Classics students acted as dramaturgs with the script. The classicists helped the actors, most of them new to the script, to carve out the meaning behind the scenes. The actors helped the classicists to view their text as a living piece designed to be seen, heard, and performed (they showed them this in practice). This kind of collaboration occurred all over tour and was sometimes not completely alien to departments. Theatre and Classics departments in certain colleges had a long legacy of working together, though often, moving this into an active classroom setting was a new opportunity.

At Skidmore College, we again combined Theatre and Classics students. What unfolded in this classroom was a prime example of the power of interdisciplinary collaboration to infiltrate a text. The actors, in trying to fathom how to portray Medea, a woman who murders her children, had to find a way to reconcile this ending with a woman towards whom they otherwise felt compassion. In their attempts to step into the character and to build the empathy needed to convincingly portray her, many were finding it impossible to understand how they could arrive at that final scene. The classicists, on the other hand, had been expertly taught about the structures of xenophobia and sexism that defined the play's context, so they had built an empathetic view of Medea, and thus were ready to defend her final choice in the play. Only through conversation between the disciplines were they able to gain an understanding of how and why the text is approached from such varied angles, and to mutually benefit from those perspectives. It seemed bizarre to me at first, but the classicists, in their turn, needed to be reminded that her final act is not eternally defensible, and it was an understanding of an actor's journey to embodying that on stage which demonstrated this. Likewise, the actors needed to investigate the complicated structures that surrounded Medea's experience in the play to grow their compassion towards her.

The real challenge and interest lay in extending this framework outside the scope of two disciplines that rather easily marry together when discussing an ancient Greek play. At Bucknell, under the extraordinary guidance of Professor Jaye Austin Williams, we brought the project to a Critical Black Studies department. How are those same points and conversations brought up in the context of those students, and how does that field of knowledge inform and challenge that text? I watched students transform the text out of its time into a contemporary setting, using *Medea* primarily as a tool to excavate current questions of the canon and constructions of whiteness. Especially when considering reception, with students unconstrained by worries about traditional Classical pedagogy or theatrical practice, their interpretation of *Medea* breathed new life into my understanding of the text. The text became flexible, applicable to a whole manner of situations, and the students were able to directly respond to their concerns, and the concerns of their field, using *Medea* as a lens.

As I interacted with students new to *Medea*, and from subjects that did not tend to address dramatic texts at all, I was able to develop my understanding of the play in a way that has absolutely transformed how I now view it. It also drastically altered my pedagogy (which was completely malleable, as this was my first experience of teaching). My approach to the work had to be permanently flexible. Apart from the standard (mis)conceptions about Classics and the supremacy-based constructions of 'Western Civilization,' I could not rely on knowledge one builds up through an affiliation with a particular subject when teaching across so many. A text to which one can refer comfortably in an English classroom is not necessarily known to Critical Black Studies students. The name of a performer or director known by a group of Theatre students may mean nothing in a Classics class. The focuses of students, their structures of learning, and their way of approaching text or teaching – they are all so different. While we often lump 'Humanities' into one monolith, it was incredible to see the huge variance in students' abilities to approach topics, and their individual sensitivities to different approaches.

There were some eye-opening instances on the tour where I was able to bring these questions outside Humanities settings. To me, these opportunities displayed how central the Humanities could be to the whole Academy if approached this flexibly. At Texas Tech University in Lubbock, I held an Honours College lunch whose attendees were primarily engineering students, many of whom were interested in the impending water crisis. These were students who in many ways saw themselves as removed from some of the issues that the Humanities are facing, not least questions of anti-racism. They felt they weren't equipped to address such questions, yet they were aware of how racialized the effects of the water crisis will be. When faced with questions of diversity and the importance of anti-racism, the students were able to explicate issues of racism in their own subjects, but they rejected the idea that they could address such structures in their own work. The act of trying to bring these supposedly 'Humanities'-based questions into these spaces allowed them to address, or at least think about, these concerns for the first time.

This manifested in different ways, both at this lunch and throughout the tour, especially when working with STEM students. As in Lubbock, I was regularly taken aback by how ready STEM students were to reject the idea that anti-racist work was directly relevant to them, while readily explicating feelings of racism or structural inequality in their own work or field. When speaking to students interested in space exploration, two students in particular claimed simultaneously that issues of race would hardly pertain to space, while in the same breath recognizing that it was likely the Global South who were going to be tossed aside when it came to both climate change and space science. When I actually brought our work, or a script, to these sessions, scientists were often able to relate their experiences directly to the characters. For example, a medical student in Pennsylvania compared Medea's struggle as a racialized woman to the struggle of young black individuals to readily be treated for skin conditions, as these were so often overlooked by doctors not taught to recognize such conditions in melanated skin. It was clear that the students were aware of these issues, but had not been given the appropriate spaces to verbalize them in the way that we regularly are able to bring them to light in the Humanities. Though it must be said that often their ways of expressing these concerns lacked the nuance and vocabulary that comes from regularly addressing these topics, regular exposure in this creative fashion would surely allow STEM students the building space to develop their explorations of these otherwise-designated 'Humanities problems,' as a Lubbock engineer framed it to me.

This can be grounded in the same work I was using to teach Humanities classes. As I started to question how the students were developing their studies and research to consider questions of social responsibility or anti-racism, I was able to frame these questions as I did all across the tour. 'Just as we at Khameleon work with a collaborative approach aimed at uplifting global majority voices' became applicable to how their research could achieve the same aim. 'As we see Medea reacting to structures that cornered her into vengeful action' allowed them to consider how structures in their own field led to disparities and to consider what the repercussions could be. As we creatively explored the implications of the play and my own work, a freedom was created for us to translate those structures into their real-world settings.

I started the tour with the generally held belief that there was no way to translate these questions to students not actively taught Theatre or Classics, but it was clear as it went on that this was an internal block which had no bearing on the reality that students from all disciplines were able to connect with the work. If we are willing to be flexible with our approach to the Humanities, and we are willing to see all disciplines as a tool with which to unlock deep conversations and disturb other practices, I believe we will make great steps forward in answering the question of how Humanities can possibly be relevant to STEM topics, which are often framed as the main centre point for solving pressing global issues. We must be willing to constantly recontextualize our texts and practice to engage with social and political issues, but not in isolation from subjects that we don't often consider to be in our purview, such as engineering (as I learnt so well in Lubbock).

We must also not be on the backfoot. We must seek out these challenges, and use the skills that we actively build in our students, and collaborate actively with partners who share different expertise. If we bring ourselves to other subjects with openness in our approach and the willingness to adapt that approach to integrate with theirs, there is fertile ground for collaboration. It is imperative to recognize that this cannot happen, however, without actively reflecting inwards, addressing the inherent structures of inequality and, frankly, delusion, in our own fields as we try to look outwards. As I recorded Khameleon Classics, the list of unaddressed issues of colonial and racial prejudice that I wanted to tackle was endless. Our institution must work proactively to tear down structures of inequality in our own fields, aligning to replace them by building systems of open collaboration, to open up and integrate the field of the Humanities with our partners in other fields.

Much of what I have said in this chapter has not been groundbreaking, and my belief in collaborative practice is not, in itself, radical. What I hope can be drawn from my writing are real examples which demonstrate that when approached with a true desire for collaboration, the potential of inter-collegiate, inter-subject, and cross-functional collaboration can be unlimited in scope. There are no restrictions on when the three ground rules, the basis of all my own work, can be put into practice in the creative and academic fields. It was something that I succeeded in doing on a unique tour I developed alone out of my bedroom during Covid, as an individual who was brand new to theatre and film, and who is no form of academic. (As graduate students regularly reminded me throughout the tour, I don't even have a master's degree!). My willingness to act as a chameleon and turn to interdisciplinary practices that were grounded in unrestricted collaboration became fertile ground for experimenting with the scope of the Humanities, which are, and have always been, entrepreneurial in their nature. The insecurity and structural inequality that plague the Humanities are at real risk of limiting their future. In response, we as practitioners and academics must be flexible, adaptable, and ready to challenge ourselves. Our willingness to confront the questions facing our students across all manner of disciplines is how we as a field can make ourselves indispensable.

Notes

1 https://www.khameleonproductions.org/khameleon-classics.
2 Visit https://www.khameleonproductions.org/about-us to find out more about our mission, aims, and the company as a whole.

Chapter 9

Healing Trauma at the Intersection of Entrepreneurship and Design

Christina Goldschmidt

It feels as if you can't have a conversation or read about business strategy or innovation without the term "design thinking" popping up. A quick search of *Forbes Magazine* for the term "design thinking" yields 1,160 results, of which the majority are gated, premium and paid content. Those articles' headlines tout, for example, that "These Days, Everyone Needs to Engage in Design Thinking" and "Design Thinking Can Deliver an ROI of 85% Or Greater." They also offer a variety of how-to guides for adopting design thinking in general and applying it to a variety of situations like artificial intelligence, ecommerce, education, banking, startups, the financial crisis, remote working and also commentaries on creating better processes for the practice itself. Why is so much content real estate and effort being devoted to this one little term? Well, it may be due to design thinking having become the go-to creative problem-solving approach to drive innovation. It allows creativity to be understood in a logical and repeatable process that also has proven its effectiveness through positive impact, business value growth and improvements to the bottom line (Tjendra 2014, par. 7).

Unlike what many of those *Forbes* articles might lead you to believe, design thinking isn't actually a tool that can solve each and every problem out there. Nor can it be used by anyone regardless of skill, training, experience and talent just as long as they follow the simple repeatable process (Baytaş 2021, par.1). It is however an attempt to codify both a larger design process and ways of working with designers and understanding designers' approaches to solving problems (Baytaş 2021, par. 10). Design thinking was productized and marketed by IDEO, a California-based innovation design consultancy (Baytaş 2021, par. 41), and is now taught by them and also popularized into infamy by other key methods like Google's Design Sprint and IBM's Enterprise Design Thinking (Baytaş 2021, par. 46). Despite all of this hype, it is still a very useful methodology, and when learned, honed and practiced, it can be very effective at driving disruption, problem-solving and business results (Baytaş 2021, par. 49).

I have been practicing design thinking techniques in my UX design practice for well over a decade. I am also an educator of design thinking

DOI: 10.4324/9781003380665-12

methods, having taught them to clients of the agencies and consultancies where I have worked and also to numerous students. Design thinking has been foundational to how I work and has been a cornerstone of my success at jobs that required me to innovate in complex industries like financial services and management consulting and especially when developing new disruptive ventures. I understand how design thinking has become synonymous with how entrepreneurship and entrepreneurial thought are practiced in today's business world because it has been that tool for me. As a practicing designer, I use it to help non-designers understand how to work with me to tackle the problem at hand (Goldschmidt and Smith 2017, 13). Employing design thinking techniques in my professional life also has had a surprise benefit: helping me heal my trauma and improving my self-image. After repeated practice and honing my skills, I believe that it has helped me to dramatically improve my own mental health and lessen the symptoms of my anxiety and posttraumatic stress disorder (PTSD). Thus, the rest of this chapter will be focused on understanding trauma and PTSD symptoms, which elements of design thinking have a positive treatment effect on those symptoms, how someone can put into practice similar techniques to improve their healing and why those techniques work to benefit healing.

Understanding Trauma and PTSD Symptoms

PTSD is possibly more common than you might think, affecting 6% of the US population at some point in their life (U.S. Department of Veteran Affairs 2021, par. 4). This is about equivalent to the number of Asian Americans in the US population as of 2019 (Ghosh 2020, par. 3). The origins of PTSD are a response to a traumatic experience such as combat, relationships with a person who is abusive, mass shootings, physical or sexual assaults, deadly accidents, political upheaval, natural disasters, terrorist attacks or a life-threatening event (Grantham and Mulholland 2020, par. 1). What happens with PTSD specifically is that a person's brain is reacting to or over-interpreting stimuli that is happening in the present and their brain is associating it with the trauma that happened in their past and only exists in their memory. They get symptoms of real-time trauma even though there is no immediate threat and oftentimes they are fully aware that the reaction is false, but they cannot do anything to intervene and prevent the reaction (Finn 2014, 6). The effect this has on the brain is that when a person experiences a traumatic event, there is a bypassing of their higher order thinking and a direct activation of their autonomic nervous system which will trigger an atomic reaction to either "fight or flight" or freeze. Then the brain saves this information to protect against the same trauma happening again as a survival tool to protect the person from a similar event in the future. But with PTSD, those memories get triggered easily and are as if the person is having a traumatic reaction to just a normal situation, and this can heavily impede someone's ability to function in the world (Finn 2014, 5). People with PTSD exhibit the following behaviors: hyper-vigilance (being alert and scanning for perceived threats), being easily startled, difficulty concentrating, emotional triggers with overreactions and being easily distracted across all of their senses (Grantham and Mulholland 2020).

Going deeper into how the brain works for people suffering from PTSD, they often have slower frontal lobe electrical activity where we see their rational brains having a lack of control over their emotional brains (Van Der Kolk 2015, 332), and the brain waves are overall less well coordinated resulting in not being able to filter out irrelevant information (Van Der Kolk 2015, 333). Both of these two brain changes show that traumatized people process nontraumatic information differently than those who are not suffering from lingering trauma. These brain changes often prevent those suffering from PTSD from being fully engaged in their daily lives as they can't actually pay attention to what's going on in the moment (Van Der Kolk 2015, 333–334). This is best summarized by what Pierre Janet said in 1889 on the subject "Traumatic stress is an illness of not being able to be fully alive in the present" (Van Der Kolk 2015, 334).

What Does Help the Traumatized Brain?

To help with the symptoms of trauma, survivors work on solving for sensitivity to sounds, improving focus and concentration, lessening anxiety attacks and improving sleep (Baidel 2020). There are many medications and therapies that help PTSD but a notable subset of such therapies are also covertly present in the practice of design thinking. That is, if you know where to look for them. When found, they materialize as the mechanism that drives the brainstorming portion of design thinking and ultimately helps practitioners think differently about a problem and generate new ideas. Let us first understand the principles behind these therapeutic techniques before we go more deeply into where they can be found in the design thinking practice:

Stress

An interesting phenomenon is that the same PTSD sufferer who is completely overwhelmed by simple choices in everyday life is remarkably able to expertly cope with extreme stress, like on the battlefield. This was well illustrated in the 2008 Kathryn Bigelow's movie *The Hurt Locker* where we see war veterans who can perform with precision on the battlefield but are overwhelmed when they return to civilian life (Van Der Kolk 2015, 334). Stress also produces adrenaline, which can result in overall good feeling and a sense of reward that helps to overcome dissociation feelings (Heacock 2019, 00:04:00–00:07:00).

Brain Wave Shifts

Mel Robins details a technique in how she has overcome anxiety through moving thought processing from her basal ganglia to her prefrontal cortex in order to rewire habits of thinking and send communication to her higher order brain to get out of the stress reactions. By counting to five backward and then saying a mantra or a statement, she can engage her prefrontal cortex and move into her higher order brain whenever she needs to. This is very similar to other techniques that PTSD and trauma-informed therapists suggest to PTSD sufferers to address their symptoms when they have a reaction to everyday stimuli (Robins 2017, 00:04:40–00:07:39).

Liminal Spaces

Developing liminal spaces, or spaces between place and time, can foster safety and a stronger ability to cope with PTSD and anxiety symptoms (Samano 2020).

Art Therapy

Art therapy may help sufferers of PTSD work through their trauma in a non-verbal fashion and be able to express themselves and process their feelings through the act of creating and through allowing deep concentration. Creating art of any kind can actually change the neural pathway in the brain and draw a deeper connection between the mind and body and the conscious and unconscious mind (Samano 2020).

Ultimately overcoming PTSD is going to always take time and any approach will be practicing techniques that both ease symptoms and also strengthen someone's overall mental outlook and are best undertaken under the guidance of a licensed therapist (Samano 2020).

The Basics of Design Thinking

While design thinking is a complex methodology, there are three basic steps for the overall repeatable process. IDEO refers to them as Inspiration, Ideation and Implementation (IDEO) but I like to translate them to Empathy, Ideation and Validation. In Empathy, you understand the people involved, their behaviors, needs, journeys and pain points and settle on the problem you plan to tackle. In Ideation, you brainstorm possible solutions using fun mind-bending techniques to find disruptive ideas and prototype possible solutions. In Validation, you test the minimal viable product with real users and review over all technical feasibility and business viability to launch the real product. If the idea fails at any of these points, you inject feedback and go back, modify and keep the cycle moving forward till you get to something viable (Goldschmidt 2021).

The process is a simple one and easy to perform, requiring minimal equipment and constraints. What does each phase roughly look like? A prolific form that many teams follow is the Google Ventures' five-day Design Sprint. I will leverage this methodology to bring shape to common steps, and so you, the reader, can have a more detailed reference guide if you so choose. Note that this approach does not take the whole process to launch into account and is only about fast learnings (GV 2019):

Empathy

- Goal setting as a team
- Mapping the complete challenge
- Q&A with the experts, including getting a deeper picture of the users
    - This often involves affinity mapping to derive insights from the conversations with the experts to analyze the larger space (Goldschmidt 2021).
- Target selection, hone in on an ambitious part of the problem that can still be solved within the week

Ideation

- Various brainstorming techniques to diverge on the idea
- Sketching ideas, focus on critical thinking not artistry
- Recruiting participants for validation testing
- Converge on an idea and weed out solutions
- Create a master storyboard for your prototype
- Create a finalized prototype for testing

Validation

- Create testing interview script and testing procedure
- Conduct testing with final prototype and actual users

(GV 2019)

With this basic understanding of the overall design thinking process, we can go deeper into design thinking's healing potential. There are several points along the design thinking journey where the healing process can be activated; however, the greatest potential lies in the Ideation step. There are as well potential secondary benefits within the Empathy and Validation steps, but we will spend the majority of our time focused on the healing potential of the Ideation step. Within the Empathy stage, trauma sufferers might have a talent for reading people and their needs, learned as a survival mechanism in response to their trauma. If a trauma survivor is able to harness this skill and not lose themselves in the process of applying it, they could enjoy professional accomplishments and see the benefits of a past bad experience. The balance here is a tricky one and in and of itself is not a sole strategy for healing. The Validation step is built on the premise of failing fast and learning that it is ok to fail and move on; this has great potential for learning personal acceptance for many trauma survivors. However, it is a secondary benefit to the potential of the brain shifts that I see possible in the Ideation step. I see the Ideation step as having the greatest potential for helping trauma sufferers heal gradually over time. An important focus area is to go deeper on brainstorming techniques that come up during the Ideation phase. There are several different processes for disrupting your thinking and looking for new ideas. Some focus on looking at the clichés that surround the problem and twisting and exaggerating them to find unobvious solutions (Williams 2010, 174). Other techniques bend reality by having you change perspectives like imagining looking 20 years in the future at newspaper headlines for the most extreme ideal outcomes and then asking your brain to work backward to the root causes to achieve those lofty outcomes (IDEO.org).

My go-to method uses a stimulus object to "mash" against your problem. When your brain uses the stimulus object and tries to make sense of how it relates to the problem, it takes a bunch of leaps and fills in the space, uncovering new ideas that you may not have thought about otherwise. I prefer to use a stimulus object that has clear physicality and also emotional meaning – good examples are an umbrella or a teddy bear. All good brainstorming techniques follow a similar process that plays with your brain. You restrict this activity to a short period of time, and include a countdown clock to induce stress and modify your brain waves. You use both individual brainstorming and also small group convergent time to help you get the most out of yourself and play off of each other and build off of each other's ideas and seek deeper meanings to the problem. This also lets you validate the solutions on the fly with partners and weed out ideas more quickly so you don't waste time. In the end, you get to viable approaches faster and are not stuck in a personal bias (Goldschmidt 2021).

Understanding the Linkage between the Ideation Step and Healing Trauma

Though the design thinking process has three complex steps and all are necessary for being successful, common shorthand often refers to the Ideation step and specifically the repeatable brainstorming step when people are talking about design thinking. It is most revolutionary for new practitioners who never thought they could generate great ideas on demand, and it is also the most fun. The very same techniques that allow practitioners to generate innovative ideas are actually how a trauma survivor can learn to get control over their thoughts and symptoms. The Ideation step continuously induces controlled states of stress to brainstorm ideas, and this helps the trauma survivor shift their brain waves. All of this has the greatest potential for learning to control PTSD symptoms because they are all within their control and have linkages to positive outcomes (Goldschmidt 2021). Trauma survivors not only learn how to practice techniques that help them reduce their symptoms but also harness the same skills for positive benefits, which leads to greater empowerment.

Stress/Brain Wave Shifts

Several of the brainstorming techniques that are used to create lateral thinking rely on the induction of stress states to speed up the excitement and shift brainwaves. This is often done with a countdown clock and the time pressure and ceremonies that come with various techniques used to generate the ideas in a repeatable fashion. By getting exposure to these stress states, in a controlled setting, and telling their brain that they are intentional, the trauma survivor learns that they are good and intentional and not a reaction to danger. The brain interprets the same physiological symptoms that one would associate with fear as good and learns to cope with them more easily when faced with PTSD symptoms in the future.

Art Therapy

Drawing is a critical practice in the prototype creation phase of Ideation. All participants are taught how to express themselves with drawing and how to practice it with regularity for communicating complex ideas. This can unlock the neuropathways that make it necessary to process their trauma and have shared experiences and a new form of expression. The repeated practicing of drawing can only serve as a positive step toward further unlocking self-expression and processing.

Liminal Spaces

Brainstorming often relies on liminal spaces to uncover unconscious ideas. By cultivating the creation and connection to these spaces, it gives trauma survivors deeper resources and control to protect themselves when PTSD symptoms flare up. Understanding the power of turning off brain activity in the shower is a classic technique that is cited by many design thinking practitioners for uncovering their best ideas (Hodkin 2019).

Solely exposing a trauma survivor to these techniques is not enough to ensure healing. I have found that repeated practice and mastery are key components of the equation. Without practice, the techniques do not actually set in, nor do they provide the trauma survivor with the necessary relief or any greater control over their symptoms. The other benefit that comes with practice is positive reinforcement. Being part of a supportive team, having professional success through uncovering solutions that actually work – these are secondary benefits that foster a supportive environment that furthers healing, trust and security.

Could Design Not Just Heal Trauma But Be the Best Place for Survivors to Thrive?

There is a larger lore linking creativity and mental illness; however, science has also started to find that creative professionals, including professionals working in digital, may be more predisposed genetically to mental illness (Gregory 2018). We also see instances of creative professionals thriving, even in the face of mental illness – including trauma and PTSD – because of their involvement in creative careers, including UX design.

Duane Topping, a former service member who suffered from PTSD, has not only found solace through sewing but also harnessed it into a successful fashion line. He recalls that "Seems I had a soft squishy side. I couldn't see it behind the PTSD. But through sewing I found it. It was so much about doing something different. It was a long way from those dark corners and the hardness my experience had spawned. I was finally able to forget those labels and PTSD and face my demons…" (Topping 2018, 00:05:34–00:06:14).

Eriol Fox, a UX designer with childhood trauma in his background, has written about his linkage between deep empathy for users and drawing unique human connections and the survival skills he needed to stay safe as a child. Though he sees it as a mixed approach because he can sometimes lose himself in the process, he also sees benefits. He talks of these here: "I'm often gleeful when I can draw complex conclusions from a small piece of information about someone during a user testing interview or field study. I find the focus on underlying issues around why humans perform actions and 'do' things inherently fascinating. Being able to solve a frustration or a need pulls deeply on that ingrained learning that kept me safe in my childhood. Making other people feel 'happier' was the condition by which I measured successful existence" (Fox 2018).

Gerry, a UX leader who has complex PTSD noted, "Because I've experienced trauma in personal and professional life, I'm hypersensitive to the emotions of others." And "I *am* wired to really care about people, and that is probably why I've been successful in UX" (Gregory 2018).

These stories give examples of how other designers and creative professionals have not only found healing through their practices but also thriving careers that benefit from how they think and approach the work differently, because of their trauma experiences.

The Future is Trauma-Informed Design

Ultimately the practice of design thinking techniques will not be effective for a trauma survivor if the work environment they participate in is triggering or perceived as unsafe. It is critical to call for the training of trauma-informed design principles in all design spaces to foster a safe, trusting, collaborative, supportive and empowering environment if someone is going to be able to leverage work to heal. This must also be inclusive of awareness of gender, cultural and historic issues so as to not cause additional trauma. As design practitioners, we should strive to reduce and remove environmental stress and negative stimuli, actively engage all individuals dynamically in our multisensory environment and foster feelings of self-reliance. Moreover, we should make sure there is a connection to the natural world, separate anyone who is distressed, foster personal identity and not only make sure we have clear opportunities for choice but also balance that with overall program needs and everyone's overall safety (Gill 2019). These core principles of trauma-informed design should help make for safer work environments where traumatized individuals, and everyone else, can hopefully start on a journey to practice in safety. But without this education and practice, overall focus on healing will always be secondary to personal safety.

I consider myself lucky to have been able to identify the connection between my work and healing and to lean into it for deeper efficacy and also share these techniques with so many. I now work to create trauma-informed spaces that allow everyone to show up as their best selves, in a trusting environment, to do our best work, thrive as individuals and help our organization and community (Moran 2021). My hope is to make the field of design a better place that embraces a truly diverse workforce and gives back by making it a sustainable field that benefits society in multiple ways, not just through what we design, but by enriching anyone who practices design, and that virtuous cycle *is* design thinking at its best.

Works Cited

Baidel, Clara. "Designing for People with PTSD." *Medium*, 2020. clarafbaidel.medium.com/designing-for-people-with-ptsd-6e8ccf5f29eb

Baytaş, Mehmet Aydin. "The Story of Design Thinking." *Design Discipline*. 15 May 2021. www.designdisciplin.com/the-story-of-design-thinking/

Finn, Matthew. "Posttraumatic Understanding: The Connections between Posttraumatic Stress and Environmental Design." *Perkins + Will*, 2014. static1.squarespace.com/static/586cf7b2be659472709cd98a/t/59f8cc9310952631f619f90f/1509477523905/PosttraumaticUnderstanding_2014.pdf

Fox, Eriol. "Can Experiencing and Understanding Abuse and Trauma Make Me a Good User Experience Designer." *UX Collective*. 31 July 2018. uxdesign.cc/can-experiencing-and-understanding-abuse-and-trauma-make-me-a-good-user-experience-designer-f9ea8ff95013

Ghosh, Iman. "Visualizing the U.S. Population by Race." *Visual Capitalist*. 28 Dec. 2020. www.visualcapitalist.com/visualizing-u-s-population-by-race/

Gill, Neha. "The Importance of Trauma-Informed Design." *Forbes*. 9 Dec. 2019. www.forbes.com/sites/forbesnonprofitcouncil/2019/12/09/the-importance-of-trauma-informed-design/?sh=7a6c8f756785

Goldschmidt, Christina. "Tackling Problems with Design Thinking." *Section4 Member Lecture*. 16 Dec. 2021. Lecture, register.section4.com/design-thinking-with-christina-goldschmidt/

Goldschmidt, Christina and Emily Smith. "A Transformation from Within." *Cake & Arrow*. 21 June 2017. cakeandarrow.com/newsfeed/2017/06/21/white-paper-transforming-digital-culture-insurance-financial-services/

Grantham, Charlie and Susan Mulholland. "Workplace Design Guidelines for Employees With PTSD." *Work Design Magazine*. 2020. www.workdesign.com/2020/01/workplace-design-guidelines-for-employees-with-ptsd/

Gregory, Brandon. "Mental Illness in the Web Industry." *A List Apart*. 18 Jan. 2018. alistapart.com/article/mental-illness-in-the-web-industry/

GV. *The Design Sprint*. 2019. www.gv.com/sprint/

Heacock, Craig. "Healing Trauma With Psychedelics – Part 1." *Back from the Abyss Psychiatry in Stories Podcast*. 5 Nov. 2019. www.buzzsprout.com/396871/1985599-healing-trauma-with-psychedelics-part-1

Hodkin, Shayna. "What Design Leadership Means to Accenture's Christina Goldschmidt." *Inside Design*. 30 Dec. 2019. www.invisionapp.com/inside-design/profile-christina-goldschmidt/

The Hurt Locker. Dir. Kathryn Bigelow. Summit Entertainment, 2008.

IDEO. *IDEO Design Thinking*. designthinking.ideo.com

IDEO.org, *Design Kit Travel Pack*. www.designkit.org/resources/9

Moran, Gwen. "Employees Say These 4 Things Can Ease the Transition Back to the Office." *Fast Company*. 7 July 2021. www.fastcompany.com/90652534/employees-say-these-4-things-can-ease-the-transition-back-to-the-office

Robins, Mel. "The Skill of Confidence and How to Take Control of Your Mind!" *Entiversal Podcast*. 2017. podcasts.apple.com/us/podcast/mel-robbins-skill-confidence-how-to-take-control-your/id1361255782?i=1000407312306

Samano, Hermann. "Home Design and Lifestyle Changes to Help With PTSD and Depression." *Porch*. 7 May 2020. porch.com/advice/home-design-lifestyle-changes-help-ptsd

Tjendra, Jeffrey. "The Origins of Design Thinking." *Wired*. 2014. www.wired.com/insights/2014/04/origins-design-thinking/

Topping, Duane. "How I Recovered From PTSD Through Fashion." *TedX Mile High*. 29 Aug. 2018. www.youtube.com/watch?v=AmFHC_IKLO4

U.S. Department of Veteran Affairs. "How Common is PTSD in Adults?" *PTSD: National Center for PTSD*. 2021. www.ptsd.va.gov/understand/common/common_adults.asp

Van der Kolk, Bessel A. *The Body Keeps the Score: Brain, Mind, and Body in the Healing of Trauma*. New York: Penguin Books, 2015. Print.

Williams, Luke. *Disrupt: Think the Unthinkable to Spark Transformation in Your Business*. New York: FT Press, 2010. Print.

Chapter 10

Liberal Arts Approaches to Teaching Women Entrepreneurship in Senegal

Narratives, Ethics, Empathy

Eric Touya de Marenne

This study on entrepreneurial humanities is based on my experience teaching business, economics, and culture in the context of French-speaking Africa. In this chapter, I will focus on three companies that are founded and managed by women in Senegal: Femme Auto, Taxi Sister, and Sooretul. I will explore specifically how students develop critical competencies through the course "French for International Business" that enable them to broaden their awareness of others through storytelling, enhance their capacity to rethink ethical issues pertaining to entrepreneurship, and become more empathetic toward gender inequalities.

Achieving gender equality in the West African nation of 17 million people is a daunting project. Women are confronted with major hurdles that include multiple constraints and a lack of access to land, finance, and markets. Although the Senegalese government has ratified in recent decades a convention on the elimination of discrimination against women and a protocol on violence against women, the struggle for parity faces sociological realities embedded in a patriarchal and deeply religious society.

The website "female-rights.com" provides major insights in that regard. Concerning female literacy rate, two-thirds of adult illiterates in Senegal are women. In the area of the labor force, the rate of participants among women is 28.56% and 61.9% for males. The gender gap is also significant in wages as, on average, men earn 82.9% more than women. Last but not least, 60% of women suffer from violence ("most of [Senegalese] women believe that a husband has the right to beat his wife if she has neglected her duties"), and 18% of girls below the age of 14 are still victims of female genital mutilation.[1]

The condition of Senegalese women has improved in recent years. According to the International Labor Organization, "female-to-male employment ratio in Senegal increased from 0.46 to 0.60 between 2006 and 2011, and women are getting more education."[2] However, Senegal's patriarchal society still demands that women should care mainly for household duties and children, and many Senegalese women are still denied

DOI: 10.4324/9781003380665-13

access to the labor market. From 1990 to 2019, female employment in the Senegalese labor force only increased from 32.92% to 35.12%.[3]

It is in this context of perpetual violation that also includes polygamy and forced marriages that the concept of entrepreneurial humanities takes on a significant importance for Senegalese women. My aim is to reflect more deeply on the subject through my experience in the classroom and the role liberal arts in general can play in the fields of business and economics.

Women Entrepreneurship and the Humanities

The question raised by Michael Bérubé in his 2013 Presidential Address at the Modern Language Association Conference is still relevant today: "Why should anyone bother with advanced studies in the humanities?" I will contend that the study of gender and culture through narratives and ethics provides essential pathways through which students can enhance their reflection about the testimonies of Senegalese women entrepreneurs and conceive, through them, alternate business and economic rationales that take into account real-life experiences.

One of the most urgent issues still confronting academia today is the perception that the humanities are unessential. The number of graduating humanities majors including foreign languages, philosophy, and history has been falling in the past decades while the number of Science, Technology, Engineering, and Mathematic (STEM)-focused majors nearly quadrupled. Anne Dennon contends that "higher education increasingly prioritizes STEM and business over the humanities" (2021). This shift calls into question the relevance of the humanities and whether they have a future. Will there continue to be a place for such studies in our universities increasingly dominated by Science, Technology, Engineering, Mathematic, and Medicine (STEMM) and business? What could be the ramifications of their reduced importance not only in academia but also for the well-being of society?

One of the aims of this chapter is to demonstrate how the answer to the question above is a definite yes. The weakening of liberal education raises fundamental concerns in a democratic society. Shifting his attention from purely theoretical issues to the realm of human praxis, French philosopher Jacques Derrida contended in one of his last publications that "the university should remain the ultimate place of critical resistance [and] thus be the place in which nothing is beyond question" (2005, 12). This reflection has pedagogical, economic, and political implications as the resistance the philosopher envisioned aimed at opposing "all the powers that limit the democracy to come" (2005, 13). In accordance with Derrida, Henry Giroux has called in his writings for a "critical pedagogy" through which students and faculty may respond to the demands of civic engagement. He underscored the necessity to "connect the acquisition of theoretical skills to the exercise of social power" (Giroux 2009, 12).

Assessing the real value and contribution of the humanities in the current context of the marketization of higher education and the reduction of state funding in public education requires us to reconsider the links that exist between higher education and society at large. It is from this perspective that I will explore how the entrepreneurial humanities challenge students' normative views by studying what it means to be a woman entrepreneur in Senegal, one of the poorest and gender exclusive countries in the world.

What Is an Entrepreneur?

According to Adam Hayes, an entrepreneur "is an individual who creates a new business, bearing most of the risks and enjoying most of the rewards" (2022). It is someone who creates and develops economic ventures and takes financial risks to make a profit. The entrepreneurial humanities, however, take on a different meaning as their main *raison d'être* is not necessarily to generate revenues or capital gains. It rather consists of creating, innovating, and thinking outside the box, as successful entrepreneurs also do. Like Steven B. Sample (2002) who contends that liberal arts education is essential in the preparation of leadership, I would argue that students and faculty in the humanities are in their own way entrepreneurs. They reveal through their creative works and innovative thinking how reality can be transformed and reconceived.

From this point of view, the humanities enable students to be social entrepreneurs as they undertake critical reflections pertaining to poverty, inequality, or social justice. According to the University of Nebraska Office of Graduate Studies website, being an entrepreneur means to "think ahead [...] working across disciplines [and] developing transferable skills."[4] Being entrepreneurial does not therefore only mean starting a business. It also signifies, through the study of foreign languages, art, literature, ethics, or social sciences, thinking differently and in broader terms, being creative, identifying new perspectives, and having a vision for the future. Furthermore, it may also mean to explore issues facing humanity today such as the environment, socio-economic inequality, violence, and poverty, which STEMM or business alone cannot examine or resolve because they are intrinsically lacking the cross-cultural, ethical, or critical dimensions which only the humanities can provide.

Coming to Clemson University, I transformed one of the two business courses offered in the French curriculum to focus entirely on the French-speaking world outside of France. Students began to study the socio-economic, cultural, societal, and political environments of Maghreb and sub-Saharan countries, among others. It is in this context that we approached issues pertaining to gender and entrepreneurship in these countries. Studying female entrepreneurs in West Africa through narratives, students deepen their knowledge about other cultures, assess the challenges faced by women in the workplace, and learn from stories of empowerment.

For example, Femme Auto is the first female garage in Senegal, a country where, as we have seen above, gender norms are being defied, while at the same time many, women are still denied access to the labor market.[5] Created by Ndeye Coumba MBoup, the shop has existed since 2006 and now employs around ten mechanics, half of whom are women. Femme Auto works on the maintenance of diverse companies' and institutions' car fleets in a sector that is predominantly androcentric. According to its founder, a woman mechanic is hardly considered in the profession. MBoup's aim in this context was to break boundaries, open the realm of possibilities for women, and show the world that female mechanics can repair cars too: "Dès le départ, j'ai voulu un garage 100% féminin pour montrer au monde entier que c'est un métier qui peut être exercé par une femme aussi bien qu'un homme." [I wanted a garage 100% feminine to show the entire world that it is a job for a woman as much as a man] (Maillard 2019).

Significantly, MBoup explains how she repeatedly asked for but never received any assistance from her government or local authorities. It is with her own savings that she decided to open her garage shop in the suburbs of Dakar. Since few schools grant diplomas for women in the profession, she has not yet reached its objective of creating an exclusively female-operated business. On the other hand, she has succeeded in initiating a system of gender parity in which women can also be supervisors. Referring to herself, she explains how "la patronne veut que son garage soit un havre de tolérance dans lequel les deux sexes apprennent à travailler dans le respect mutuel" [The female boss wants her garage to be a haven of tolerance in which the two sexes learn to work in mutual respect] (Maillard 2019).

Through her project, MBoup provides at her level a counter-narrative to not only conventional entrepreneurship but also mainstream economics. Confronted by prejudices and faced with models and methods that are biased toward the masculine, she partakes in the creation of a community that is economically more gender-inclusive. She contradicts through her action the laissez-faire notion that economics should operate outside of human control. From a theoretical and pedagogical standpoint, Julie Nelson who has published extensively on economics and gender contends that "the idea that economic systems are inanimate machines [...] has harmful effects" (2006, 4). She argues in this respect that her field of study (economics) has been largely analyzed and understood through a logic that is masculine and therefore abstract and exclusive, while a feminine approach of the discipline would emphasize practicality and inclusion.

Feminists like Julie Nelson, Amartya Sen, and Marylin Waring challenge the notion that economics is a positive science, contending that the issues economists study and debate result from a belief system that is influenced by various ideological, cultural, or social factors. In this respect, economic research itself is founded on constructed narratives resulting from power relations. Coumba MBoup and Nelson offer counter-narratives which undermine male-dominated economic systems that put women at a disadvantage in both Western and non-Western societies. Given the inferior status of women in many societies, they both contend through practice and theory that gender, as well as the social conditioning of citizens, should be taken into account in economic analyses.

Femme Auto's counter-narrative, like the feminist opposition to mainstream economics, has major pedagogical ramifications pertaining to course content and students' understanding of entrepreneurial humanities. The students have a broader understanding of what it means to be female in Senegal. They learn about the prejudices and inequalities women experience daily. Beyond geographic boundaries, they examine how socioeconomic discourses are constructed, as well as theories, norms, and values, and how the latter inevitably inform citizens and policymakers everywhere including in France and the United States. Like French sociologist Pierre Bourdieu, MBoup's gender parity system challenges the hypothetical *homo economicus* that is mainly interested in the accumulation of wealth and the maximization of profit to support *homo reciprocans* which privileges collective cooperation.

What Can a Woman Do?

Learning from the struggle of female entrepreneurs like Coumba MBoup in Senegal, students ponder how the question raised by Simone de Beauvoir ("What is a woman?") is still relevant today and leads to an additional crucial question associated with women's rights and freedom: "What can a woman do?" "Taxi Sister" is a female taxi driver organization that epitomizes this question. It exemplifies how Senegalese female entrepreneurs are confronted with prejudice, ostracism, and masculinist views and expectations of women. The Taxi Sister project was started by the Senegalese government in 2007 to encourage female entrepreneurs. Ten women were initially offered the opportunity to obtain a driver's license, and there are today 15 women taxi drivers in Dakar. The city has a population of 4 million and 15,000 taxi drivers. Through her interview, taxi driver Mabelle Alssafa Gueye attests to the verbal abuse of which she is a victim, but she stresses at the same time the importance of not letting sexism and patriarchal values dictate what women can or cannot do in their career.

The Taxi Sister project seeks to pull women out of poverty. According to the UN Human Development Index, Senegalese women fall behind men in development indicators. Less than 30% of adult women are literate, compared to 50% of men; and on average, women earn just over half the income men do.[6] As the Taxi Sister video (same as Femme Auto video link above, see footnote 8) demonstrates, the *Direction de l'Entrepreneuriat Féminin* [Department of Women's Entrepreneurship] based in Dakar is taking steps to combat stereotypes and defend women's rights. According to its director, Marème Cisse Thiam, several initiatives including strategies of development and information sessions are raising awareness among the population so that female taxi drivers may be respected.

The entrepreneurial humanities and the experience of Senegalese women entrepreneurs and workers are considered here in the context of global economics, including the French-speaking world situated in West Africa. During the last decade of the twentieth century, according to Oxfam International, about 1.3 billion people had at their disposal less than a dollar a day to survive; global income increased by an average of 2.5% per year while the actual number of poor people increased by more than 100 million; and the number of people living on less than $2 a day was in the order of 2.8 billion.

More recent data from 2020 is no less alarming when it comes to gender inequality and lack of women's rights:

> The world's 2,153 billionaires have more wealth than the 4.6 billion people who make up 60 percent of the planet's population [...]. The 22 richest men in the world have more wealth than all the women in Africa [...]. Women and girls put in 12.5 billion hours of unpaid care work each day, a contribution to the global economy of at least $10.8 trillion a year.[7]

In this context, the narratives featuring the courage and determination of women entrepreneurs gain a broader significance. They contribute to humanizing economics and putting a human face on globalization. At the same time, they demystify and deconstruct the discourses of mainstream economists that are only based on scientific and mathematical foundations. To the latter, the feminist economist Julie Nelson has opposed a study and interpretation of economics that is more social and gender-focused.

The first two videos focusing on Femme Auto and Taxi Sister (see link footnote 8) enable us to consider the impact the entrepreneurial humanities can have on students majoring in business or economics, among others, by transforming their own narrative imagination. They foster their critical ability to envision the socio-economic, ethical, and political ramifications of their studies. The two stories also broaden students' awareness so that they not only become better informed about social inequality worldwide, but also the need for women empowerment and alternative ways of conceiving of entrepreneurship.

Entrepreneurship, Citizenship, Empathy

The third video featuring Sooretul[8] also introduces students to alternative economic rationales that take into account people's real-life experiences. I will focus on how learning from this company's activities and their impact on women's lives is conducive to developing the students' senses of empathy.

Launched in 2014, Sooretul is a Senegalese start-up devoted to helping women deliver their organic agricultural products to urban consumers. It promotes the work of women living hundreds of miles away from Dakar. According to Awa Caba, a Senegalese woman CEO and co-founder of Sooretul, the company advances rural women's economic empowerment through digital and mobile technologies, providing groups of women with new means to market their products such as material support, visibility, and access to an urban clientele. Most of the women working have no access to the technology or sales outlets needed to sell their products.[9]

The e-commerce platform also improves the traceability of the commodities, allowing customers to make their purchases online and have them delivered to their home. The platform brings together more than 15,000 women working in the agricultural sector through a virtual local market. It responds to the demands of urban consumers who seek local, healthy, and quality-controlled products.

Pedagogically, when students learn from Sooretul's mission and engage with the work of women in rural Senegal, they deepen their appreciation for what it means to be a female farmer with limited access to the market. They also measure the disastrous consequences of economic policies solely privileging big businesses and corporations in urban centers and ignoring small entrepreneurs in peripheral areas. Further examined in the classroom through the video segment are the uncontrolled and irrational effects of unbridled capitalism through which an oppressed humankind can easily become itself an ordinary commodity, a tool at the service and mercy of profit-making.

Through the study of Sooretul, students also develop a capacity of listening to other people's story along with the burden it carries. According to Cathy Caruth, "our ability to listen to the trauma of others [...] is enabled by our ability to listen through the departures we have all taken from ourselves" (2013, 170). Hearing and learning from these stories implies inhabiting different subject positions experiencing the stigmas associated with prejudice, poverty, and socio-economic injustice.

Through their classroom experience, students imagine new paths of understanding other socio-economic realities in different contexts and through empathetic intercession, thus reaching out toward the lives, works, and histories of others. This ethical and political action "entails the imperative of giving voice to another person, place, or period and setting the stage in their interest and from their perspective" (Bhabba 2010). This action alludes to the necessary renewed encounter with and understanding of the other as foundation of our humanity. It invites us to better appreciate the primary importance of alterity (in all its forms), as Emmanuel Lévinas contended, through the living relation with and responsibility for the other. To be an entrepreneur, in this instance, means to be responsible before others, to put oneself in the place of others, not observing someone from the outside but bearing the burden of her existence and responding to her demands.[10]

Conclusion

Studying the experience of female entrepreneurs in Senegal challenges and calls into question the pedagogical methods generally used in economics instruction, predominantly taught through mathematics and deprived of human or social consideration. Studying entrepreneurship from the perspective of Senegalese women provides critical paths through which students can explore the works of feminist economists mentioned above such as Julie Nelson and Marylin Waring who foreground the social construction of traditional economics and challenge the masculine-associated methods of its teaching. The Senegalese women's creative initiatives introduce a counter-discourse to the normative socio-economic narratives and policies which lead to greater inequality, instability, and constitute a menace to the future of democracy, the environment, and peace in the world.

Jean-François Lyotard's concept of "libidinal economy" (2004) constitutes for example a path through which students can reconsider women entrepreneurship and economic growth in a male-dominated world. He notably reveals how hidden unconscious forces under the guise of rationality determine economic policies. According to the French philosopher, libidinal energy constitutes one of the main driving forces of any theoretical fiction and the foundation of all economic systems, rationalizations, and justifications.

Ultimately, the notion sheds light on the shortcomings and biases of economic rationales that promote growth at all costs, weaken the equal sharing of resources, and leave answers to the following questions incomplete and unsatisfactory: Who can access the market? For whose benefit? What constitutes economic growth? What does equal sharing among men and women mean, locally and globally? How can we reconcile economic growth with the preservation of the environment? The entrepreneurial humanities envisioned here constitutes an essential process that must be enriched and transmitted not only because they inspire us and give meaning to our lives, but also because they make us think about how to construct a better world for ourselves and others.

Notes

1 See https://www.female-rights.com/senegal.
2 See https://www.imf.org/en/Countries/SEN.
3 See https://www.theglobaleconomy.com/Senegal/Female_labor_force_participation/.
4 See https://www.unl.edu/gradstudies/connections/learn-think-entrepreneur-0.
5 To watch the Femme Auto and Taxi Sister videos, see https://www.youtube.com/watch?app=desktop&v=e16ukHcFjck&feature=PlayList&p=A151939F787E2A9C&index=0&playnext=1.
6 See http://hdr.undp.org/.
7 See https://www.oxfam.org/en.
8 See https://shop.sooretul.com/en.
9 To watch the Sooretul video, see https://www.youtube.com/watch?v=tmI45CpSFUc.
10 "J'ai à répondre devant l'autre en son altérité. Je suis responsable de tous les autres devant tous les autres. [...] être responsable devant l'autre, se mettre soi-même à sa place, non pas observer quelqu'un du dehors, mais porter le fardeau de son existence et répondre à ses demandes" [I have to respond to the other in his otherness. I am responsible for all others before all others. [...] to be responsible in front of the other, to put oneself in their place, not to observe someone from the outside, but to carry the burden of their existence and respond to their requests] (Lévinas 1993, 166).

Works Cited

Bhabba, Homi: "Affects and Interests: Some Thoughts on the Culture of Human Rights", *John F. Kennedy Institute*. 5 Nov. 2010. https://www.jfki.fu-berlin.de/en/graduateschool/events/archive/videos/Bhabha/index.html

Caruth, Cathy. *The Routledge Companion of Critical and Cultural Theory*. Eds. Simon Malpas and Paul Wake. New York: Routledge, 2013, 170.

Chalier, Catherine et Miguel Abensour, eds. *Emmanuel Lévinas*. Paris: Cahiers de l'Herne, 1993.

Dennon, Anne: "Colleges Cut Liberal Arts Majors Due to Covid 19." *Best Colleges*. 10 Nov. 2021. https://www.bestcolleges.com/blog/colleges-cut-liberal-arts-majors-covid-19/

Derrida, Jacques: "The Future of the Profession or the Unconditional University." *Deconstructing Derrida: Tasks for the New Humanities*. Eds. Peter Pericles Trifonas and Michael A. Peters. New York, Palgrave Macmillan, 2005, 11–24.

Giroux, Henry: "The Attack on Higher Education and the Necessity of Critical Pedagogy." *Critical Pedagogy in Uncertain Times: Hopes and Possibilities*. Ed. Sheila L. Macrine. New York: Palgrave Macmillan, 2009, 11–26.

Hayes, Adam. "Entrepreneur: What It Means to Be One and How to Get Started." *Investopedia*. 19 July 2022. https://www.investopedia.com/terms/e/entrepreneur.asp

Lévinas, Emmanuel. "Préface à l'édition américaine d'*Autrement qu'être ou au-delà de l'essence*." *Emmanuel Lévinas*. Eds. Catherine Chalier and Miguel Abensour. Paris: Cahiers de l'Herne, 1993.

Lyotard, Jean-François. *Libidinal Economy*. Trans. Iain Hamilton Grant. London: Bloomsbury, 2004.

Maillard, Matteo: "Un garage automobile de femmes démonte les préjugés au Sénégal." *Le Monde.* 28 Mar. 2019. https://www.lemonde.fr/afrique/article/2019/03/28/un-garage-automobile-de-femmes-demonte-les-prejuges-au-senegal_5442762_3212.html

Nelson, Julie A. *Economics for Humans.* Chicago: University of Chicago Press, 2006.

Sample, Steven B. *The Contrarian's Guide to Leadership.* San Francisco: Jossey-Bass, 2002.

Part III

The Humanities@Work

Chapter 11

The Humanities at Work

Internships and the Entrepreneurial Act

Ken S. McAllister and Judd Ethan Ruggill

Typically, the humanities are not the first port of call when talking about entrepreneurship. Rather, the spirit of "one who undertakes or manages" (from the Old French root *entreprendre*) is most often cultivated and elevated in the business, engineering, and science archipelagos of the university. The humanities, however, are actually an ideal locale for training entrepreneurs, as they prize and promote the creative, interpersonal, and intercultural intelligences crucial for materializing new ideas. In this chapter, we focus on the ways that humanities internship programs can drive the entrepreneurial act, discussing in particular two successful initiatives we helped start—one for the Department of Public & Applied Humanities (University of Arizona), and one for the Learning Games Initiative. For each of these cases, we explore how their structures and organizational vision contributed to the strengthening and expansion of the entrepreneurial humanities in their respective contexts.

Key to this exploration is the understanding that interns tend to occupy a liminal space in an organization. Neither students nor employees entirely, interns must often bend or hack the work culture they are immersed in to create opportunities that are meaningful for their lives and careers. This is especially true for humanities interns, who can sometimes be underappreciated on both sides of the equation: employers may not be sure how exactly to capitalize on someone with a humanities education, and humanities advisors may be unfamiliar with how to mentor a humanities major seeking to develop humanities-inflected work skills for a non-academic context. But while the interpersonal and organizational negotiations that accompany new humanities internships are sometimes awkward, they are also part of why internships are an ideal proving ground for humanities students: they challenge students' abilities to assess organizational surroundings for potential change, design interventions into standard operating procedures, and to advocate for their ideas among audiences ranging from encouraging to oppositional. Humanities internships are, in short, fantastic for training entrepreneurs.

DOI: 10.4324/9781003380665-15

Public & Applied Humanities: Building Career Readiness

The Department of Public & Applied Humanities was established in 2017 and a year later launched the Bachelor of Arts in Applied Humanities, an undergraduate degree offered in collaboration with four colleges on campus.[1] The degree has grown rapidly since, and as of Fall 2022 has 277 majors spread across its eight curricular emphases—Business Administration, Fashion Studies, Game Studies, Medicine, Plant Studies, Public Health, Rural Leadership & Renewal, and Spatial Organization & Design Thinking—and two modalities (in-person and online).

Unusual in the humanities, the BA in Applied Humanities features what we term the "career readiness sequence." This sequence, which is required for the degree, consists of three three-unit courses: (1) a pre-internship, where students learn the fundamentals of communicating their transferable skills to the professional realm and prepare to put those skills to use in an internship; (2) an internship homed anywhere in the world and in any job sector of interest; and (3) a senior capstone designed to help students develop an understanding of the importance of regular and skillful reflection for an engaged, satisfying, and meaningful work life. In other words, the career readiness sequence is meant to provide what scholar Kenneth Burke (1941) terms "equipment for living." Initiating and flourishing through the change and transformation that defines the information age demands mundane skills as well as exceptional ones, and the career readiness sequence is focused on helping students develop such day-to-day abilities. Cultivating a generosity of spirit, accommodating and even encouraging dissent, acting professionally regardless of circumstance—these are the rudiments of entrepreneurialism, the building blocks for new ways of operating, envisaging, and manifesting.

From our perspective, the entrepreneurial spirit undergirds the entirety of the career readiness sequence, as students are consistently asked to imagine themselves into the world of work as a way to also imagine the work they want to do for the world.[2] They are mentored to integrate career planning/readiness into their everyday lives so that they not only know how to start their career but also progress through it in a steady and rewarding way. Just as importantly, students are taught to recognize the significance of their educational and personal experiences, and how to communicate those experiences to a range of audiences. Along the way, students learn about and practice active listening and other strategies for enticing attentiveness and trust, techniques often essential for discovering new opportunities. Put another way, the career readiness sequence teaches interactive storytelling, a vital humanities tool that combines listening, sharing, and inventing. Not coincidentally, interactive storytelling is also an engine of entrepreneurialism.

Importantly, we see career readiness as different from job readiness; for us, career readiness signifies much more than that a student is ready for an entry-level position post-graduation. Rather, career readiness encompasses (1) the ability to understand and shape the relationship between work and life, and (2) the capacity to act in ways that promote a meaningful career as an integral part of a meaningful existence. Career readiness signals not only capacity but also possibility, the ability to spot opportunities for innovation and change within a working life, and the skills to manifest these latencies in the workplace throughout one's career.

The entrepreneurial spirit is arguably most apparent in the internship itself. Students must not only find and secure an internship, but also engage directly with the concept of what it means "to intern." Adjacent to both pursuits is each student's unique challenge to discover what makes for a "good fit" personally, professionally, and for prospective partner agencies. Such career calculus can be extraordinarily difficult, especially for students with little job experience; this is precisely why we created a pre-internship course, which introduces these concepts *before* jobs and lives are on the line. Interning is, on the one hand, a for-credit educational experience; internships are graded and appear on the student's transcript. On the other hand, interning is real-world work experience; students work in and are supervised by partner agencies, and may even be paid as part of the experience.[3] Interning thus demands that students occupy two distinct but related subject positions: initiate and apprentice. As Applied Humanities majors, our students become acquainted with the work world (i.e., they are initiated) through the coursework of the internship. As interns, they learn how to apply their budding knowledge in a professional setting to directly shape the world of which they are now a part (i.e., they apprentice). In both contexts, students are mentored in how to see, size up, and (where advantageous) seize opportunities that are likely to bridge professional ambition, personal satisfaction, and organizational benefit.

Moreover, some students take the opportunity to create their own internships. While this route requires more work, self-created internships enable students to invent new businesses, rebrand existing ventures, and develop innovative service and financial opportunities for organizations they may already work for. In effect, students learn to see the internship process itself as creative and entrepreneurial, an opportunity to explore and experiment under the guidance of faculty they must seek out and establish relationships with, and through opportunities they create in their courses. This is a kind of low-stakes entrepreneurialism in which especially motivated students can test their ideas safely in a real-world setting.

Regardless of whether students intern with a partner agency or create an individualized experience, the job market confirms at least one measure of the program's success: a good chunk of our students are offered paid positions during the course of the internship.[4] While most students turn down these offers—they have yet to graduate and the idea of beginning a career while still enrolled in school full time is daunting—such offers give students a tremendous boost of confidence, one that often carries over into their coursework, which becomes more engaged, concrete, and generative. Internship-based entrepreneurialism, in other words, frequently leads to academic entrepreneurialism, a development that students report makes coursework more productive and rewarding.

Learning Games Initiative Research Archive

The career readiness sequence is a good example of how an academic unit can strengthen its entrepreneurial impact through the curriculum. This is especially true if the curriculum already includes elements that are key to entrepreneurial thinking: core course modules focused on collaboration, teamwork, and innovation; community outreach projects that situate students in non-academic learning contexts (e.g., interviewing local business leaders or community members); developing content for media that are new to the students (e.g., ArcGIS StoryMaps, AR/VR); and so on. Most colleges and universities have another institutional sector, however, that can site entrepreneurial internships: centers, laboratories, libraries, galleries, and other research or service units which, while not directly connected to an academic department, are tightly integrated with the mission of higher education. These units are often inhabited by a variety of academic personnel, from faculty and senior researchers to specialized support staff guiding everything from grant getting to marketing to payroll. Such units can be ideal internship locations because they approximate non-academic organizations in their structure while maintaining close ties with the institution's educational and research mission. This combination can provide entrepreneurially minded interns with an enviable opportunity to learn and practice conventional workplace skills in an employment context underpinned by such values as curiosity, fact-driven discovery, a long view on innovation, and the privileging of learning over producing.

Consider, for instance, the Learning Games Initiative Research Archive (LGIRA) headquartered at the University of Arizona. Begun in 1999 to help scholars in the emerging field of computer game studies, LGIRA is essentially a massive lending library for people who study digital games. It houses more than 2,50,000 items, including not only thousands of games and game consoles, but also a wide assortment of peripherals and paratexts, from handmade curios and original concept art to prototype controllers, memorabilia, and industry documents. Between 9,000 and 11,000 items are processed into the collection annually, and hundreds of items each year are circulated for study worldwide to individual researchers, schools of all levels, museums, galleries, and industry partners. And while not a museum, LGIRA regularly hosts tours of its facilities for schools, community organizations, and other groups interested in digital games, software preservation, and the workings of a very unusual archive.

The bulk of the day-to-day work of LGIRA is done by interns, some paid, some volunteering, some earning course credit. Each year's intern cohort is overseen by LGIRA's regional directors—the archive has seven physical locations in the US, plus one in Germany and another in Australia—and together they collaborate on all aspects of the archive's management, growth, and globally oriented public-facing presence.

It was not always this way. For the first decade or so, LGIRA interns primarily did the tedious work of data entry, which is to say, the essential archival work of gaining intellectual and physical control over the collection. From the beginning, it was the interns who most consistently saw opportunity where the directors often only saw a Sisyphean task. Those of us in administrative positions were driven by one basic truth: for the archive to be beneficial to the growing community of game scholars, we needed to know exactly what we had and where it was. Plodding through the accessioning of objects one after the other was how the directors saw the process as needing to unfold. The interns played along, at least for a little while.

Fortunately for everyone, the fact that LGIRA had little in the way of financial resources meant that one of the few things we could offer our hardworking interns was a high degree of freedom in when they worked and what they did (as long as it got accurate records into the database), as well as a promise that we would write them strong letters of recommendation—especially if they made unique contributions to the enterprise. It thus did not take long for our interns to begin exercising their entrepreneurial muscles. Two early interns saw that one of the things keeping new interns from achieving high levels of accuracy in data entry was a lack of process standardization. We had taught the interns how to accession (an archivist's term for the process of adding new items to a collection) donations with a hands-on tutorial, but had never had the opportunity to document the approach in a manual that could be shared with and followed by new archive personnel. Those two interns undertook this task and within a semester had written a ten-page how-to guide giving step-by-step instructions for how to enter objects—from games to movie adaptations to food items—into the database. Later entrepreneurially minded interns have undertaken important revisions and expansions to this guide.

Other interns have expressed their entrepreneurial instincts by streamlining aspects of the intake and cataloging processes, customizing server-side scripts for the website, writing grants to expand LGIRA's community presence, engineering collaborations with other archives, establishing the archive's social media profile, and curating in-house mini-exhibits designed to help visitors understand the scope and import of LGIRA's work. They have introduced us to software tools that make it easier to scan fragile multi-page documents, put their newly acquired knowledge about materials preservation—learned in school—to work with collections of papers contributed by influential game designers, and remapped the archive's physical layout to optimize the process of finding requested items. In short, a large number of LGIRA's innovations over the years have been introduced by interns, and there is no question that the archive's success and impact today is due to their creativity, determination, and capacity to see opportunity.

After witnessing many times first-hand the relationship between interning and entrepreneurialism, it occurred to us that we were seeing a pattern, not a coincidence. Interns, when they are told on Day 1 that they are expected to do the quotidian work of archive maintenance *and* the creative work of using their extant knowledge and skills to make the archive better, almost invariably make interesting contributions. Much of this success—at LGIRA, we count all new ideas and approaches as successes even if they do not contribute to a measurable improvement of the archive—can be traced to our belief that ignorance is a potent catalyst for innovation. Permeating LGIRA is the understanding that there are infinite ways of understanding games and innumerable ways of arranging data to tell different stories and reveal new truths. Interns quickly become steeped in this way of approaching the archive, and almost immediately begin to practice using their ignorance as a tool for generating rather than arresting innovation.

This ignorance training takes a variety of forms, but generally unfolds in two ways. First, interns become accustomed to more experienced LGIRA personnel (including advanced interns) expressing ignorance without shame. The nature of every archive is that it raises more questions than it answers: what is this thing and where did it come from? How many were there? Did it differ from year to year and place to place? How many are left? Why does it look like this and not some other way? What other objects are similar, and how can we explain the differences? How old is it? Were the parts all made in the same place? Who worked on it? How did it get distributed? How well did it sell, who bought it, and why? Did the producers understand well what the object was and how it would be received by consumers? What are the dimensions of the object and why? What's the object made from and why? Can the object still be acquired today? If so, from where? If not, why not? Did the object generate or engage a cohesive fan base or user group? And so on. Archives are great places to practice being comfortable with not knowing, a skill that when juiced with curiosity leads to wonder…*and sometimes even innovation.*

It may seem fortuitous, in the context of thinking about humanities internships and entrepreneurship, that a game archive, above all, hosts an infinite bundle of questions. Where better to encourage people to put new ideas to the test than in a shrine to play, a place where trying, failing, and trying something else is the most fundamental rule of engagement? Consequently, for years LGIRA has taken advantage of the ways humanities students are trained to think critically, globally, and connectionally to extend and expand the archive and its services. Because they understand that, where people are involved, "truth" is complicated and facts often have a multitude of faces, humanities interns are ideal for an archive containing objects from all over the world that were designed for a multitude of audiences and are connected to a medium that, at its center, is for storytelling.

Thus, we have realized over time that it is not the archive and its wild aggregation of oddities that inspires entrepreneurial thinking in interns. Nor is it the pro-ignorance mentoring that interns receive from the archive's culture that brings out their entrepreneurial tendencies. Rather, we have come to believe that it is interns' work in the humanities that makes them especially susceptible to habits of creative association and theoretical promiscuity, and that these habits may be usefully and imaginatively deployed at any internship site or in any employment context—especially if innovation is a desirable outcome.

Humanities Internships and Entrepreneurship

As much as we have come to appreciate how readily humanities interns take to entrepreneurialism, we have observed one common impediment to their development that in both cases above must be frequently addressed: humanities students often have an internalized sense of disciplinary inadequacy that discourages them from giving free rein to their entrepreneurial impulses. This condition, combined with the fact that "entrepreneur" (despite its origins in arts management) is now generally understood as a business term, means that a key component of humanities internships (and humanities education generally) must include the process of disabusing students of the belief that the humanities are antiquated, inconsequential, non-impactful, or in any other way peripheral to one's life and career, *whatever that career may be.* We have found that when students truly begin to realize that physicians could not practice medicine, engineers could not design systems, and geologists could not understand rocks if it were not for the humanities training they all received, a window of entrepreneurial possibility begins to open for them. As it does, their capacity to see connections both in *and beyond* the humanities increases, a slow epiphany that empowers them to envision not only career paths as editors, translators, and academics, but also as inventors, executives, consultants, and collaborators in virtually any employment sector, from fintech to bioengineering.

Internships are a tremendously effective way for students to begin applying the growing sense of possibility that this type of humanities education is affording them. In both PAH and LGIRA, double (and even triple) majors are now commonplace, a development attributable to the fact that our College's leadership has long advocated the importance of interdisciplinary collaboration, not just with the arts, social sciences, and adjacent humanities fields, but everywhere on campus. The College's faculty regularly collaborate with colleagues in optical science, public health, integrative medicine, lunar and planetary science, agriculture, architecture, law, business, and elsewhere precisely because they themselves have remembered and realized that the university rests on a foundation built and sustained by the humanities.

Such faculty awareness makes for excellent student career mentoring, and has also led to a proliferation of internships within the College (and PAH especially), including in fields that sometimes leave people with more conventional understandings of humanities work scratching their heads. Through opportunities listed by tech start-ups, natural resource management, research labs, fashion and architectural design studios, and international banking (among many others), our humanities students quickly discover just by reading each semester's list of available internships that the strangulating myth that humanities degrees are worthless could not be more wrong. And once these students begin their internships, this discovery is made concrete. They realize that their foreign language and culture training makes it easy to pick up computer languages, parse complex policy documents, and conduct business in global contexts. Their regular exercises in evidence-based argumentation means that they fit right in at legal firms, humanitarian aid agencies, and government and corporate think tanks. And their nearly instinctual inclination to mistrust anything that is characterized as simple, easy, or obvious makes them particularly valuable colleagues in contexts where ambiguity, change, standardization, and advocacy are everyday tools of the trade (e.g., work in the government, lobbying, marketing, and nonprofit sectors). Such posts, even at the internship level, almost immediately make it clear to students that their humanities training is essential—not peripheral—to success, not only in their careers but also for the organizations themselves. Their ability to be fearless in the face of change, shameless about moving from ignorance to familiarity, and imaginative in places where most others are constrained by practicality and convention means that they see opportunity everywhere. Internships are key to helping humanities students go from seeing to seizing opportunities, giving them the skills to be entrepreneurial wherever they go.

Notes

1 Launch partners included the Eller College of Management, the Mel & Enid Zuckerman College of Public Health, the College of Agriculture &

Life Sciences, and the College of Architecture, Planning & Landscape Architecture. The number of partner colleges has since expanded to include the College of Applied Science & Technology, the College of Medicine-Tucson, and the College of Social & Behavioral Sciences.

2 We fully recognize the complexities and problematics of training students to think of work as a fundamental way of being in the world, particularly given that such work today is done in the context of capitalism's many supporting isms (i.e., racism, sexism, classism, and ageism). At the same time, we owe it to our students to help them prepare for, thrive in, and effect change on this system. *Praemonitus, praemunitus*, as the saying goes.

3 Recent PAH internships have positioned students at the Tucson Center for Black Life; Washington, D.C.-based public relations firm 314 Action; Monarch Coffee Farm in Hawaii; the DUSK Music Festival; Mac Duggal, a fashion design firm; PepsiCo; the YWCA; and many other organizations.

4 As of January 2022, 21% of Applied Humanities students who completed internships were offered full-time paid experiences, and 46% were offered paid experiences to continue past the original internship timeline (inclusive of full- and part-time paid experiences).

Work Cited

Burke, Kenneth. "Literature as Equipment for Living." *The Philosophy of Literary Form: Studies in Symbolic Action*. 1941. Berkeley: University of California Press, 1973. 293–304.

Chapter 12

Mastering the Art and Science of a Humanized Employee Experience

Leah N'Diaye

> Leaders must either invest a reasonable amount of time attending to fears and feelings or squander an unreasonable amount of time trying to manage ineffective and unproductive behavior.
>
> Brené Brown[1]

In today's Silicon Valley "dream-big-or-go-home" ethos, organizations owe a return on investment to their shareholders. The focus for business is usually the bottom line, the ability to expand. Beat the competition. Get bigger, get better, and get faster. But the entrepreneurial journey continues past big dreams. In series A to C funding, investors are not just looking for dreams and ideas. They are looking for companies with the ability to turn a great idea into a flourishing business. Successful businesses must have a strong product or service, a solid customer base, and the follow through to produce a copious return on the investment.

Great ideas aren't just great because they are innovative. They are great because they uncover customer needs – problems people didn't even know they had yet. Solutions to these types of forward-thinking problems equate to dollars. The product and customer experience (CX) are designed, and tested through a proof of concept, funding is secured, the business is launched, and then executives manage it like their livelihood depended on it.

Traditionally, businesses relentlessly focus on the CX to drive value. They focus on their Net Promoter Score (NPS) to ensure their business is moving in the right direction. NPS is a trusted measure of customer loyalty. It can help companies understand their audiences by quantifying customer sentiment toward products and services. Businesses listen determinedly to customer feedback, make course corrections, improvements, and enhancements all in the spirit of delighting their customers and shareholders.

However, for long-term success, a business must also focus on the employee experience (EX). Unfortunately, this area is often overlooked

DOI: 10.4324/9781003380665-16

in the early phases. Start-ups typically focus on attracting a certain culture and employee base so that all employees can easily produce the product or service on a tight timeline with a small number of resources. However, once they start to scale, they need to create an EX that will attract, retain, and engage the masses.

The EX encapsulates the full employee journey at any organization. From "interview-to-exit" – every moment, every interaction, every touch point and transaction in the employee lifecycle constitute their entire experience.[2] How engaged or "happy" a workforce is largely depends on how well an organization acts on what is important to its employees.

An EX must also be one that is *humanized*, to highlight the basic need for respect and dignity in the workplace – to not just treat people as workers with tasks to be done or service to produce but as people with social and cognitive needs that must be met at a very deep level. How engaged a workforce is largely depends on how well an organization understands human needs in today's context of intersectionality,[3] a global pandemic, and sociopolitical unrest.

As defined by Medallia, the company which declares itself the pioneer and market leader in Experience Management, "Employee Experience is not about what companies do; it's about how companies make employees feel throughout the journey."[4] This essay is about making the workplace – EX – more humanized, especially in today's post-pandemic world.

"Feelings... Nothing More Than Feelings." Morris Albert

Feelings are squishy. Feelings are gray. Feelings are not "corporate". Feelings are "unprofessional." The organizations of the 1980s and 1990s hadn't been concerned with feelings as they were relentlessly focused on their product or service and expanding their markets. "Leave your personal life at the door" was a common expression I heard when I started out as a recent graduate in the corporate world. This perspective is changing. With globalization, the Internet, and mass commoditization, people had to identify creative ways of differentiating themselves, consequently creating the need to focus on CX which is a body of work that attempts to understand and even visualize customer "sentiment" or feelings in the form of the quantitative metric called the Net Promoter Score (NPS).

Thanks to this shift in customer centricity, perspective on being more employee-centric started to emerge once leaders realized the symbiosis between happy customers and happy employees in that together these aspects could positively impact the bottom line. Quantifying employee sentiment has typically been done through employee engagement surveys and focus groups. Measuring sentiment is one thing, doing something about what organizations are hearing is another. It's more than putting the basic employee benefits, performance management, and compensation programs into place. It's about creating an environment which allows people to be human, providing employees a sense of purpose and belonging. In a work environment transformed by disruption, leaders must reinvent their Employee Value Proposition (EVP) to deliver a more human deal that focuses on the whole person, their life experience and ultimately, the feelings the human deal creates (Gartner 2021, "Reinvent Employee").

We all know the axiom, "It's not personal, it's just business." This phrase implies that logic is more material than feelings. Yet, feelings are part of the human experience and leaving them out of decision-making, judgment, and interaction is unrealistic (Zigarmi 2018). One company recognizes that feelings are material and is making the employee sentiment of happiness part of the EX dialogue. Humu – a California-based employee survey company – is revolutionizing employee surveys using algorithms and behavioral nudges to drive change. Happiness is defined as "employees who frequently experience positive emotions at work, recognize their organization as a great place to work, feel immersed in and passionate about the work they do, and experience a strong sense of belonging to their company."[5]

Although this empirical data helps to make Human Resources professionals more strategic with insights into how employees are feeling, it's just the tip of the proverbial iceberg. Recommendations and nudges are valuable but it's not enough. Managers must subscribe to the belief that their role is more than "telling people what to do," or "role modeling the right behavior," they must see themselves as leaders who are creating an environment for organizational performance *through* others and are responsible for creating an environment where individuals feel **seen, valued, and heard** (my emphasis). According to Project Oxygen conducted by Google, Inc. in 2008, managers must be good coaches and listeners. In 2018, this study was updated with good managers "create an inclusive team environment, showing concern for success and well-being" (Harrell and Barbato 2018). As prior research shows, psychological safety is a precursor to performance – which is needed in today's rapidly changing environment – at the individual, team, *and* organization levels.

Professor at the Harvard Business School Dr. Amy Edmondson originally coined the term "psychological safety," which she defines as "a shared belief that the team is safe for interpersonal risk taking" (2018). A psychologically safe environment creates the space for people to have respect for another's skill sets, to care about others as individuals, and to trust each other's intentions. The more psychologically safe people feel, the more people will be apt to share resources, knowledge, and skills. This environment fosters a focus on employees as people, not just producers of a service or product. As Simon Sinek, a speaker and optimist who shares his perspective on how the greatest leaders and organizations think, act, and communicate, astutely pointed out on LinkedIn in Feb 2022, "100% of employees are people, 100% of customers are people. 100% of investors are people. If you don't understand people, you don't understand business." Understanding business and people are critical components to avoiding unnecessary costs which are, most recently, due to the organizations' lack of adapting to new employee needs.

Most recently, according to a Gartner study among women, 65% report the pandemic has made them rethink the place work should have in their lives. The unbalanced distribution of work and household responsibilities has created challenges for women in the remote and hybrid work environments that have taken shape during the COVID-19 pandemic. In this study, women expressed needing environments which provide flexible and healthy work environments which also allow them to thrive in their career on all levels (compensation, satisfaction, purpose, etc.) (Gartner 2022, "HR Research"). Recent research by Microsoft, the 2021 Work Trend Index, showed that 41% of the workforce (men and women) was considering leaving their employer at the time of the survey. Not only is this due to the Great Resignation – a term coined by Anthony Klotz, an organizational psychologist and professor at Texas A&M University, to describe the wave of people quitting their jobs due to the ongoing coronavirus pandemic – it has been an ongoing challenge companies have faced due to employees having a poor experience at their jobs (Smith 2022). Megan Neale, Co-Founder and COO of Limitless, explains that companies in 2021 "were dealing with gaps in their CX supply chains because they cannot fill customer service roles or retain staff" ("2022 Customer Experience"). Poor employee retention is usually a symptom of a poor EX, which in turn, leads to a negative CX because there are no people, or only *unhappy* people, to serve customers. The employees who are left behind inherit the burden of taking on the work of others due to the lack of resources and burn out. This resource gap creates a vicious circle that can negatively impact businesses' results.

Employees who are left behind and who are coming in as new recruits have basic needs that have changed due to the pandemic and the blending of work and life. The definition of "basic needs" has moved from the standard Maslow's Hierarchy of needs[6] which are typically physical to a more intricate definition which includes psychological, cognitive, and social needs.

According to Ardeshir Mehran, Ph.D., performance leadership coach and owner of the Bay Area consultancy Human Work Studio, people have a requirement to express their emotional needs. He refers to this requirement as "The Bill of Emotional Rights" which details lifelong principles that have existed in all people across societies, cultures, and history. He asserts that these rights are as elemental as our DNA and should be nurtured in the organizational setting. He writes, "We feel in flow and alive when we live a life rooted in these rights. Conversely, we feel anxious or depressed when our Bill of Rights is violated, dismissed, or fragmented" (Human Work Studio).

When people feel like their Emotional Bill of Rights has been violated, fear comes into play. These new requirements are difficult for organizations to incorporate because they are more accustomed to focusing on corporate culture which *Harvard Business Review* refers to as, "cognitive culture or the shared intellectual values, norms, artifacts, and assumptions that serve as a guide for the group to thrive" (Barsade and O'Neill 2016). Cognitive culture sets the tone around how people should show up at work – customer centric, collaborative, competitive, etc. Another side of culture coin is an organization's "emotional culture" which is the shared affective values, norms, artifacts, and assumptions that govern which emotions people have and express at work and which ones they are better off suppressing. Cognitive culture is conveyed verbally whereas emotional culture tends to be conveyed through body language and facial expression. Emotional culture is rarely managed, and the effects can be demanding during times of transformation or disruption.

Forward-thinking companies such as Salesforce, Zappos, and Warby Parker have embraced and recognized not only on building cognitive culture but also skill building to enhance its emotional culture (Abmann 2016). I recently heard at the 2022 Change and Transformation Conference in New York that even the behemoth company, Microsoft, is taking steps toward helping managers be more attuned to emotional culture. These companies know that there is a direct correlation between allowing emotions to coincide in the workplace with high financial performance because they know that when organizations manage emotional culture, it reduces burnout and increases employee retention. For example, the German multinational software corporation – SAP – reported improving its Business Health Culture Index from 69% in 2013 to 78% in 2018 and with each 1% change in the Index they reported delivering a \$90–\$100 Million (EU) impact on their operating profit. Let the numbers speak for themselves, a concerted focus on the EX will render a significant return on the investment.

Cisco, a multinational high-tech corporation headquartered in San Jose, California, has established the practice of introducing Learning Labs to teach vulnerability. Cisco introduced this practice because they realized that leaders were increasingly engaged in vulnerable conversations with employees, often on topics outside of traditional work concerns, and they felt unprepared to navigate these situations, particularly in a remote setting (Gartner 2021, "Case Study"). Preparing leaders for these conversations and engaging in these moments that matter with employees creates a more positive EX. Cisco is now top on the list of Fortune top companies to work for list for 2022 (Klooster 2022).

As part of my tenure at the Silicon Valley Bank, I had the privilege of conceptualizing a management development program teaching managers to serve as coaches to their employees – introducing case studies and role plays allowing managers to practice engaging with employees through difficult emotions. Managers learn how to become more emotionally intelligent – the capacity to be aware of, control, and express one's emotions and to handle interpersonal relationships judiciously and empathetically – through a series of experiential and immersive learning with peer coaching feedback. Additionally, managers learned how to coach employees to tie their values, strengths, and interests to achieve their greater purpose.

These innovative companies mentioned above make work a place where employees feel like they are part of something bigger than themselves, where they will feel like their talents can contribute to the purpose of the organization, where they feel that they can be authentically human. As a management consultant and change practitioner for the past 20 years, I have pulled from philosophy, neuroscience, linguistics, and my own experiences to inform and adjust my techniques in supporting internal organizational change.

My most recent work consisted of leading the cultural aspects of integrating 800 employees from a private bank into a larger financial institution. The biggest challenge was determining how to integrate an organization during a global pandemic, 100% digitally. We thought about how we could make them feel connected to the parent company without the ability to walk into an office and have an actual human to talk to. We also knew they weren't going to be switching to our technology systems on day one of integration, so we had to account for employees feeling like they are part of a new organization even though they weren't yet doing anything differently yet. The approach we took was based on preparing managers and leaders to have empathetic, transparent, and informed conversations. We took this approach because intuitively we knew it was the right thing to do but also it was backed by research. According to Gartner research, "The Future of Work Needs a New, Humanized Employment Deal" (2021), employees need to feel deep connections and purpose, so we created digital "moments that matter" to provide them the opportunity to connect and engage. We put employee pulse checks into place allowing employees the opportunity to express how they feel about the integration and then respond accordingly. We introduced forums to enable managers with tools and talking points and encouraged one-on-one meetings with new managers to help establish strong connections. It all came down to preparing managers to deal with difficult conversations around the future ahead and easing their anxieties with not only concrete information around the change but also with tools on how to help employees through the change. This work reminds me that there is both an art and a science to managing a human EX.

The Art

The concept that people and business are inextricably linked came to me when I was a graduate student in the French Literature Master's program at the University of New Mexico while also working in Telecom. I enjoyed learning and teaching language because it brought new ideas and new perspectives to my students. I reveled in seeing the smiles on my students' faces when they discovered, for example, that French people don't stand "in the shower" they stand "under the shower." This "ah ha" moment is called perspective taking. It is temporarily walking in the shoes of another (or in this case the shower of another) and understanding their point of view without judgment. It is also recognizing emotion in another person and having the ability to communicate the understanding of another person's emotion. The culmination of these attributes is known as "empathy." To quote Brené Brown, "Empathy is feeling with people."

This perspective-taking ability was helpful to me on the sales floor when managers would accuse employees of being "lazy" or not working hard enough to make sales. In this instance, I would encourage the sales managers to speak one-on-one with their team members and ask them with curiosity to level the playing field between manager and team member, "I have noticed that your sales numbers have gone down, is there something getting in the way that I could help you with?" One plausible answer to this question is, "Well, yes I have been having a hard time hearing as my headset isn't working and no one has gotten me a new one and I've asked IT about it ten times already."

According to *Forbes* magazine, empathy has always been a critical skill for leaders, but it is now becoming a priority. Since the COVID-19 outbreak, life as we know it has changed. And with those changes has come increased mental health issues. According to a mental health study conducted on 2,000 employees by Qualtrics at the end of March and early April 2020 in Australia, France, Germany, New Zealand, Singapore, the United Kingdom, and the United States, the following has been reported:

53.8% report being more emotionally exhausted
53.0% report increased feeling of sadness in day-to-day life
50.2% report being more irritable
42.9% report feeling generally more confused
38.1% report increased insomnia
32.3% report increased anger
24.4% report increased feelings of guilt.

("The Other COVID-19 Crisis: Mental Health")

When employees have difficulty completing tasks, are mentally exhausted and generally sad, it is no surprise that the EX is impacted. According to this report, "The data show that companies' and managers' actions can improve wellbeing and mitigate some of the negative effects of the COVID-19 outbreak on workers. They must be willing to listen and then act."

Unlike cognitive intelligence (IQ), emotional intelligence (EQ) is said to be learned and improved upon. Daniel Goleman, an internationally known psychologist who wrote the book "Emotional Intelligence" which was on *The New York Times* bestseller list, explains that while our IQ may get us a job, it is our EQ that determines how quickly we advance and are promoted. The argument is that after technical skills are accounted for, it's "our ability to work with and connect with others that determines how successful we are at work." Many companies, like Cisco mentioned above, took the cue teaching empathy through leadership-development programs. However, there are other methods to learning empathy as well – for example reading novels by allowing the reader to transport into another character's mind, allowing them to see and feel as the character does. The words on the page expose the audience to life circumstances that are very different from their own. Through fiction, it is possible to experience the world as another gender, ethnicity, culture, sexuality, profession, or age. Reading is virtual reality before virtual reality. Words on a page can introduce the reader to what it feels like to be in another land, to be born into homelessness, to lose a loved one. And this new information can influence how readers relate to others in the real world. According to *Gulf News*, literature has "shaped civilizations, changed political systems and exposed injustice." Literature also helps people understand other walks of life. Narratives inspire empathy and give people a new perspective on their lives and the lives of others (Staff Writer 2020).

Be assured there are other ways to learn empathy if literature isn't of interest. Tips include, attending someone else's church, mosque, synagogue or other houses of worship for a few weeks or spending time in a new neighborhood, or striking up a conversation with someone you wouldn't normally speak to and learn about them. Be curious and show no judgment. Practicing empathy is a start. Being authentically caring is another. According to the Qualtrics survey mentioned above, 64% of workers say their manager cares about them as a human being. The remaining 36% who report their manager doesn't care about them as a human being are "twice as likely to be extremely worried about losing their job." It is important to understand what people are worried about and what could help them ease their concerns. As an example, many health-care workers have resigned, because with the current staffing shortage, they are burning the midnight oil and in extremely difficult and sometimes unsafe conditions.

No matter how much empathy and compassion you provide health-care workers, what they really need is people, twice as many people to get the job done. They also need time for rest and recovery. One physician I recently spoke to, Dr. Sophie Peterson, shared with me that, "Being physically tired is a major problem and rest is a basic physiologic human need." For Peterson, many of her nurses resigned because there wasn't enough flexibility in the workplace. According to Ed Yong, about one in five health-care workers has left their job since the pandemic started. Yong's article states that, "Health-care workers aren't quitting because they can't handle their jobs, they are quitting because they can't handle being *unable to do their jobs*" (Yong 2021). The pandemic pushed them past their limits. According to a survey, 37% of employees feel emotionally drained (Gartner 2021, "What Is Work"). When organizations are agile and respond to employee needs so that they can do their jobs, workers will be more inclined to stay. For example, putting in place flexible work arrangements, sabbaticals, hybrid work from home during return to office are all good steps forward. These interventions need to be inclusive of all types of needs. To appropriately assess the needs, it takes an organizational consultant and leadership to use the power of observation and empathy to identify the right solution. According to Strategy.business.com, "Feelings are messengers of needs. Meeting needs unlocks positive feelings and energy; neglecting needs does the opposite. By integrating business objectives with meeting people's needs, companies can make sure the strong wind of a positive emotional force is at their back" (Katzenbach et al. 2020). Before introducing any new solution to address needs, it's equally important to ensure the leadership capabilities are in place to support the sustainability of the solutions.

One of those leadership capabilities is being an inclusive leader, and it starts with the words people use. As Mark Twain once wrote, "The difference between the almost right word and the right word is really a large matter, 'tis the difference between the lightning bug and the lightning." Adopting inclusive language is not about being politically correct, it's about being allies to people who have been historically marginalized (due to their race, ethnicity, gender, sexual orientation, age, disability status, and/or other aspects of their identity) (Brodzik 2021). Word choice can be used, intentionally or unintentionally, to include or exclude other people. Using inclusive language as outlined by Kathie Snow (2009) allows communication with people in a way that is respectful and brings everyone into the conversation. Language is constantly changing and should be considered within its historical context. "People First Language" teaches us that while the meaning of the word may change, it is challenging to disassociate words from their original meaning. For example, the expression "peanut gallery," which some may use to mean "observers," refers to the cheap seats in a theater where Black patrons were obliged to sit. This term is used quite often in the corporate setting and is charged with negative meaning.

People First Language centers on the individual rather than their descriptor, for example, using "people with disabilities," rather than "disabled people." It is important to consider the historical context of words and phrases. There are many that have colonialist roots and using this language can undermine collaboration and transparency. For example, the term "divide and conquer," a term commonly used in the business place to indicate "sharing duties and working together" has connotations from the oppressions of colonialism, and "grandfathered in" has roots in Jim Crow-era voting laws[7] that discriminated against Black individuals. Even as a language and cultural studies major, I still managed to miss how oppressive this term is. It can be surprising to learn that the origins of seemingly neutral idioms are based on oppression or cultural insensitivity.

There are people who believe that using "inclusive language" is just being politically correct. By using inclusive language, and being an inclusive leader, everyone is more likely to feel valued and respected. This language makes for a happier work environment, resulting in employees who feel more comfortable – more psychologically safe – to contribute and apply their talents. This, in turn not only drives organizational performance but it's also just basic human decency.

The Science

You have been provided some examples and evidence around how organizations introduce more humanized approaches to the EX, now let's look at the science – the brain. What happens when people feel excluded or feel like they are in a dehumanized experience? Studies by Naomi Eisenburger at UCLA found that being excluded activates our pain system, suggesting that it is a threat to our very survival (Hills 2018). When we don't get invited to key meetings, when our ideas are ignored, when we don't feel heard, the pain we feel is experienced in the same areas of the brain as physical pain.

So, what is happening in the brain when people feel excluded? Experimental neuroscience research has shown that social exclusion damages mood, self-esteem, and sense of belonging (Blackhart et al. 2009). The brain releases an enzyme that attacks the hippocampus, which is responsible for regulating synapses. As a result, the brain "myopically focuses on a narrow field of view to survive. Myelin sheathing increases on existing neural pathways, and we are less likely to consider or try new solutions" (Comaford 2019). In other words, the brain temporarily shuts down in a way that causes a decrease in creativity, collaboration, and innovation which negatively impacts productivity. Organizations have a compelling case to focus on inclusion. Inclusive language is one way in which organizations can take steps to create an environment where employees feel safe to be themselves.

Another aspect of the science of the EX is Neuroscience – the branch of science concerned with the study of the nervous system. Neuroscience has become incredibly pertinent because in the past organizational change focused only on the structural aspects of organizations without considering the people's side of change; change doesn't happen without individual people changing their thinking, beliefs, and behavior. Changing behaviors takes time and planning and requires employees to flex their resilience muscle. The Merriam-Webster dictionary defines "resilience" as "the capability of a strained body to recover its size and shape after deformation caused especially by compressive stress." Research from the University of Michigan suggests the brain processes rejection like it does physical injury (Comaford 2019). Resilience for us refers to the mind's ability to "bounce back," or to recover from pain. Resilience is developed through a myriad of ways such as positive thinking, using relaxation techniques, and learning from failures.

Many organizations are calling upon neuroscience and the many great philosophers who understood the brain as a powerful tool. Attributes of this thinking has been incorporated into employee development programs at many organizations to build resilience. One such company is Google, Inc. which created a program called "Search Inside Yourself" with the aim of "helping people develop the skills of mindfulness, empathy, compassion and overall emotional intelligence to create the conditions for individual and collective thriving."[8] This program incorporates aspects of Buddhism and Stoicism into their curriculum.

Stoicism is a school of philosophy that comes from ancient Greece and Rome in the early parts of the third century, BC. Some say that "it's a philosophy of life that maximizes positive emotions, reduces negative emotions and helps individuals to hone their virtues of character."[9] Many Stoics – such as the famous Seneca and Epictetus – emphasized that because "virtue is sufficient for happiness," a sage would be emotionally resilient to misfortune. This belief is different to the modern definition of the term "stoic calm." In terms of building resilience, the traditional Stoic, Marcus Aurelius, famously wrote to himself: "Choose not to be harmed and you won't feel harmed. Don't feel harmed and you haven't been." Learning the skill to rewire the brain to perceive emotional pain differently builds mental toughness and resilience to anything that happens in our lives. It doesn't mean that one won't feel pain. But the length of time it takes to rebound from the pain determines how quickly you will return to the path to happiness and high performance. Additionally, it's worth noting that a Stoic philosophy doesn't give managers a hall pass to inflict pain. They still need to be transparent, clear, candid, and compassionate with their teams.

Another area of the humanities business professionals have already been pulling from is Buddhist philosophy. Buddhism offers methods of purposeful thinking and techniques to practice happiness or enlightenment.[10] One of the eight Tenets of the Noble Eightfold Path[11] – mindfulness – is probably the most applied Tenets in the business world today. This Tenet is particularly helpful, and hundreds of studies have proven that mindfulness and meditation can positively impact mental and physical health, whether by reducing stress, improving sleep, increasing focus, or improving relationships. According to neuroscience research, mindfulness practices dampen activity in our amygdala and increase the connections between the amygdala and prefrontal cortex. Both of these parts of the brain help us to be less reactive to stressors and to recover better from stress when we experience it. Companies like Headspace and Calm have capitalized on this research and offer meditation apps to support employees navigate through anxious times.

Conclusion: What Can Organizations Do With All the Feelings?

Organizations owe a return on the investment to their shareholders and owners. An exceptional CX and EX are a recipe for success. When employees are happy, customers are happy, and vice versa. However, there is not a one-size-fits-all EX. It is important to balance the culture(s) you wish to create and the impact you wish to have on your people. It is possible to have a return on investment *and* have a humanized EX. Utilizing teachings from the language arts, linguistics, literature, philosophy, and neuroscience show us that it is possible to focus both on business results and on people.

It is important to note that employees working in a psychologically safe and inclusive environment won't be immune to rejection or exclusion. There are those who won't get the promotion they are seeking, or those whose ideas aren't accepted, those who don't feel like they are at the table in a strategic discussion. It's important to remember that a human experience is not about appeasing every idea or every employee – it is about having candid and transparent conversations based on trust and making sure employees are seen, valued, and heard. It is also about being sensitive to the personal needs of individuals – using language that is appropriate for them, not placing judgment on them, and leading with empathy and compassion. This approach allows for a resilient workforce that can "bounce back" and improve when challenged, and grow, expand, and thrive as a business.

You might be thinking that you don't have time for all these conversations. Substantial team research detailed by Charles Duhigg in his book *Smarter Faster Better* (2017) validates the fact that high-performing teams offer both emotional safety and ways for their members to productively express themselves. This means it's up to leaders to find the right emotional tone that builds the communication and rapport needed to engage in effective collaboration. For example, being empathetic and holding people accountable is the right balance. Empathy can be ruinous, unhelpful, and damaging if overused. For example, saying nothing to a direct report about how their observed behavior is undermining their performance is not caring because you are withholding information that could help them succeed. It turns out to be harmful. Engendering a humanized EX is about understanding that business is about people and people are key to high performance.

In this post-pandemic and ever-changing world, organizations need to prepare themselves to navigate through constant disruption and change. Here are eight key areas organizations can focus on to increase their probability of success and create an environment in which humans thrive in the workplace:

1 **Have clear organizational purpose, mission, and values which not only clearly characterize the product or service delivered and incorporate the human element:** Most statements and values lack inspiration and lack defining how employees can contribute to the bigger picture. Ensure employees are part of the process in creating purpose, mission, and values. You might be surprised what attributes are important to them.
2 **Update (or create) the Employee Value Proposition (EVP):** The EVP is the set of attributes that the labor market and employee perceive as the value they gain through employment in the organization (Gartner 2021, "Reinvent Employee"). It must foster connections in a way that help employees feel understood by strengthening their family and community connections, not just work relationships. Elements of the EVP must include:
   - **Radical Flexibility** – How leaders help employees feel autonomous by providing flexibility on all aspects of work, not just when and where they work
   - **Personal Growth** – How leaders help employees feel valued by helping them grow as people, not just as professionals
   - **Holistic Well-Being** – How leaders help employees feel cared for by ensuring employees use holistic well-being offerings, not just ensuring they are available
   - **Shared Purpose** – How leaders help employees feel invested in the organization by helping the organization take collective action on purpose, not just make corporate statements
3 **Invest in leadership-development experiences that are emotional, sensory, and immersive experiences:** Weave in cultural

competence, curiosity, mindfulness, resilience, and awareness of self-bias into development programs. Learning and development are not enough. It's critical to drive behavior and mindset shifts across the organization through role modeling and holding leaders accountable.

4 **Make inclusion, diversity, and equity a non-optional imperative:** This work is done through transparent policies and procedures, but also by getting a diverse group of people into the right roles to bring a broad set of views and perspectives. Self-evaluation of diversity within leadership and other workforce groups can offer insight about voices that are missing at the table and give direction toward recruitment.
5 **Acquire talent which has already demonstrated cultural awareness competencies and brings diverse perspectives:** It's important to recruit and onboard leaders who have already demonstrated these new competencies – ensure interview guides appropriately evaluate these competencies. Consider case studies or behavioral interview guides to assist with this evaluation.
6 **Consider the neuroscience aspects of managing organizational change:** Instead of concerning ourselves with "pulling" employees along, seek ways to create moments for employees to "let go" of the past and welcome new experiences. An example of this is through facilitating group coaching sessions with leaders and employees to address and reframe concerns. Provide concrete examples of what is changing instead and being specific around what you need from them is a simple yet powerful way to help create the inertia around change. Provide employees with a path to learning new mindsets, processes, and technologies. Be ready to constantly make course corrections in your plans as you learn about how the organization is responding.
7 **Consistently evaluate, prioritize, and balance workloads:** Whether your organization has the appropriate workforce bench or not, it's critical to be precisely focused on the most important priorities. Otherwise, talent effort is wasted and there is a higher risk of burnout. The cost of re-recruiting and onboarding is unbelievably substantial.
8 **Keep learning and improving:** Organizations which are mindfully and purposefully learning and improving are not only listening to customer feedback but also employee feedback. They create rhythms in the organization to foster reflecting on learning and introducing areas for continuous improvement.

Reminding ourselves that employees are people is a good start but it's just the beginning. Most executives already understand that employee engagement directly affects CX and vice versa. According to Gallup, just 33% of American workers are engaged in their jobs. Fifty-two percent say they're "just showing up," and 17% describe themselves as "actively disengaged" (2022). To put it simply, organizations have a lot of work to do if they want to optimize the full potential of their investments. Imagine the possibilities of unleashing all this human potential. Imagine the innovation, creativity, and hope for the future that could come to fruition through a more human EX. Imagine how much more ready your organization would be for future disruption and change.

Notes

1 Brené Brown is an American research professor, lecturer, author, and podcast host. Brown is known for her research on shame, vulnerability, and leadership.
2 What is Employee Experience?|Medallia. https://www.medallia.com/what-is-employee-experience/.
3 The interconnected nature of social categorizations such as race, class, and gender as they apply to a given individual or group, regarded as creating overlapping and interdependent systems of discrimination or disadvantage. (Oxford Language).
4 "The Definition of Employee Experience." *Medallia.* https://www.medallia.com/what-is-employee-experience/
5 https://www.humu.com/.
6 For Maslow's hierarchy of needs, see https://en.wikipedia.org/wiki/Maslow%27s_hierarchy_of_needs.
7 The Jim Crow laws were a series of segregation laws enacted as early as the 1890s, primarily in the southern and border states. Jim Crow laws were designed to create a "separate but equal" status for black Americans and other non-white racial groups. The enactment of Jim Crow began shortly after Reconstruction, but the most stringent restrictions were established following the Supreme Court case *Plessy v. Ferguson,* which created the "separate but equal" doctrine.
8 See https://siyli.org/about/.
9 On stoicism, see https://www.holstee.com/blogs/mindful-matter/stoicism-101-everything-you-wanted-to-know-about-stoicism-stoic-philosophy-and-the-stoics.
10 On Buddhism, see https://www.pursuit-of-happiness.org/history-of-happiness/buddha/.
11 The eight tenents are Right View, Right Intention, Right Action, Right Speech, Right Livelihood, Right Effort, Right Mindfulness, and Right Concentration.

Works Cited

"2022 Customer Experience (CX) Trends Revealed." *The European Business Review.* 21 Dec. 2021. https://www.europeanbusinessreview.com/2022-customer-experience-cx-trends-revealed/

Abmann, Tim. "5 Forward-Thinking Companies Shaping the Future of Work." *Jovoto.* 14 Dec. 2016. https://www.jovoto.com/blog/creatives/knowledge-know-how/forework-initiative-5 forward-thinking-companies

Barsade, Sigal and Olivia O'Neill. "Manage Your Emotional Culture." *Harvard Business Review*. Jan.-Feb. 2016. https://hbr.org/2016/01/manage-your-emotional-culture

Blackhart, Ginette C., Brian C. Nelson, Megan L. Knowles, and Roy F. Baumeister. "Rejection Elicits Emotional Reactions but Neither Causes Immediate Distress nor Lowers Self Esteem: A Meta-Analytic Review of 192 Studies on Social Exclusion." *Personality and Social Psychology Review* 13. 269–309 (2009). https://pubmed.ncbi.nlm.nih.gov/19770347/

Brodzik, Christina. "The Power of Inclusive Language. Building Inclusion and Diversity in the Workplace." *Deloitte*. 29 Jun. 2021. https://www2.deloitte.com/us/en/blog/human capital-blog/2021/inclusive-workplace-language.html

Comaford, Christine. "What Being Exkuded Does to your Brain." *Forbes*. 16 Mar. 2019. https://www.forbes.com/sites/christinecomaford/2019/03/16/what-being-excluded-doesto-your-brain/?sh=1d47178f76d6

Duhigg, Charles. *Smarter Faster Better. The Secrets of Being Productive in Life and Business*. New York: Random House, 2017.

Edmondson, Amy C. *The Fearless Organization: Creating Psychological Safety in the Workplace for Learning, Innovation, and Growth*. Hoboken, NJ: John Wiley & Sons, 2018.

Gallup. "State of the Global Workplace: 2022 Report." https://www.gallup.com/workplace/349484/state-of-the-globalworkplace.aspx?utm_source=google&utm_medium=cpc&utm_campaign=gallup_access_banded&utm_term=&gclid=Cj0KCQjwwfiaBhC7ARIsAGvcPe7cJwlvonGLyKaPEkDppZaAWNiO7EjemPmSAqm1DgL_ETmjsYXxDoaAnZCEALw_wcB

Gartner. "HR Research Finds That 65% of Women Report the Pandemic Has Made Them Rethink the Place of Work in Their Lives." 23 March 2022. https://www.gartner.com/en/newsroom/press-releases/03-23-22-gartner-hr-researchfinds-sixty-five-percent-of-women-report-the-pandemic-has-made-them-rethink-the-placeof-work-in-their-lives

———. "What is Work Really Like Today? Leaders and Employees See Things Differently." 11 Aug. 2021. https://www.gartner.com/smarterwithgartner/what-is-work-really-like-today-leadersand-employees-see-things-differently

———. "The Future of Work Requires Executive Leaders to Embrace Radical Flexibility." 11 June 2021. https://resources.igloosoftware.com/campaigns/b2to-gartnerreport/?utm_source=google&utm_medium=cpc&utm_campaign=1-es-gartner_futurework_report&utm_term=gartner%20future%20of%20work&cid=&lmr=advertising&gclidCj0KCQjwwfiaBhC7ARIsAGvcPe5iWLTS8KkrPBvApIKaqav77PJJ9_XZJhSYkz4WnY0B11Ie8hojeAaAgqeEALw_wcB

———. "Case Study: Empathy in Action – Leader Learning Labs (Cisco)." 10 June 2021. https://www.gartner.com/en/documents/4002451

———. "Reinvent Employee Value Proposition to Deliver a More Human Deal." 25 May 2021. https://www.gartner.com/en/newsroom/press-releases/2020-05-25-gartner-hr-research-shows-organizations-must-reinvent-their-employment-value-proposition-to-deliver-a-more-human-deal

Harrell, Melissa and Lauren Barbato. "Great Managers Still Matter: The Evolution of Google's Project Oxygen." *re:Work*. 27 Feb. 2018. https://rework.withgoogle.com/blog/the evolution-of-project-oxygen/

Hills, Jan. "Diversity at Work: The Business Case for an Inclusive Culture." HRZONE. 31 May 2018. https://www.hrzone.com/lead/culture/diversity-at-work-the-business-case-for-aninclusive-culture

Human Work Studio. https://www.humanworkstudio.com/

Katzenbach, Jon, Chad Gomes, and Carolyn Black. "The Power of Feelings at Work." Strategy. 14 Sept. 2020. https://www.strategy-business.com/article/The-power-of-feelings-at-work

Klooster, Alison. "Cisco Tops Fortune's 25th Annual 100 Best Companies to Work for List in 2022." *Fortune Media*. 11 Apr. 2022. https://www.prnewswire.com/news-releases/cisco tops-fortunes-25th-annual-100-best-companies-to-work-for-list-in-2022–301522364.html

"The Other COVID-19 Crisis: Mental Health." *qualtrics.XM*. 14 Apr. 2020. https://www.qualtrics.com/blog/confronting-mental-health/

Smith, Morgan. "Professor Who Predicted 'The Great Resignation' Shares the 3 Trends That Will Dominate Work in 2022." *CNBC*. 14 Jan. 2022. https://www.cnbc.com/2022/01/14/thegreat-resignation-expert-shares-the-biggest-work-trends-of-2022.html

Snow, Kathie. "People First Language." 2009. http://www.inclusioncollaborative.org/docs/PersonFirst-Language-Article_Kathie_Snow.pdf

Staff Writer. "How Does Literature Affect People." *Reference*. 28 March 2020. https://www.reference.com/world-view/literature-affect-people-3f0e73dbd37d24ce

Yong, Ed. "Why Health-Care Workers Are Quitting in Droves." *The Atlantic*. 16 Nov. 2021. https://www.theatlantic.com/health/archive/2021/11/the-mass-exodus-of-americashealth-care-workers/620713/

Zigarmi, Lisa. "Why Are Feelings Forbidden in Business?" *Forbes*. 17 Apr. 2018. https://www.forbes.com/sites/forbescoachescouncil/2018/04/17/why-are-feelings-forbidden-in-business/?sh=9f4aa375dd83

Chapter 13

An Agora for the Medical Student Community

Creating Innovative Spaces for Medical Trainee Reflection and Collaboration

Aleena Paul and Ajay Major

We are more than just medical students.

The members of the medical student body are not scholars merely fixated on the long-sought title of "MD" or "DO." We are distinct individuals with passions, curiosities and insurmountable complexity.

As future physicians, to share these complexities with each other is to engage with the broader medical community. in-Training, the online newspaper for medical students, will be a forum for this collaboration.

in-Training is the agora for medical students, the Grecian intellectual center for news, commentary, and the free expression of the medical student voice. It is of medical students, for medical students, and by medical students.

When in-Training was conceived, the publication was seen as an opportunity for medical students to share in their common experience. Today, it has the opportunity for much more: a community for medical students to contribute their unique perspectives and opinions on medicine, the health care system and the world at large.

Whether you have an inspiring experience or lesson to share with your peers, are interested in a career in physician-journalism, or simply want to have your voice heard, in-Training is for you. We look forward to working with you.

In 2012, as first-year medical students at Albany Medical College, we emailed out the preceding call for contributions to a new publication we called *in-Training*, first to our personal friends and acquaintances, and then through a listserv to Deans of Academic Affairs at medical schools across the United States. Slowly at first, and then in leaps and bounds, we received responses from medical students who were excited at the prospect of a new online platform for trainees to read, write, and edit. Since our launch, *in-Training* has now published over 2,000 works by medical students across the globe, from narrative medicine reflections to poetry to opinion pieces, with over 6 million page views in that time. In this essay, we outline our entrepreneurial framework in founding *in-Training*, the decisions we made to enable organic evolution of the publication to meet the changing needs of the medical student community, the steps we took to ensure long-term

DOI: 10.4324/9781003380665-17

sustainability, and the impact of the publication on the intersection of the humanities and medical education.

Conceptualizing *in-Training*: From Vision to Mission to Execution

Incidental Inspiration for in-Training

The original idea for *in-Training* stemmed from a combination of personal interests and a defining moment of inspiration. As chief editors of our undergraduate college's student newspaper who spent many long hours in the proverbial trenches with our fellow writers and editors, we sought to recreate this nurturing peer community as we matriculated to medical school and entered the great unknown of medical training. At first, we sought advice on revitalizing the defunct student newspaper at Albany Medical College. As we pondered over the small details – how to recruit writers among our medical school class, whether we could obtain funding for publication costs from student affairs – we had the chance to attend a workshop entitled "Lights, Camera, Action: Careers in Medical Journalism" at the Student National Medical Association (SNMA) Annual Medical Education Conference in April 2012. Led by physician-journalist Dr. Tyeese Gaines, the discussion centered on the importance of physician-journalists in patient advocacy and communicating health information to the public. When we solicited Dr. Gaines' advice on revitalizing our medical college's newspaper, her advice was striking: "We're in the online era of journalism. Why not go bigger?" Dr. Gaines encouraged us to look toward serving a larger audience with our new publication, outside of the small sphere of our medical school.

With this inspiration in mind, we began outlining an online publication that would sit at a novel intersection of the humanities, student publishing, and medical education. We were fortunate at that early stage to have had experiences that we could draw on to bolster our entrepreneurial vision. Our time leading the college newspaper had given us a structure for crafting the publication's editorial workflow and relationships with writers and editors. We were both in the process of completing MBA degrees in healthcare management, which gave us the language to incorporate organizational structures, market analysis, financial sustainability, and ethical guidelines into the foundational underpinnings of *in-Training*. And as brand-new medical students, we had the real-life experience of being a physician-*in-Training* to guide the development of a niche publication by and for medical students.

Finding Our Niche

Prior to conceptualizing the vision and mission of our new publication, we conducted a market analysis of the current medical student publication landscape, to identify areas where our publication would be most fruitful. In our search of online medical student newspapers, magazines, publications, journals, blogs, and their various permutations, we discovered four general types of publications: anonymous medical student blogs, particularly on free platforms like Tumblr and Blogspot; medical student publications sponsored by large national organizations in which non-medical-students sat on the editorial boards; formal research journals, in which medical students submitted their scientific research; and small publications at individual medical schools, which generally were not online and were frequently out of date or defunct.

The only online publication we found that was written, edited, and managed entirely by medical students was *The Medical Student*, a monthly newspaper in print and online published by medical students by the five medical schools in London in the United Kingdom. We drew inspiration from the publication's ability to remain editorially independent, with control over content and editorial appointments vested in the medical student editors-in-chief, and used it as a model for the original organization of *in-Training*'s editorial board duties. While the publication curated a broad array of content, including news, opinions, art, and humanism in medicine, its primary audience was the medical education community in London, and thus was not considered a direct competitor in our vision.

The ultimate result of our market analysis was that there were no online non-research publications that were dedicated to the medical student community and that served a broad United States-based audience. The only publications that served national or international audiences were traditional academic journals focused on research, which often presented significant barriers to publication for medical students and generally were not medical student-driven.

As such, we identified a potentially large unfilled arena in medical student publishing, particularly for non-research-related works. Given we had not yet discovered the specific topics that the medical student community would write about for our new publication, we elected to establish *in-Training* as a broad publication accepting a diverse range of medical student writing, with a prespecified plan to permit organic evolution of the publication as we received content and identified new unfilled niches.

Creating the in-Training "Voice"

Our original intent for *in-Training* was to create an online publication that represented the authentic voice of the medical student community. At that very early stage in our creation, we had only two concrete conceptions about the publication: it would be entirely focused on the medical student community, and it would be run and managed entirely by medical students. In our handwritten notes from April 5, 2012, the day after our meeting with Dr. Gaines at the SNMA conference in Atlanta, we described our medical student audience as follows:

> Idealistic, hopeful, youthful, maybe a little naïve … future leaders of medicine who are pioneers at the forefront of medicine.
>
> [Handwritten notes, 4/5/2012]

With those character traits in mind, we then began to imagine the type of place where those "idealistic, hopeful, naive" students would create their community. We decided to characterize our virtual space as an "agora," a Greek term meaning "gathering place" or "assembly" that described the central meeting place in ancient Greek city-states that served as the center of artistic, spiritual, and political life of the city.

> *in-Training* is the agora for medical students, the Grecian intellectual center for news, commentary, and the free expression of the medical student voice.
>
> [Handwritten notes, 4/27/2012]

We chose the name *in-Training* on April 27, 2012. We felt the name fully encapsulated all members of our medical student agora – our doctors "*in-Training*" – while firmly anchoring the publication in the realm of undergraduate medical education.

Our initial recruiting messaging captured key elements of our vision. With the statements "we are more than just medical students" and "we are distinct individuals with passions, curiosities and insurmountable complexity," we hoped to speak to the "idealistic, hopeful...future leaders of medicine" that we had identified as our intended audience. Further, we wished to encourage medical students who had previously been involved in the humanities, the arts, and other fields intersecting with medicine to reignite such interests in their contributions to *in-Training*. Our messaging also laid the foundation *in-Training*'s role as a gathering place and space for collaboration for the medical student community, a goal that we were personally passionate about as members of the community.

The Ethics of Medical Student Publishing

As a publication by and for medical students, it was inevitable that stories about interactions with patients would form the basis for many submissions. Thus, it was vital to consider potential liabilities that could be incurred by us as the founders, writers, and members of the editorial board, as well as their associated medical schools. In consultation with the Student Press Law Center (SPLC), a nonprofit organization that aims to protect freedom of the press for student journalists through free legal counsel, we discussed issues of patient privacy and personal liability. Based on conversations with the SPLC and detailed analysis of guidelines maintained by other medical publications, we wrote formal ethical guidelines for *in-Training* that included obtaining consent from patients, never glorifying the vulnerability of patients, and omitting all protected health information. These guidelines are a part of an electronic contract that each writer and editor signs prior to joining the publication and are prominently displayed on the website.

Designing the Website and Social Media

The *in-Training* website, in-Training.org, was built by founder Ajay Major utilizing the WordPress content management system, a free and highly-customizable platform for blogs. WordPress was chosen because it could be easily modified and customized as the publication changed and grew over time, and because there are copious free plugins available to enhance its features and streamline operations. For example, plugins were installed to create a note system that allowed editors to indicate the status of an article within the editorial cycle, as well as to automatically notify writers about edits to their articles. Further, website hosting was purchased from a WordPress-managed hosting provider to enable daily website backups, traffic monitoring, and website support, the latter particularly important for busy medical students.

As early adopters of social media ourselves, we recognized that social media would play a vital role in amplifying *in-Training*, particularly among young medical students. As such, we created social media accounts across all major platforms, particularly Twitter and Tumblr which had very active physician communities, and we researched medical education influencers and relevant hashtags to advertise our published articles.

The Foundational Years of *in-Training*

The first year of *in-Training* was one of rapid growth and adaptation to the first articles we received from the medical student community. While we had been confident that we had uncovered an unfilled niche when we founded *in-Training*, we were surprised by the numbers and speed with which interested medical students approached us to contribute. Inundated by new writers, it was quickly clear that we would need to expand our editorial board beyond the two of us. With the recruitment of our first three medical student editors, our editorial board was officially born and we began using a shared Gmail and Google Drive account for centralized coordination of interested writers and their articles. In retrospect, the conscious decision by our early editorial board to perform all peer review of articles on the cloud, rather than by emailing documents back and forth, was paramount to our ability to quickly review and publish articles. With respect to the type of content we initially received, we had expected submissions to be mostly "news," factual or opinion articles written by medical students on advances in medicine or on new medical discoveries, as informed by our previous experiences in traditional newspaper journalism.

We were stunned – and elated – when the vast majority of pieces received in those early days were narrative accounts of medical students' experiences, and emotions as they navigated the transformative experience of medical school. Our inbox was filled with reflections on every stage of the medical school experience, from white coat ceremonies, to the first time in anatomy lab, to seeing first patients, to deciding on a specialty for residency. In these narrative pieces, we discovered that there truly was a space for *in-Training* in the medical student community, a rich niche for medical students to write about the shared, grueling experience – including the good and the bad – of becoming a physician-*in-Training*. As first-year medical students ourselves during the first year of *in-Training*'s existence, we realized that, prior to the founding of *in-Training*, the medical student community as a whole did not have a communal place to reflect on medical school and seek catharsis and camaraderie on its trials and tribulations. As we continued to receive reflections from medical students across the nation, we embraced our vision for *in-Training* as the agora of the medical student community.

Developing a Sense of Self and Physicianhood on *in-Training*

Within two years of its founding, *in-Training* had grown to an editorial board of 16 active editors, a managing editor to supervise the flow of all articles through the entire editorial cycle, social media managers, and us as the editors-in-chief. As we continued to receive predominantly personal narratives from medical students, we began discussing as an editorial board the importance of self-reflection in medical education and the role of *in-Training* in fostering reflective capacity among medical trainees. We started to notice trends and themes in the reflections we were receiving from our writers, who were predominantly from the United States but with a growing number of international writers. First-year medical students most commonly wrote about the paths that brought them to the field of medicine as well as experiences in anatomy lab with the cadaver as one's first patient. These themes continued from second-year students, writing about the pride, sense of wonder, and anxieties of navigating the large volumes of didactic knowledge and brand-new history-taking and physical examination skills needed to become a doctor.

The transition to the third year of medical school brought with it new elements in submitted articles that pointed to our writers' professional identity formation into physicians. The third year of undergraduate medical education is the time when students at most United States medical schools become members of the clinical care team and are learning through direct interactions with patients and with the health-care system at large. Their submissions often spoke of personal lessons learned from caring for individual patients and grappled with inconsistencies between the ideals of physicianhood and the complexities of the health-care system. In these reflections, the student writers highlighted the impact of the "hidden curriculum" of medicine – the unintended and unwritten lessons and values perpetuated by the hierarchy of medicine – on their professional identity formation. By the fourth year, many medical students had clarified the type of physician they aimed to be, and many of the articles highlighted excitement for the transition to residency and personal goals for executing change within medicine. In direct conversations with our writers and editors on regular conference calls, and through comments on social media, medical students conveyed the value they found in sharing their transformations and growth during medical school with each other, and the sense of community that built in a peer-managed space by and for medical students.

Enabling Medical Student Advocacy through *in-Training*

As *in-Training* gained legitimacy and recognition as a publication dedicated to the medical student voice, we noted a slow shift in the content of submissions from narrative reflections to opinion pieces about advocacy and policy in medicine. Medical students transitioned to using *in-Training* as a platform to call for improvements to medicine and medical education and to respond to current events. At that time, *in-Training* began to evolve into a platform for medical students to practice their advocacy work and writing for the lay public, as well as to call for a greater appreciation among medical students for the social determinants of health and the need for humanism in medicine. In addition, editors and writers brought forth the idea of hosting an *in-Training* Mental Health Week in response to reports of increasing rates of burnout, poor mental health, and suicide among physicians and physicians-*in-Training*. With this annual series of articles, *in-Training* as a publication and editorial board was transforming into a robust, active voice for the current concerns of the medical student body.

Publishing in *in-Training* as Academic Scholarship

For medical students as for others in academics, publications are a core component of scholarship which can create opportunities for further research and career advancement through improvement of one's academic portfolio. Publication on *in-Training*, an online peer-reviewed publication, has intrinsic scholarly merit as an addition to one's curriculum vitae, in addition to free online access to articles in bolstering a medical student's personal academic brand. However, we recognized that creating a formal training program would enhance our scholastic merit and would further expand our conception of *in-Training* as a space for medical students to experiment with writing and editing.

In that vein, we founded the *in-Training* Writers-in-Training Program in our third year to train the next generation of physician writers. Each year, a cohort of budding writers are chosen after an application process, and the writers – called our "interns," a nod to the term used for new physicians in residency – are paired with *in-Training* editors for a year-long mentored intensive writing internship. The program has continued every year since 2015, and graduates from the program have gone on to publish in *New England Journal of Medicine*, *Academic Medicine*, and *American Medical Association Journal of Ethics*, as well as found their own podcasts and be published in medical humanities books. A letter is sent to the medical school Deans of all of our interns to enable incorporation of their internship accomplishments into their recommendation letters for residency applications. In discussion with our writers and editors, many have been asked about their *in-Training* articles or their roles on the *in-Training* editorial board during interviews for residency, a reflection of the impact of *in-Training* on the evolving recognition of online publications in academic scholarship.

Developing Financial and Organizational Sustainability for *in-Training*

Although *in-Training* began as a self-financed publication, the start-up costs were relatively small, as online publications are very inexpensive relative to print publications with essentially no initial capital costs. For *in-Training*, our initial costs only included purchasing the domain name in-Training.org and paying for a web hosting company for WordPress server space. All other necessities for the publication were obtained for free through the Google suite of products, including Gmail and Google Drive. When the initial period of rapid growth and web traffic increased our website hosting costs, we were sustained with a grant from the Albany Medical College Alumni Association. However, as we approached the fourth year of *in-Training*'s existence and with our own time in medical school coming to a close, we reached a stage where we needed to establish financial and administrative structures to ensure sustainability of the publication.

Given the large numbers of medical students and future physicians who accessed our online platform, we recognized that *in-Training* could serve as a potentially lucrative source of funding from advertising and monetization. In our initial market analysis, we noted that many online medical publications relied on affiliated links or advertisements on the website site for revenue generation, and we easily could have collaborated with test prep book publishers and apparel stores for scrubs and other physician-targeted commodities. As medical students ourselves, and having developed personal connections with many of our writers and editors, we were intimately aware of medical students as a potentially "vulnerable population" when it came to this type of advertising, especially noting medical students writing for *in-Training* about financial challenges with loans and costs of living during medical school. At that stage, we definitely decided that advertising, sponsorships, and affiliated links would detract from the educational mission of the organization and would be deleterious to our mission to serve as the voice of the medical student community

To ensure financial and organizational sustainability, we founded a literary corporation and publishing house called Pager Publications, Inc. – an amalgam of our last names – in 2014 and secured nonprofit 501c3 status, to provide students and educators with dedicated spaces for the free expression of their distinctive voices. Per our bylaws, Pager Publications, Inc. maintained ownership of *in-Training* and was responsible for its financial needs. With this structure, the day-to-day operations of *in-Training* would remain in the hands of its medical student editorial board with complete editorial independence, but the editorial board would not be responsible for fundraising and could therefore focus on their specific vision for the publication as well as their own medical training. Nonprofit status allowed us not only to collect tax-deductible donations to support the website hosting costs of *in-Training*, but also to apply for grants to further empower our mission. As an example, we applied for and were awarded a grant by The Arnold P. Gold Foundation to curate and publish our first print book, "*in-Training*: Stories from Tomorrow's Physicians," a compendium of 102 articles published on *in-Training* with discussion questions written by the medical student editors. Book sales enabled us to continue support of *in-Training* after we had left the publication, with all proceeds going to support our website hosting and publication costs.

Matriculating and Moving on from *in-Training*

From the outset, we committed to creating *in-Training* as a publication that would forever be by medical students and for medical students. As such, when we prepared to start our own residency training in 2016, we prepared to transition the publication to a new set of editors-in-chief and a new editorial board. After codifying all of our institutional memory into documents for the new editors-in-chief and hours of training on all aspects of the organization, we wrote our final letter from the editors and stepped back from our roles, now serving as advisors for the publication through Pager Publications, Inc.

Now over seven years later, *in-Training* has continued to grow and change with each new cohort of editors while staying true to our initial vision to create a publication that evolved with the current needs of the medical student community. In these seven years, the 12 editors-in-chief have overseen the publication of nearly 1,000 new articles by hundreds of medical schools across the globe, multiple citations of *in-Training* articles in the academic literature, the creation of new columns and podcasts, a refined mission statement in 2020, and the publication of two print *in-Training* books, including "*in-Training*: 2020 In Our Words," a print compendium of peer-edited narratives written by medical students about their experiences throughout the COVID-19 pandemic.

Since we stepped down as the editors-in-chiefs of *in-Training*, we have continued our mission at Pager Publications, Inc. of creating new peer-edited publications for the medical education community. We have supported the founding of the new online publications *in-House*, *The Palate*, *Mosaic in Medicine*, and *Intervene Upstream*, as well as assisting the United Kingdom-based medical student publication *North Wing Magazine* with their transition from print to online. As a publishing house, we have published six print books by medical students, resident physicians, and educators. And in 2021, in collaboration with colleagues at Rice University, we executed and published a study in the *Journal of Medical Humanities* in which we demonstrated that incorporating *in-Training* articles into undergraduate medical humanities coursework may be a novel pedagogical method for fostering peer-to-peer learning in academic medicine.

The growth and success of *in-Training* occurred concurrently with increasing integration of the humanities into medicine and medical education. Many institutions have centers and institutes dedicated to the study and implementation of the health humanities, and the field of narrative medicine has entered daily medical parlance as an academic as well as practical tool in enabling connection between patients and their physicians, as well as to combat burnout and improve physician well-being. In December 2020, the American Association of Medical Colleges published findings from the Fundamental Role of the Arts and Humanities in Medical Education initiative, asserting that "the integration of the arts and humanities into medicine and medical education may be essential to educating a physician workforce that can effectively contribute to optimal health care outcomes for patients and communities." The report pointed to the importance of integrative experiences with the arts and humanities to improve the "education, practice, and wellbeing of physicians."

By providing a platform for medical students to express their distinct voices since our founding in 2012, we believe that *in-Training* has played a fundamental role in this growing passion for the humanities throughout medicine and medical education. Through our peer-managed online space, future physicians have engaged with and explored the humanities, as well as developed skills in writing, editing, and advocacy that will augment their vocations. We aspire to continue our entrepreneurship in providing platforms for medical trainees to induce paradigm shifts in medicine and to enable them to innovate for a better future for patients and prospective trainees.

Chapter 14

Perfection Fatigue and the Resurgence of Humanist Microentrepreneurs

Matthew M. Mars and Hope J. Schau

Introduction

Global mega-brand businesses leverage rapid manufacturing processes reliant upon exact technological replication and marketing strategies premised on planned obsolescence. Product developers diligently work to design products and services that align with ever evolving, yet explicit, standards, which with each permutation render the last obsolete. Examples of such precise engineering range from the molded uniform bodies of each new line of dolls and action figures to franchised hamburgers that are prepared and served in the same exact way no matter where in the world they are ordered. The appeal of rigorous standardization is amplified by marketers who through their branding and advertising campaigns create and broadcast the latest ideal. These market-promoted standardized ideals range from professional tools to entertainment technology, from fashion styles to home designs, from food choices to exercise regimes. Indeed, marketing messages heavily influence the images that consumers have of (and for) themselves and others. Very often at the center of such messages is the grand notion of perfection (Hackley 2000, 225). Consumers' obsession with perfection is characterized by an unattainable ideal of performance based on unrealistically high expectations and hyper-critical assessment standards (He 2016, 198; Kopalle and Lehmann 2001, 387).

Our present research is anchored on the assumption that perfection through consumption is elusive, a mythical ideal that by design is a perpetually moving target which can only be fleetingly attained. In short, the myth and ideals of perfection keep consumers in an unending state of longing. This perpetual pursuit of perfection is at the core of mega-brand strategies that embed in products and service features that ignite consumer desire for their newest, most innovative devices and technologies that are destined to become obsolete as even newer, sexier models burst onto the scene. This recursive cycle affords consumers brief bursts of contentment and longer periods of yearning for the newest shiny object that corporate creatives have engineered for them.

DOI: 10.4324/9781003380665-18

Our research reveals that the chronic state of yearning realized in consumers' never-ending pursuit of perfection is resource intense and exhausting. We term this phenomenon, "perfection fatigue," which in conjunction with more constant states of economic, social, and environmental uncertainties inspires consumers to seek out idiosyncratic, imperfect, potentially more authentic products and experiences. A revival of humanism is afoot. There is amplified consumer appetite for local microentrepreneurs offering an array of distinctive goods that through production histories and place-based connections align with values and motives for more conscious and intimate consumption.

In the coming sections, we conceptually develop the notion of consumer perfection fatigue from production replication and planned obsolescence through the authenticity of idiosyncrasy and the rise of the humanist microentrepreneurs. We provide evidence from a five-year field engagement with local microentrepreneurs who cast the mainstream emphasis on mass scale aside in favor of market goals associated with community wellness, economic localism, environmental stewardship, and social justice.

Production Replication and Planned Obsolescence

For more than a century, technological advances along industrial assembly lines have increasingly enabled the production of near infinite numbers of replicas, objects produced within almost imperceptible deviation thresholds (Benjamin, 2014, 145). Production replication coupled with global mega-brand strategies encourages product obsolescence through rapid incremental product changes. While production replication is evidence of technological progress, it has negative implications. Manufacturers engaged in mass production and short-term planned obsolescence deplete natural resources and create manmade unrecyclable materials to meet increasingly rapid market cycles (Cox et al., 2013, 21), with abundant waste becoming a global crisis.

Some consumers revere their new market acquisitions so much that they video document their unboxing (Ramos-Serrano and Herrero-Diz 2016, 95). Many others continue to purchase replicas but work to curate sets of identical objects (e.g., espresso machines, smartphones) in a paradoxical effort to assert uniqueness (Zaggl et al. 2019, 205). Others still recognize that replicas almost entirely emanate from global firms at the expense and potential extinction of local, small-scale producers (Gereffi and Christian 2009, 576) and respond by seeking more humanist, intimate consumption experiences within alternative markets like swap meets, craft fairs, farmers' markets, and thrift stores (Belk et al. 1989, 4; Isenhour and Berry 2020, 298–299; Mars and Schau 2017, 419).

Perpetual Pursuit of Perfection

Products that can be flawlessly produced and distributed on a mass scale (e.g., smartphone devices) become objects of consumer desire. Consumers, encouraged and perpetuated by market systems of rapid replication, in conjunction with planned obsolescence (Guiltinan 2009, 20), get trapped in an endless, unyielding, quest for perfection that over time is exhausting and in conflict with one's well-being (Berg 2004, 130; Rothman and Rothman 2011, 130). Rapid consumption cycles are recognized as having steep environmental tolls as objects that drop from peak performance or lose their sheen are cast aside in favor of newer and closer to flawless replacements. Consider, for example, Apple's iPhone production cue that pushes out a new suite of models almost every year.

The newest versions of the device line sometimes offer profound and other times more pedantic performance upgrades and stylistic features (e.g., facial recognition security, improved camera lenses, enlarged screens). Regardless of how the product is redesigned, Apple maintains a consumer culture that is driven to have the newest devices in their hands, pockets, and bags (Vichiengior et al. 2019, 130). Consumers at times become disenchanted with experiences tied to mass-produced replicas and are uncomfortable with the economic, environmental, and social consequences of global production and consumption. From discarding nutrient dense but unattractive produce while people go hungry (Stuart 2009, 4) to outsourced toxic landfills (Moore 2011, 137), waste has hit epic proportions with staggering consequences. Environmentally, the amount of energy used, and emissions released to produce iPhones is notably high, whereas the recycling of the finite materials used is troublingly low (Suckling and Lee 2015, 1182). Socially, the wages paid to the factory workers who assemble and package the devices are egregiously and unjustly low (Chen 2016, 123).

Consumers exhausted by the grind of mainstream consumption and/or inspired to invigorate local economies and foster community connectedness, economic justice, and environmental sustainability are increasingly turning to alternative markets. Despite these pernicious externalities, the consumer pursuit of perfection keeps what is otherwise an unsustainable cycle turning.

Further, while mass production of homogeneous item-lines makes perfection more accessible, consumer individuality is lost. The impersonal nature of perfect replication pushes some consumers to seek out idiosyncratic, customized experiences. Putting aside the temporary pleasure one may derive from their new acquisition and the massive profits realized by Apple (and other producers), the long-term consequences of these evolving production cycles of near perfection to obsolescence are environmentally and socially devastating.

Authenticity of Idiosyncrasy

Authenticity can be intrapersonal or interpersonal in nature (Leigh et al. 2006, 483). Intrapersonal authenticity involves individual consumers seeking out products or services that foster self-reflection and self-actualization. The tourist who challenges themselves during a rock-climbing excursion is an example of an intrapersonal authentic experience (Mody et al. 67). An antique or oddity that conjures childhood memories is illustrative of intrapersonal authenticity. Interpersonal authenticity involves consumers looking for products or services that bring groups of individuals together in collectively meaningful ways. A group that works collectively to solve an escape room challenge is an example of an interpersonal authentic experience (Mody et al. 2019, 67), while classic car clubs point to product-based interpersonal authenticity. According to Leigh et al. (2006), regardless of its nature "authenticity is a consumer perception that occurs through a filter of one's personal experiences" (482).

Authenticity is also a source of nostalgia for many consumers. Nostalgia provides individuals with connections to the past and notions of better, more certain times, as in the case of local food consumers who through shopping at farmers' markets conjure up recollections of a "period in time when 'real' food existed" (Autio et al. 2013, 568). The power of nostalgia is especially strong during times of hardship and intense uncertainty, providing consumers with what Gammon and Ramshaw (2021) refer to as "a palliative tonic in times of crisis" (132). For instance, many have turned to nostalgic products and/or activities to help counter fears and loneliness brought on by the COVID-19 pandemic and subsequent lockdowns (Cho et al. 2021, 5; Gibbs and Egermann 2021, 1). Consumer craving for nostalgia undoubtedly ebbs and flows along with the rise and fall of crises. Yet, we contend that consumer demand for authenticity and nostalgia should *not* be viewed as being entirely dependent on crisis. Rather, consumers acknowledging environmental and social implications of their ceaseless quest for perfection, experience perfection fatigue, and seek more humanist and idiosyncratic consumption products and services.

Humanist Microentrepreneurs

Entrepreneurial ventures can be classified into four distinct types: survival, lifestyle, managed growth, and aggressive growth (Morris et al. 2018, 454). Each venture-type is characterized by degrees of innovation and market disruption, investment sources, and economic motivation. At one extreme are aggressive growth ventures that involve high degrees of innovation and market disruption, are backed by venture capital, and view success through the lens of wealth accumulation. Aggressive growth ventures are seen as the gold standard in entrepreneurship literature (Aldrich and Ruef

2018, 459). On the other extreme are survival ventures, portrayed in the literature as inherently involving low degrees of innovation and market disruption, largely entrepreneur-funded, limited to day-to-day or week-to-week persistence and modest income generation, and often dependent upon singular entrepreneur labor, e.g., craftsmanship (Mars 2020, 639; Wong 2012, 243).

Whereas aggressive growth ventures are highly structured and ready for rapid replication and scalability, survival ventures presumably have little structure with entrepreneurs constantly changing approaches in response to daily shifts in market conditions (Morris et al. 2018). Consequently, survival ventures typically lack the operational consistency needed for scaled production and market expansion. Such inconsistency originates from the environments in which survival ventures operate, which are fiercely competitive, highly uncertain, and remarkably transient due to low barriers to entry. Like survival ventures, microentrepreneurship is dependent on singular labor (Prügl and Tinker 1997, 1472) which can only be scaled to an individual's maximum capacity (Mars 2020, 631) and lacks the operational facility needed for sustainable expansion. We contend that microentrepreneurs are engaged in survival ventures.

We use the term microentrepreneur to focus our research on market actors and ventures that limit the scope of their growth to household subsistence rather than regional expansion, and to avoid potentially pejorative nomenclature like "street entrepreneurs." We examine humanist microentrepreneurs in alternative markets that celebrate singularization in ways distinctly absent within dominant markets that privilege homogenization and perfection.

Field Work and Interviews

Through a 5-year field engagement and interviews with 42 microentrepreneurs, we find that an emerging set of humanist microentrepreneurs cater to consumers who seek relief from "perfection fatigue"; a sense of discontent brought on by various effects and consequences of technology-enabled replication that is firmly embedded in mainstream markets. Our data show that humanist entrepreneurs flourish largely in opposition to omnipresent corporate markets featuring predictable arrays of identical global offerings that are produced, distributed, and sold in ways that challenge conscious and intimate consumption.

Data Evidence of Embracing Imperfection

We find that microentrepreneurs in alternative markets foster the continuation of the past by emphasizing renewal over replacement, or idiosyncrasy over exactitude. The types of microentrepreneurs who participate in alternative markets range from produce growers to egg farmers, jam and jelly purveyors, to soap and lotion makers, and artisans and craftspeople to food truckers serving dishes out of renovated school buses, restored airstreams, and other ingenious rolling kitchen contraptions. Microentrepreneurs individually and collectively illustrate the sense of idiosyncrasy that characterizes humanist marketing. Consider vendor-farmers who lay claim to heritage lands and practices, who boast of multi-generation histories of working the same land using the same techniques to produce the same crops season after season from ancestral, oftentimes heirloom, seeds. Our multiple site visits to generational farms confirm these claims with farmers directly demonstrating the use of longstanding pesticide-free weed control techniques (e.g., cover crops), planting multiple crops closely together in loose rather than precise patterns, and relying on seeds and tools that are passed down generation to generation. Leo, a squash farmer, explains maintaining heritage practices in the following way:

> I was taught by my father, mother, grandfather, and grandmother how to work the land in good and honest ways. The food we produce is delicious and healthy for us and nature. I am sure we could grow a lot more if we used chemicals, lots of new technologies, and industry seeds. But, this would change how we grow and what we grow. People [customers] crave the quality and trust of what we sell. They don't want the boring grocery store dime a dozen tomato. They want a story that they can believe!

Leo's quote encapsulates how authenticity and heritage displays contribute to the sense of whimsy and distinctiveness that serve as primary draws to the markets. Farmers' market consumers don't just want a common tomato from the commercial grocer, but a singular storied tomato with heritage narrative (Epp and Price 2010).

A more obscure, yet powerful indicator of the renewal over replacement theme, is the consistent participation of blade sharpening experts at all the markets in our analysis. With slogans such as "are things dull around your place" and self-proclaimed titles such as "blade advocate," the sharpening experts work to extend the lifespan of old and well-used tools rather than push for their replacement by new and perfectly polished and edged cutting technologies. These craftspeople use simple tools to perform their long-developed trade on-site, immediately bringing new life to blades that would otherwise be discarded in favor of new, perfect alternatives. Further, we see heritage underpinnings of humanist entrepreneurs through the practice of a craft and trade at risk of extinction and in the renewal of well-used tools.

The use of longstanding practices, such as heritage growing and handcrafted artistry, undoubtedly involves variation in product esthetics and uncertainty in product availability. Greg, a produce farmer, says with a degree of amusement,

> Sometimes my tomatoes are all fat, sometimes they are all not, and sometimes they are a mish mash of size. Some are really firm and others are a bit smushy here and there. Sometimes I have no tomatoes at all! [laughs] Customers find not knowing what they are going to get when they come to see me is fun and maybe even exciting. It's the experience, man. You know what I mean?

This quote underscores the marked difference between shopping at conventional grocery stores, where produce-types are primarily homogeneous in appearance and nearly always available through massive global supply chains, versus at farmers' markets, where esthetics and availability are likely to vary product to product, week to week, and market to market. Market setups involve idiosyncratic patterns of booths that are sometimes overly stocked and other times sparsely supplied with common, yet individually unique items. Uniqueness is seen in cucumbers of the same type that vary widely by length, diameter, and texture with some smooth and others bumpy, bottles of goat milk lotions with haphazardly placed labels, handcrafted bowls with seemingly unplanned, but visually appealing design blemishes, and so on.

In the microentrepreneurship context, novelty results in imperfections that are not only tolerated but also celebrated. As Greg notes, blemished fruits and vegetables that would be discarded or hidden in the produce sections of conventional supermarkets are showcased as symbols of authenticity and localness,

> I am proud of the bumps and bruises. They mark the journey of my stuff [naturally grown produce] from my field to their [customers] cutting boards. Me making the not-so-pretty stuff visible shows I stand by the taste and safety that comes along with my veggies, which is so much better than the mass-produced garbage that is at [specific supermarket chain]. That shit is fake and no good for us or the environment.

We find that what a conventional market rejects as being ugly and flawed is seen as bold and beautiful in the alternative markets. The celebration of novelty, imperfection, and variation further illustrates vendors passionately asserting, with the support of the market managers, their own ways of producing and packaging goods and services as opposed to quietly seeking or wishing for belonging in highly rationalized, mainstream marketspaces.

By embracing and promoting the inexact and varied nature of their goods and services, microentrepreneurs illuminate a powerful, but before now overlooked factor: "perfection fatigue." Humanist microentrepreneurs highlight community development, economic and social justice, environmentalism, and overall health and wellness to illustrate perfection fatigue. The quotes provide evidence of a pervasive view held across those in our study that sees imperfection as a remedy to the symptoms of the perceived ills caused by the homogeneity of products and services that dominate mainstream markets.

Perfection fatigue is fueled by intersecting notions of idealism and longings for more unique wares, just and sustainable products, and genuine and intimate experiences. Humanist microentrepreneurs support a multi-agenda (e.g., environmentalism, localism, social justice) that converges in part on perfection fatigue. Humanist microentrepreneurs are relieved of the burden of competing within conventional grocers that demand both consistency and scalability. Izzy freely acknowledges the inconsistency of her goat soap and lotion products and explains the inconsistencies in a very pragmatic way,

> I don't have a factory. I am the farmer, mixer, bottler, labeler, shipper, and seller. I do my best to ensure the highest quality possible under whatever conditions are thrown my way. Things change constantly and I am always adjusting. My customers know that the only certain thing about my products is that they are all natural and locally and humanely produced. This is what they really want. Not high-end lotions and soaps that are boring, expensive, and come with no story or sense of place, person, or animal. And let's be honest, if they didn't accept me and my products for who and what we are, I'd have been out of business a long time ago!

Izzy highlights that she is proud of her ability to perform multiple market roles and adapt to uncertainty and change, while offering singular, storied self-care products. She believes that her customers value the idiosyncratic nature of the products she offers and the stories that accompany them over global, predictable skin-care offerings. Likewise, Annette, a microentrepreneur, identifies unpredictability as a core feature of her market,

> We haven't given up on trying to offer the same things each and every week. Why? Because we never wanted this in the first place! [laughter] Our farmers can't guarantee anything other than how they grow and harvest their produce. Same for our entrepreneurs who source and use the same produce in their products. Customers support and seek out this reality for whatever number of reasons. There is an unspoken agreement between the vendors and customers and that is acceptance and loyalty. It is so special.

Annette underscores that predictability is not only impossible with microentrepreneurs but was never a goal of the market. She clearly articulates that her clientele seeks variability as a compelling value. Christine echoes this philosophy, "scale and standardization would be a death sentence for [microentrepreneurs]... [offering and product variance] that is [what] our customers come to expect."

Comments provided by Bill, an ecologically minded fruit farmer, underscore the overall theme of microentrepreneurs enthusiastically embracing rather than helplessly accepting unpredictability as a core feature of local food production,

> If I wanted a predictable life I'd work for a factory farm. My knowledge, work ethic, heritage, and courage all go into everything I grow and sell. It doesn't matter what it looks like or how much of it I can harvest. It is all stamped by me. My customers see it, too. Thankfully I do not have to worry about meeting the unreasonable expectations of chain stores, which would either kill my spirit or kill my business. Probably both.

Bill finds synergy among work styles that favor heritage preservation, produce that varies with local weather and seasonal rainfall, and the consumers' expectations.

In stark contrast to dominant market notions of continuous growth and technological innovations, humanist microentrepreneurs do not dream of becoming global,

> I chose to stay small so that I can build and control my brand based on my own expectations and whatever capacities I have. I know as soon as I try to expand beyond the [farmers'] markets, expectations of what my products look like and taste like and how much I can offer and when are no longer in my control. My identity and personal touch, no matter how flawed it can be from batch to batch, would be gone.

Thus, humanist microentrepreneurs have turned unpredictability and the limited capacity to scale into value levers, which would otherwise be seen as significant constraints in the conventional marketplace. This strategic perspective and approach further illustrate the power of perfection fatigue as a unifying, yet to date underlying key driver of humanist microentrepreneurs.

Curated Diversity of Goods

The mix of microentrepreneurs in alternative marketspaces (e.g., farmers' markets, swap meets, bazaars) ensures a wide variety of unique products and services that are unlikely to be routinely available through more mainstream retail channels. Heirloom melons and squashes, mesquite bean flour, and prickly pear cactus candies are examples of the novel items that are specific to the field site regions and regularly available at farmers' markets. Artisans and craftspeople further contribute to the markets by offering one-of-a-kind creations, such as handmade, desert-scented candles and handcrafted wooden bowls, and furniture and frames made from native trees. While similar types of products, whether foods or handicrafts, can be found across competing farmers' markets, it is impossible to find exact reproductions of nearly any of the individual items found at any one of the markets at any specific point in time. Moreover, no one market is exactly like the next.

Novelty is central to the overall value proposition that humanist microentrepreneurs offer to consumers. Annette says, "people are proud of the things they buy here [specific market] that can't be found elsewhere and that nobody else has. It makes a trip here an adventurous experience instead of boring errand." Annette touts the novel curation of materiality as creating an adventure rather than a market errand to restock supplies. Equally important, novelty is a critical element of accessibility for microentrepreneurs who do not maintain standardized production models that churn out hundreds and thousands of exact replicas. Izzy, goat milk purveyor, remarks,

> the dimensions of my [soap] bars are never precise, and my lotions never have the same consistency. I tell my customers this right up front. They need to know that I am a small-time, artsy entrepreneur – not a factory owner!

For her, it is important to communicate the idiosyncratic nature of her production practices and her offerings in contrast to the replication-based practices and standardized goods sold in the dominant markets; she is an "artsy entrepreneur – not a factory owner." She goes on to later say,

> I could never get my products on the shelves of a big store. I couldn't meet their demands and expectations. My stuff is awesome. People love them as [sic] for how they are made with love as much as how great they make them feel when using them. Really, I am not sure I could do this my way if the farmers' markets shut me out.

Izzy confesses that while her products are of high quality, she could not meet the specifications required of the commercial stores. She asserts that her products are made with an intimate ingredient not found in "big store" offerings – "love." In general, product novelty combines to make the farmers' markets both distinct and accessible to humanist microentrepreneurs, as well as consumers who are seeking local, just, and/or sustainable products and experiences.

The compositions of farmers' markets are generally varied with microentrepreneurs selling a wide span of product-types that include baked goods, candies, eggs, fruits and vegetables, prepared foods (e.g., jams, sauces, salsas) and meats, as well as many types of artwork, crafts, and household items (e.g., candles, linens, solar lighting). Service providers, ranging from blade sharpeners to masseuses, are often present at the markets. The assorted nature of the markets is mostly by design with the underlying intent being to draw in as many customers as possible. Yet, the compositional parameters vary across markets with the most rigid of those observed capping non-food purveyors at 20% of the total booths and preventing the sale of foods grown or produced outside of the 250-mile radius of the market. The most pliable market allows 40% or more of purveyors to be non-food providers and has no formal definition of what is considered to be local production. Bryce explains that,

> the market has to sustain itself. We need critical mass to continue. The customers regulate who does and does not sell at the market. The purveyor will stop coming if people don't buy their products. People vote with their dollars.

Bryce leaves it to consumers to set standards, while Christine recognizes the delicate tension between selection availability and profit viability but is unwilling to compromise the established identity of her enterprise: People want choice. Without it, they will stop coming. But they also want to know what they are buying is what a farmers' market should promise to provide first and foremost – fresh, locally grown and made foods! In general, humanist microentrepreneurs aim to strike a balance between the enticement of the markets as enchanted cathedrals of consumption[1] and the pragmatic realities of supporting economically viable intimate enterprises.

Theoretical Implications

We find the aura of wonder that surrounds humanist microentrepreneurs is created through an embodiment of imperfection that offers respite from the continual chase of flawless products, idealized upgrades, spotless produce, commodified cuisine, etc. While others have shown a growing pattern of consumer flight from, and pushback against, the relentless pursuit of flawless replication,[2] we are the first to conceptualize the notion of "perfection fatigue" and identify humanist entrepreneurship as a potential, multi-dimensional path to relief. The various motives that lead microentrepreneurs to engage in humanist entrepreneurship, and in so doing bring life to alternative markets, all aim to counter ills born from, and sustained largely by, the manufactured quest for perfection. Humanist entrepreneurship is an alternative set of market-based strategies that has a common primary target: the fetishization of perfection.

The presumed healing from perfection fatigue by way of the intimate consumption experience echoes previous theoretical arguments that assert enchantment offers an escape from the rigid, rationalized underpinnings of modernity.[3] In particular, Thompson and Coskuner-Balli (2007) indicate that alternative marketspaces represented in our study engross consumers in "experiences of magic, wonderment, spontaneity and transformative feelings of mystery and awe" (280). Relative to perfection fatigue, enchantment comes from the release of pressure to seek out the flawless, fall in line with commodified masses, and/or sacrifice environmental and social values for the next must-have item. Humanist microentrepreneurs foster distinct agendas motivated by the reduction of perfection fatigue.

Conclusion

Providing consumers with alternatives to the tedium of replicable perfection, humanist entrepreneurs provide an alternative market. Humanist entrepreneurs engender immersive and sometimes abiding engagement by consumers who wish to support their local economy *and* acquire singular objects that are uniquely and comfortably their own. Items like hiking boots that mold to your specific foot and cadence through wear become singular (Godfrey et al. 2018, 121) and singularly valuable for their fit and the memories of prior use that attach to them (Epp and Price 2010, 822). Likewise, heirlooms and antiques that become more valuable when bearing unique markings from and the overall aura of past users (Türe and Ger 2016, 1). Alternative markets emerge in no small way to cater to consumers who are disenchanted with global brands and retailing, and who, inspired by perfection fatigue, have a desire to invigorate local economies, and preserve heritage and the environment may turn to alternative markets. Crafting and craft fairs featuring the works of everyday artisans form a $38B industry as specifically Millennials born and raised in the era of fetishized perfection seek singular objects as expressions of autonomy, activism, and connectedness (Danziger 2018). To capture this singular object focus, antique stores have become art studios where custom-made pieces by living artisans are 70–80% of sales, and resellers evolve from antique experts to artist agents (McKeough 2018). In short, humanist entrepreneurs operating outside the dominant paradigm of ideal perfections are currently thriving.

Notes

1 See Thompson and Coskuner-Balli (2007) for an in-depth theoretical articulation of the allure and enchantment of contemporary marketspaces.
2 See Belk et al. (1989), Berg (2004), Isenhour and Berry (2020), Ramos-Serrano and Herrero-Diz (2016), and Rothman and Rothman (2011) for evidence and theoretical discussion of consumer response and resistance to cycles of mass production and product and experience homogeneity and flawlessness.
3 See Lears (1994), Saler (2006), and Schneider (1993) for a greater perspective on the quest for enchanting experiences and products as antidotes to the massification effects of modernity.

Works Cited

Aldrich, Howard E. and Martin Ruef. "Unicorns, Gazelles, and Other Distractions on the Way to Understanding Real Entrepreneurship in the United States." *Academy of Management Perspectives* 39.4 (2018): 458–472.

Autio, Minna, et al. "Consuming Nostalgia? The Appreciation of Authenticity in Local Food Production." *International Journal of Consumer Studies* 5 (2013): 564–568.

Belk, Russell W., et al. "The Sacred and the Profane in Consumer Behavior: Theodicy on the Odyssey." *Journal of Consumer Research* 16.1 (2013): 1–38.

Benjamin, Walter. "The Work of Art in the Age of Mechanical Reproduction." *Historical Perspectives in the Conservation of Works of Art on Paper.* Ed. Margaret Holben Ellis. New York: Getty Publications, 2014. 144–147.

Berg, Maxine, "In Pursuit of Luxury: Global History and British Consumer Goods in the Eighteenth Century." *Past & Present* 182 (2004): 85–142.

Chen, Sibo "The Materialist Circuits and the Quest for Environmental Justice in ICT's Global Expansion." *triple C: Communication, Capitalism & Critique. Open Access Journal for a Global Sustainable Information Society* 14.1 (2016): 121–131.

Cho, Heetae, et al. "Compensatory Consumption During the COVID-19 Pandemic: Exploring the Critical Role of Nostalgia in Sport Consumer Behaviour." *Journal of Marketing Management* 37.17–18 (2021): 1736–1763.

Cox, Jayne, et al. "Consumer Understanding of Product Lifetimes." *Resources, Conservation and Recycling* 79 (2013): 21–29.

Danziger, Pamela N. "Millenials are Ready for Crafting, But Is the $36B Craftig Industry Ready for Them?" *Forbes.* 8 July 2018. https://www.forbes.com/sites/pamdanziger/2018/07/08/millennials-are-ready-for-crafting-but-is-the-36b-crafting-industry-ready-for-them/#53ca9b8b3a2c (accessed 2022, April 2).

Epp, Amber M., and Linda L. Price. "The Storied life of Singularized Objects: Forces of Agency and Network Transformation." *Journal of Consumer Research* 36.5 (2010): 820–837.

Gammon, Sean, and Gregory Ramshaw. "Distancing from the Present: Nostalgia and Leisure in Lockdown." *Leisure Sciences* 43.1–2 (2021): 131–137.

Gereffi, Gary, and Michelle Christian. "The Impacts of Wal-Mart: The Rise and Consequences of the World's Dominant Retailer." *Annual Review of Sociology* 35 (2009): 573–591.

Gibbs, Hannah, and Hauke Egermann. "Music-evoked Nostalgia and Wellbeing During the United Kingdom COVID-19 Pandemic: Content, Subjective Effects, and Function." *Frontiers in Psychology* 12.647891 (2021). doi: 10.3389/fpsyg.2021.647891

Godfrey, Matthew, et al. "The Embodiment of Repair: Consumer Experiences of Material Singularity and Practice Disruption." *Advances in Consumer Research (Vol. 46)*. Ed. Andrew Gershoff, et al., Association for Consumer Research, 2018. 121–126.

Guiltinan, Joseph. "Creative Destruction and Destructive Creations: Environmental Ethics and Planned Obsolescence." *Journal of Business Ethics* 89 (2009): 19–28.

Hackley, Christopher. "The Panoptic Role of Advertising Agencies in the Production of Consumer Culture." *Consumption, Markets and Culture* 5.3 (2002): 211–229.

He, Xin. "When Perfectionism Leads to Imperfect Consumer Choices: The Role of Dichotomous Thinking." *Journal of Consumer Psychology* 26.1 (2016): 98–104.

Isenhour, Cindy, and Brieanne Berry. "'Still Good Life': On the Value of Reuse and Distributive Labor in 'Depleted' Rural Maine." *Economic Anthropology* 7.2 (2020): 293–308.

Kopalle, Praveen K., and Donald R. Lehmann. "Strategic Management of Expectations: The Role of Disconfirmation Sensitivity and Perfectionism." *Journal of Marketing Research* 38.3 (2001): 386–394.

Lears, T.J. Jackson. *Fables of Abundance: A Cultural History of Advertising in America*. New York: Basic Books, 1994.

Leigh, Thomas W., et al. "The Consumer Quest for Authenticity: The Multiplicity of Meanings within the MG Subculture of Consumption." *Journal of the Academy of Marketing Science* 34.4 (2006): 481–493.

Mars, Matthew M. "From Within the Shadows of the Everyday: Localized Entrepreneurship and the Dilemma of Scale." *Community Development* 51.5 (2020): 628–645.

Mars, Matthew M., and Hope Jensen Schau. "Institutional Entrepreneurship and the Negotiation and Blending of the Southern Arizona Local Food System." *Agriculture and Human Values* 34.2 (2017): 407–422.

McKeough, Tim. "How Low Will the Market for Antiques Actually Go?" 3 Mar. 2018. *The New York Times*, https://www.nytimes.com/2018/03/03/style/how-low-will-market-for-antiques-actually-go.html (accessed 2022, April 2).

Mody, Makarand, et al. "Parallel Pathways to Brand Loyalty: Mapping the Consequences of Authentic Consumption Experiences for Hotels and Airbnb." *Tourism Management* 74 (2019): 65–80.

Moore, Sarah A. "Global Garbage: Waste, Trash Trading, and Local Garbage Politics." *Global Politcal Ecology*. Eds. Richard Peet, et al. New York: Routledge, 2011. 33–144.

Morris, Michael H., et al. "Distinguishing Types of Entrepreneurial Ventures: An Identity-based Perspective." *Journal of Small Business Management* 56.3 (2018): 453–474.

Prügl, Elisabeth, and Irene Tinker. "Microentrepreneurs and Homeworkers: Convergent Categories." *World Development* 25.9 (1997): 1471–1482.

Ramos-Serrano, Marina, and Paula Herrero-Diz. "Unboxing and Brands: Youtubers Phenomenon through the Case Study of EvanTubeHD." *Prisma Social: Revista de Ciencias Sociales* 1 (2016): 90–120.

Rothman, Sheila, and David Rothman. *The Pursuit of Perfection: The Promise and Perils of Medical Enhancement.* New York: Vintage, 2011.

Saler, Michael. "Modernity and Enchantment: A Historiographic Review." *American Historical Review* 111.3 (2006): 692–716.

Schneider, Mark A. *Culture and Enchantment.* Chicago: University of Chicago Press, 1993.

Stuart, Tristram. *Waste: Uncovering the Global Food Scandal.* New York: WW Norton & Company, 2009.

Suckling, James, and Jacquetta Lee. "Redefining Scope: The True Environmental Impact of Smartphones?" *International Journal of Life Cycle Assessment* 20 (2015): 1181–1196.

Thompson, Craig J., and Gokcen Coskuner-Balli. "Enchanting Ethical Consumerism: The Case of Community Supported Agriculture." *Journal of Consumer Culture* 7.3 (2007): 275–303.

Türe, Meltem, and Güliz Ger. "Continuity through Change: Navigating Temporalities Through Heirloom Rejuvenation." *Journal of Consumer Research* 43.1 (2016): 1–25.

Vichiengior, Tunyaporn, et al. "Consumer Anticipation: Antecedents, Processes and Outcomes." *Journal of Marketing Management* 35.1–2 (2019): 130–159.

Wong, Stanley Kam Sing. "The Influences of Entrepreneurial Orientation on Product Advantage and New Product Success." *Journal of Chinese Entrepreneurship* 4.3 (2012): 243–262.

Zaggl, Michael A., Markus A. Hagenmaier, and Christina Raasch. "The Choice between Uniqueness and Conformity in Mass Customization." *R&D Management* 49 (2019): 204–221.

Index

Note: *Italic* page numbers refer to figures and page numbers followed by "n" denote endnotes.